THE LIVING WILDERNESS

A Partial List of Books by Rutherford G. Montgomery

WILD LIFE AND NATURE

Amikuk : Kildee House : Broken Fang : Carcajou : Gray Wolf : High Country : Husky : Trail Of The Buffalo : Troopers Three : Wapiti The Elk : White Mountaineer : Yellow Eyes : White Tail : King Of The Castle : Klepty : Monte, The Bear Who Became A Celebrity : Cougar : Odyssey Of An Otter : Weecha : The Defiant Heart : In Happy Hollow : Big Brownie : Midnight : The GOLDEN STALLION Series : Crazy Kill Range : Adventure : Beaver Water : Hill Ranch : Claim Jumpers Of Marble Canyon : Ghost Town Adventure : Ice Blink : McGonnigle's Lake : McNulty's Holiday : Mister Jim : Mountain Man : Mystery Of Crystal Canyon : Mystery Of The Turquoise Frog : Rough Riders Ho : Sea Raiders Ho : Silver Hills : Stan Ball Of The Rangers : Timberline Tales : Trappers Trail : Snowman : Capture Of West Wind : Tim's Mountain

FLYING

Tom Pittman, USAF : Hurricane Yank : Jets Away : Jet Navigator : The KENT BARSTOW Series : Out Of The Sun : Thumbs Up : War Wings : Warhawk Patrol : The YANKEE FLIER Series by "Al Avery"

SEA (By "Everitt Proctor")

Last Cruise Of The Jeanette : Men Against The Ice : Thar She Blows

OTHER NOVELS

Call Of The West : Black Powder Empire : Bride By Legacy : Sex Isn't Everything : Posted Water : The Tracy Twins in Japan, and The Tracy Twins South Of The Border by "E. P. Marshall"

THE LIVING WILDERNESS

AS SEEN BY

Rutherford G. Montgomery

Illustrated by Campbell Grant

A TORQUIL BOOK

Distributed by
DODD, MEAD & COMPANY
New York

Printed in the United States of America

This book is dedicated to a lifelong friend whose shadow has fallen across many of my books, this one in particular. While he was creating a rangy, redheaded detective who has since become world famous, I settled for a smaller audience, readers who might not feel at home on the streets and boulevards of Miami. If you have one friend like him, you are successful beyond measure.

FOREWORD

Some of the wild animals that roamed the plains and mountains of this country when our forefathers landed and started building a nation have vanished, unable to cope with the white man and his guns and hunting dogs, or because man has leveled their forest refuges; but a surprising number still manage to live much as they always did, having adapted themselves to the changed conditions. The gray wolf, smartest of all the wild dogs, has been exterminated except in the far north and on certain islands in the Great Lakes area; but its little brother, the coyote, has managed to increase in number. One pair lives in the Hollywood Hills in the midst of a densely populated area. The little songdogs of the dawn can't read KEEP OUT signs. The wolverine has practically vanished, except in the far north. There are few grizzly bears left, but the black bear, clown of the woods, still frolics in North American forests.

It is probably your own fault if you haven't seen much of this wildlife. Many people watch birds; they have banded themselves into clubs and groups, they have books which describe birds, and tell the watcher what to look for and how. Looking for other animals is a much more difficult task, but it can be as rewarding as bird watching. Birds are abroad in the daytime and generally do not keep to cover while many wild animals frolic and hunt only during the night. You can see most of them, however, at dawn or just before dusk. Many of them are about during the day, but unless you know how and where to look, you do not see them. Some trappers have caught thousands of pine martens without ever having seen one free of the jaws of a trap. Milt Holt of Gunlock, Utah, has been hunting cougars for years and has taken hundreds of them. He told me that he had never observed a cougar in the woods until after his hounds had treed the big cat. But many naturalists have watched cougars and martens. It can be done if you know how.

The procedure is really simple. You do just as the predators do when they stalk game; move silently, keep to cover, stop often, freeze, listen and look around. Anyone who walks through the wood snapping twigs, kicking stones, never pausing, will be seen by hundreds of forest dwellers, but you may be sure that such a hiker will not see any of them, except for an occasional flash of fur here and there; a chipmunk with tail elevated, dashing across a trail, the white patch on the rear of a cottontail rabbit as it ducks into a thicket.

A rock or a stump at the edge of a meadow is a fine place to spend an hour. If you sit still you become a part of the rock or stump to the eyes of wild creatures. The meadow will come to life before your gaze. Wild animals do not recognize a person by looking at him, they depend upon scent and sound, and movement. Over the years these creatures have learned that the smell of man means danger. You should pick a rock or stump where the breeze blows from the meadow toward you. Down-wind is the term hunters use. If you move, all of the wild creatures in that meadow will vanish.

Learn from the cougar and the bobcat who know that movement will betray them. The cougar glides through the meadow grass on his belly. He moves forward a few feet, then freezes. The deer he is stalking may catch a flash of tawny color and lift its head to look, propping its big ears forward, listening, but the deer sees nothing because the cougar has frozen and will not move until the head is lowered and the deer starts browsing. Watch any house cat stalking a bird, it will use the same tactics. Of course, the deer often does spot the cougar moving. It may have to stalk many deer before making a kill. In nature survival is a matter of wits matched against wits.

This book sets out to tell where to look for the different animals. Take your time and have patience to stake out and wait; you will see many wild creatures doing things they never do in a zoo. Camping out is best, of course. You will be surprised at the number of wild friends you can make. Leave the air rifle and twenty-two at home, take a camera instead. Learning the way of life of a raccoon is more rewarding than shooting this delightful fisherman.

The terrain you are in will tell you much about what you can expect to see. As you move toward the mountains you will pass through belts of brush and timber which will change as you climb upward. The coastal mountains may have only scrub brush on one slope with oak and other hardwood trees on the other. There may be scrub oak, then a belt of quaking aspen and then the conifer belt with its pines, spruce, hemlocks, and lodge-poles. In the Rocky Mountains and the High Sierras of the West, barren, naked cliffs and peaks will rise above the timberline, but even high in the barren country you will find wildlife. You may meet a bear on the oak slope, while on the brush slope you may see a coyote or a desert fox, or a bobcat.

In the national and state parks you can get a close look at many of the larger animals as well as some seldom-seen smaller ones, like the ringtail cat. If you visit one of the national parks like Yosemite or Yellowstone you should avoid hotels and motels, if possible. In Yosemite sleep in a bedroll in one of the campgrounds. During the day and at night you will have visitors. The blue-coated crested jays will find you first. Feed the first visitor a few crumbs, and he will announce loudly that a soft touch has arrived. In a few minutes all of the jays in the vicinity will be hopping about your camp, chattering loudly. This chatter will bring gray squirrels, chipmunks, and striped ground squirrels as well, and a white-tailed deer or a mule deer or two. They are all beggars and very lovable rogues. Deer in parks become very tame and friendly, but they lose the lithe grace and alertness of wild deer. They will eat anything from watermelon rind to bread crusts.

Night brings a different kind of visitor. The real show starts after the campfire dies down and you are tucked into bed. The bears announce their arrival with a loud clattering of garbage-can lids. After they have looted the cans they are sure to visit the camps. One precaution should always be taken; the grub box should be securely locked inside the car trunk. A bear can smell bacon at a great distance, and will go to a lot of trouble to get it. One lady thought she could protect her slab of breakfast bacon by hiding it under her bedroll. Bruin simply rolled her bed over, with her in it, and made off with the bacon.

If you are lucky enough to be sleeping out on a moonlit night you may be able to lie and watch a black bear seat himself at your camp table and start sniffing for grease spots. Your visitor may step carefully over you in order to reach the table. We once left a stew kettle to soak on the camp table. It attracted a mother bear and her two cubs. In the morning we found the kettle licked clean. Rangers watch the bears closely, and if one becomes too much of a pest it is caught and hauled high into the mountains. No attempt to handle or hand-feed park bears should ever be made. They have sharp claws and may insist on a bigger handout than you wish to give them. Mother bears with cubs should be watched from a safe distance. Yellowstone Park is a fine place to observe bears. There the grizzly is making his last stand.

Raccoons usually come at night. You can be sure the little bandit wearing the black mask will investigate everything in camp. Latches on supply boxes won't stop him. East or West you'll find him. The same is true of meadow and jumping mice. I have had them perch on the toe of my boot as they nibbled a bit of cheese or a crumb.

The fliers will be out at dusk. In timbered areas you can see flying squirrels flash out of the shadows of tall trees and sail through the moonlight as they glide down for a landing. Bats will be out and there are few places East or West where they cannot be seen.

There are certain identifying characteristics about wild animals which will tell you a lot about how they live. Roughly the wildlife world is divided into two classes, the hunters and the hunted. The mark of the killer is the eyes placed well toward the front of the head, as man's eyes are placed. The hunted have eyes placed more toward the side which helps the animal see behind it as well as ahead at all times.

Before man entered the picture there was a balance of nature. Man has upset this to a great degree. In some areas where coyotes and foxes have been destroyed, plagues of rabbits have appeared. Streams where beavers were trapped out have eroded, and rain now runs off without being checked and so does not sink into the ground, thus lowering the underground water table. Extermination is a nasty word and a dangerous one when applied to wildlife.

My own interest in wild animals began when I lived on a farm in North Dakota more than half a century ago. As I recall it started when I was in the fourth or fifth grade. We lived in a hill country just south of the Canadian border which was drained by the Souris River. A meandering creek ran through our homestead. Money was something a Dakota farmer in those days saw very little of. The only way I could think of to earn a little pocket money was to run a trap-line along our creek.

I managed to save up enough money to buy six number one Newhouse steel traps. And that was when I started studying wild animals. I found there were many fur-bearing animals living along the creek but in order to catch them I had to know something about their habits. I knew there was no use trapping during the summer, so I spent most of my time tramping along the creek, watching for muskrats, mink, weasels, wolves, and coyotes, trying to find out their habits. Before the summer was over I had extended my interest to badgers and even flickertail gophers. I wasn't very expert at first and failed to learn much that I could have learned if I had known what I now know about observing animals.

Along that creek with its hazel-nut thickets, its plum groves, its tall ash and elm trees, and its heavy growth of willow, I met and watched the dwellers of the wild, the hunters and the hunted. They interested me from the start and after a time they fascinated me. For a number of winters I trapped, but finally I stopped catching and killing. I think it was because I found myself killing animals I had watched during the summer; they had become friends, even the bloodthirsty weasel aroused my admiration because of his courage.

Since those summer days trapping along the banks of that Dakota creek or sitting for hours watching a muskrat at work or a coyote stalking gophers, I have observed wildlife in many states and have written many books about animals big and small. I keep on seeking to learn their way of life. There is much I do not know about many of them, but I have learned some things which I enjoy sharing with others who have not had the opportunities I have had to watch creatures of the wild. This book describes many I have known.

TABLE OF CONTENTS

PHOTOGRAPHS

THE LIVING WILDERNESS

Blood on the Trail

Along the North Dakota creek I met a tribe that has ever since interested me: the weasel family. At first I knew only three of the tribe, the weasel, the mink, and the marten; later as my range widened I came to know the rest of them, the fisher, the wolverine, and the otter.

At first the weasel was of interest to me only during the winter when its brown summer coat had turned to pure white with a black tip on its long, slender tail. They were easy to watch because they seldom kept to cover and would defy me if I disturbed one of them. You could chase one of them down a gopher hole, but within minutes he'd pop out and hiss at you.

A weasel's favorite drink is the warm blood of its victim. I soon came to believe that a weasel kills for the sheer lust of killing. I have found muskrat dens where the whole family had been killed, but not even one eaten.

The weasel has always fascinated me. Its body is equipped for the profession of murder. It is slender and supple, every muscle and nerve is perfectly coordinated. It is so powerful that it can overcome animals many times its size. Its sharp teeth make its jaws fearsome weapons.

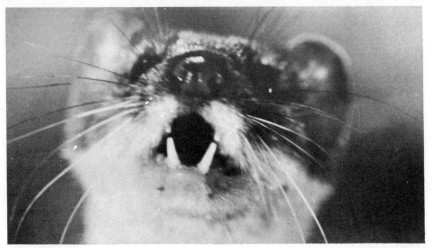

WEASEL   *Roy E. Disney*

I have seen a weasel strike down a big flickertail gopher before the terrified rodent could move a muscle. The sharp teeth flashed out so fast as they bit into the jugular vein that it was impossible to count the number of bites.

The weasel is certainly a game hog, but he does not lack courage. He kills by direct attack and not by stealth, exposing himself to fangs and claws. I have never seen a weasel turn tail and run away from a fight. Woe be to any big snake that tries to swallow him. His slashing fangs will cut through the head of the snake and the weasel will be free in a few seconds. He may not survive the ordeal but neither will the snake.

Many large animals are terrified when a weasel appears. Small brush rabbits have been known to drop dead of fright when faced by a weasel. In snow time I have checked the tracks of a weasel pursuing a large rabbit. In one case the rabbit escaped by making a maze of tracks, circling, doubling back, jumping sidewise. The weasel trails with his keen nose and not by sight, and if the rabbit is not panicked or paralyzed by fear, it sometimes escapes.

The weasel's lack of fear of man many times brings disaster to the little killer. I remember one night on the farm when we were all sitting down to supper. We suddenly heard a commotion

SHORT-TAILED WEASEL   *James R. Simon*

in the henhouse, loud squawking and excited cackling. We dashed outside with Dad in the lead.

When he burst into the henhouse, he found a weasel there. It had already killed four hens and was attacking mother's old brown rooster who weighed at least eight pounds as against the weasel's probable eight ounces. Dad had no weapon, but he didn't intend to let that weasel kill the rooster. He grabbed it with a bare hand and jerked it away from the rooster's neck, intending to hurl it against the henhouse wall. The weasel was too fast for him; it sank its fangs into his thumb and hung on. Dad came dancing out of the henhouse waving his arm wildly, jerking it in an effort to dislodge the weasel. It hung on until he twisted its head around and broke its neck.

I once had an experience illustrating this lack of fear of man. I had been fishing for brook trout on Mill Creek in western Colorado. I had caught quite a few fish just above the legal minimum of seven inches. Gourmets know that there isn't a tastier morsel than an eight- or nine-inch brook trout. I sat down on a grassy hummock to smoke my pipe, laying rod and creel on the grass beside me. A weasel came out of a thicket and stood sniffing eagerly. At the time, I thought it was a very young weasel; later

I was to learn that it was a least weasel or pigmy, which would never weigh over three or four ounces.

The little fellow suddenly darted to my fish basket and started trying to get inside it. I waved him off with my dip net. He backed away a few feet, and stood staring at me, hissing sharply. Thinking to have some sport with it, I took a fish from my basket, picked up my rod and fastened a fly hook into the mouth of the trout, then dangled it above the head of the weasel. It promptly leaped into the air. On the third try it sank its fangs into the gills of the fish, and with a big tug jerked it loose from the hook. I don't remember just how high that weasel jumped, but it was twice as high as I thought any weasel or other small creature could jump. I sat down and watched the weasel drag away a trout bigger than himself. I figured he had earned his meal.

A weasel probably should be considered a somewhat dull-witted fellow. When I was trapping I used a simple device for catching weasels. They were sure to follow the ice and snow-covered surface of the creek, making side trips in search of mice. I would gather a small bundle of twigs and make a V-shaped fence across the creek bed, one arm of the V facing up stream and one down. Where the points met I left an opening where I set my trap, not bothering to dust snow over it, just leaving it in the open. If a weasel came along, he just followed the fence to the opening and stepped into the trap. Few wild animals would be that dumb or careless, except the marten.

In seeking a home where a family can be raised, the weasel has little trouble. He does not dig or burrow, but can dispossess any digger who has labored to make a den.

Not much is on record regarding the weasel's mating habits, but ferrets have been closely observed and they are close kin. Their courtship is a savage affair. However, the pairs I have observed in the wood, and supposed were on their honeymoon, seemed to get along with no friction.

The weasel litter will be from one to ten. Though a blood-thirsty killer, the father seems domestically inclined. I found one den containing pink, wrinkled, toothless, and almost naked babies, being cared for by both mother and father.

Weasels undoubtedly do more good than harm to farmers. Their diet in winter is meadow mice, white-footed and other varieties. In summer they may add a few birds to this list and some rabbits.

The weasel pelt has always been much in demand. When I was trapping I got sixty cents for a prime weasel pelt while receiving ten cents for a prime muskrat pelt. Today prices of both are much higher.

Most of our North American weasels belong to the long-tail species. They have a wide range, although some naturalists doubt the least weasel is to be found on the Pacific Coast or west of the Rockies. However the one who stole my fish was living on the Western Slope of Colorado.

From my grade school days until today, I have been meeting weasels. The weasel is one wild animal you are apt to meet often. If you do take the time to watch him, he is a restless creature and something is bound to happen if you follow him and observe him.

The Crafty Killer

The prize pelt back in my boyhood trapping days was the mink. I was paid nine dollars for a prime pelt. When I caught a mink, which wasn't very often, I sharpened my pocket knife to a razor's edge, and spent a lot of time skinning my prize. That knife, a birthday gift from Dad, was an I.X.L. stock knife with a flesh blade of surgical steel, an expensive knife even in those days.

Skinning weasels and minks was a rugged job. I had to do it in our woodshed which, in winter, was a cold and draughty place. Mother refused to allow me to work in the warm kitchen.

"They stink," she would say. "And don't come into the house wearing your hunting clothes." I guess I did smell pretty strong when wearing my hunting pants and mackinaw. I often stuffed weasels into my coat pocket. They always died fighting a trap and froze stiff. My warm pocket helped thaw them out.

Both the mink and the weasel have a strong musk odor, more offensive than that of a skunk to many people. After I finished skinning my catch I had to change clothes in temperatures which often got down to forty below zero.

The mink is not a fast mover compared to the weasel, but its deadly thrusts are far from slow, and it is crafty and cunning, an aggressive killer who is trap-wise and difficult to take. In addition to being an expert hunter on land, it can catch many fish by outswimming them. In this it resembles the land otter.

The mink is larger than the weasel. I have caught mink that measured up to thirty inches over all, and weighed two pounds. This extra weight allows them to kill bigger animals than the weasel can handle and their bodies are as lithe, supple, and as well-coordinated as the weasel's.

A solitary mink will travel far and have many dens. It likes its meat fresh, and is very fond of muskrat. After breaking into a rat house and eating the inmates who are not lucky enough to escape, the mink is likely to make the house one of its dens.

You will easily identify the mink if you see one, by its long, slender body, its uniform russet color, and its long neck and upraised head.

I soon learned that minks like to run along fallen logs, especially if the end of the log is in the water. I also learned that this was no place to set a trap, for you can't conceal a trap from a mink if it is placed on a log. Nor was I any more successful in setting traps in mink dens. Traps had to be smoked, handled with gloves and well-concealed. I'd say that nine-tenths of the minks I caught were taken by accident, not through any cleverness on my part. I suspect I caught only the careless fellows, and there are always a few careless and unwary individuals who never die of old age. This is true of any species.

Because of its valuable pelt, minks are now raised on farms, but a domesticated mink tells us very little about the way of life of a wild mink. Born in captivity, they never get a chance to learn the ways of the wild. After a few generations their instincts become dulled; only the beautiful fur remains the same.

Minks like to drag their kill home and eat it in their den. As there is usually a spare den near any spot where the mink might make a kill, this offers little inconvenience. I once had a mink steal a big sucker I had tossed out on the bank. He did it without my seeing him and while I was seated fishing not a yard from where the fish lay. I later found the tail and part of the head in a den under a stump not more than fifty yards from where I caught the fish. I knew a mink had stolen my fish because he did not bother to cover up his tracks, he just padded along a muddy bank dragging my sucker. I lost his trail when he entered a thicket to reach his den. It was several days later when I found the den, and by that time the mink was probably miles away.

The mink is a graceful creature. I would not say it is shy, rather it is wary and very careful. Its mind seems to work much like that of its cunning big brother, the wolverine. A mink does not avoid people, except to make sure he is not seen. He may set up housekeeping in a shed or a barn if rats are plentiful. This will be a boon to the farmer unless the mink finds a way to get into the henhouse. Minks are as efficient rat killers as ferrets.

The musk of the mink is very offensive, but he does not spray it as the skunk does, so that it is not noticeable along streams or swamps. I do not recall that it bothered me any when I removed a pelt. Perhaps I was only thinking of the small fortune I was going to acquire when I shipped the skin to St. Louis.

During the mating season, which lasts for a couple of months, a male mink travels far and has many love affairs. He finally settles down with his last conquest and becomes a devoted father, just as the weasel does.

The family will consist of mother, father, and from four to eight youngsters. As they grow up they play rough games, scratching, biting, and mauling each other, spitting and snarling savagely. The parent minks like to play with the youngsters in the water, teaching them to catch fish and crawdads and to dig clams. The fighting play is probably "boot camp" training for later life. Young minks are well able to take care of themselves after they leave home.

Aside from trappers, the mink has few enemies who care to challenge it. His defense is a ripping, slashing attack.

Sanctuaries, parks, game refuges and the decline of trapping for fur have assured the continued existence of this elusive hunter. This is to my liking. It makes it possible for me to sit on the bank of a stream and dress out my catch of trout or bass or pike, keeping an eye open for a graceful brown creature who, if he is in the vicinity, will be sure to visit me. I know if there is a mink down-wind, he'll come to investigate, he just can't resist the smell of fish being dressed out. I'll probably see him, and I'll leave him a small feast.

The Solitary One

Another deadly killer of the weasel tribe is the fisher. This brownish black animal may weigh as much as twelve pounds or more (the record weight is eighteen). Few fishers remain except in the far north and perhaps in Pennsylvania and some of the New England states. If you do see one it will be where there is swampy ground, shallow lakes or slow-flowing streams. Its range once covered all of the United States, Canada, and Alaska. It was common on both coasts and in the mountains.

This forest hunter resembles the wolverine in build, but has all of the characteristics of a weasel in its broad head which tapers to a point, small eyes, long neck, and a slender body which ends in a bushy tail.

There has been some controversy over the popular name. The fisher does not actually fish though it does relish fish and will eat any it can find stranded on shoals or dead on banks.

The fisher is the swiftest member of the weasel clan; it can overtake the pine marten, who is faster than a red squirrel, and it can outrun a snowshoe rabbit. It is a good swimmer and will cross rivers and lakes which interfere with its pathway.

Ordinarily a fisher will not stand and fight, but if cornered it will whip any dog, even a tough bear-dog. Its climbing ability and agility in tree tops keeps the fisher safe from cougars and wolves but not from trappers and hunters. It is easy to spot in a tree and can be shot without any effort.

Like most members of the weasel tribe the fisher is not sociable or gregarious. But it has a voice. It may cry mournfully like a child or utter a short, sharp whistle or make a series of put-put sounds which cannot be heard more than a few feet away.

In many ways the fisher resembles the pine marten, possessing many of the marten's tricks and manners. It has musk glands which it never seems to use. It is probably the most active of the tree-climbers. It can leap forty feet in a descending jump, but usually comes down the trunk of a tree head first. If it could swim as well as the land otter it would be the most wonderfully equipped animal in the woods. It has plenty of courage and has been known to attack boys with dogs who annoyed it. Like the wolverine, the fisher has been known to follow a trap-line and destroy the catch. Once having found a trap-line, the fisher has to be destroyed or the trapper will be forced to change to a new locality. Catching a fisher in a trap or dead-fall is not easy. They are sure to examine the set made for them and refuse to approach the bait. They know that a trap with an animal caught in it is not dangerous to them. If they find a trap with a live marten in it they will kill the marten and eat it.

It does little good to bury a trap set to catch a fisher. The fisher is too clever to be tricked by a hidden trap, but like many smart ones, it can be caught. It may steal the fish used as bait a dozen times and then get careless or decide the trap is not dangerous and step into it, even though the trap has not been buried or hidden. The fisher cannot profit by this experience; he has never learned to sever a leg above the trap jaws as some fur-bearers do, which is the only way to escape from the cruel jaws of a steel trap.

The fisher is mostly a night hunter which is fortunate for the squirrels and the martens. Few squirrels or martens escape if the fisher sees them. A red squirrel may save himself by staying in a tree top and leaping from twig to twig, always picking branches too slender to support the weight of the fisher, but very few squirrels will do this; they panic and leap to the ground where the swift fisher soon overtakes them. The pine marten is too heavy for twig-hopping and has to leap from limb to limb and from tree to tree. At this game it is no match for the fisher and is soon caught.

The fisher is credited with being one predator who will kill and eat a porcupine with no ill effects. The fisher simply flips the porcupine over on his back and attacks the belly, which is un-protected by quills, and the fisher does not devour the quill-studded skin as does the wolverine.

The fisher will devour anything it can catch and kill, but mice furnish a large portion of its diet, which is in keeping with the habits of all predators big and small. There is always an in-exhaustible supply of mice of various varieties everywhere the fisher goes. By night and day they swarm through the meadows and thickets. Catching a mouse is easy for an animal as agile as a fisher. But to satisfy the needs of an animal as active as a fisher requires the catching of hundreds of mice in a single night.

The fisher kills foxes, raccoons, and occasionally a lynx. As is usually the case with members of the bloodthirsty weasel clan, when there is a fight the victor devours the vanquished. In the case of the swift-running fox, the chase will be long, perhaps last-ing a full day. The greater endurance of the fisher will finally force the fox to enter a den or hole which the slim-bodied fisher can easily enter. Then the chase ends very quickly.

In a fight between a raccoon and a fisher the fight may be a long one, because the raccoon is not an easy opponent to over-come. There will be a desperate, slashing encounter on the ground because the raccoon is a slow tree-climber. Nor has the raccoon the speed to get away from his attacker. He will make a running fight out of it, making a stand when overtaken, slashing and ripping until he shakes loose for another short run. In the end the relentless fisher will win.

There is one trait the fisher shares with all of the big cats; it dislikes clamor and noise. A small yapping or howling dog will tree a fisher the same as it would tree a cougar. But cornered on the ground, no dog has any business tackling a fisher. Ernest Thompson Seton has recorded a story in his *Lives of Game Animals* about an Indian who owned a bulldog he thought could lick any animal it met. One day the Indian saw a fisher enter a hollow log. He sent the bulldog into the log and laid his rifle aside while he sat on the log waiting for the bulldog to emerge with the fisher in his mouth. The bulldog burst out of the log with the fisher raking his rump. The fisher vanished into the woods before the Indian could reach his rifle. And the bulldog refused to take up the fisher's trail.

Little is known of the mating habits and den of the fisher. It has been established that the mother leaves her blind and helpless babies when they are less than a week old to go out and find a new mate. However, she will be away from them for only one night or two.

The youngsters' eyes open at the age of seven weeks, at which time they leave the den and follow their mother. Her brood will number from one to four. After two years of wandering the youngsters will seek mates.

The story of the fisher, like that of the weasel, is pretty much a recital of killing. There is no time for play or lazing on grassy banks; the romance period lasts only three days, for there is no time to waste at all. The fisher just lopes on and on, looking for game.

The Tree-minded Weasel

The pine marten is a deadly enemy of the squirrel. It is a weasel that has taken to tree-hunting and it is an expert; only the fisher can outclass it in a tree. When it meets a fisher it suffers the same fate as a squirrel does when it meets a marten. Perhaps this is poetic justice.

The marten has a coat of rich yellowish or deep brown fur which is a staple in the fur trade. The marten has all of the features of the weasel tribe and will measure up to twenty inches in length and may weigh as much as three pounds. It may be found wherever there are conifers. The range preferred by the red squirrels is the range preferred by the pine marten. In my youth I did not see many martens because few pines grew in the Dakota hill country. Later I found them in the forests of the West; the same is true of the eastern forests.

My first experience with a family of martens was when I spotted two furry little heads poking out of a woodpecker's hole high up on the trunk of a dead tree. I tried to climb the tree but wasn't able to reach the den. I was probably lucky. If the mother marten had caught me stealing her babies, I would have been in trouble. But I wanted one very much for a pet.

The pine marten population varies, rising for a few years and then declining. There will be eight years of increase, then they begin to decline in numbers. This is a mystery which has not been solved. No known plague descends upon them, nor can the decline be attributed to lack of food.

A marten has the deceptively big-eyed look of a squirrel, but none of the squirrel's temperament; it is a savage soul and seems to hate every other animal, except its mate during the mating season. Thus it shows only a couple of weeks of amiability during a year, and that is sure to be broken if the male meets another male at that time.

The marten moves like the mink and the fisher, taking thirty-inch bounds, only slowing to a walk when it wants to investigate something. When a marten sets off on a hunt he will leap from tree to tree, but will descend to the ground if the trees are scattered.

The marten is not quite as single-minded as the fisher. It occasionally takes time out for a few tricks. One marten was seen playing tag with a coyote that was trying to catch it. It did not take to a tree where it would have been safe, but ducked around logs and through them, making the coyote look foolish. The pine marten seems to be one weasel who upon occasion has a sense of humor. Young martens certainly play together constantly.

In many areas of the country the marten has vanished along with the forests. Only the parks and the refuges, along with forested areas where conifers still grow, offer refuge for this small hunter. I am sure Pennsylvania has a marten population in its forests. The Pennsylvania Game Commission has one of the finest game management programs in this country.

As with the fisher, mice are an important part of the marten's diet, but it kills many squirrels, chipmunks, birds, frogs, toads, and insects. But mice are in biggest supply in mother nature's cupboard.

The marten dislikes water as much as a domestic cat does and avoids taking a bath. They dislike it so much that they will stay in their dens for days if it is raining. Only hunger forces them out into the rain for a fast foraging expedition. But they like to take sun baths. Trappers have been heard to grumble because the fur was sun bleached, or so they thought.

Man, of course, is the chief enemy of the marten. Few men meet a marten in the woods without trying to kill it. This attitude, I feel, is slowly changing, but no animal wearing so valuable a coat can escape being hunted. Another way man acts as an enemy is in starting forest fires. The majority of such fires are started because of carelessness on the part of man. With large areas denuded of pine, fir, hemlock, and spruce the marten is homeless, even if he escapes the flames. The fisher is a deadly enemy of the marten, but there are not many fishers in a given area. The lynx and great horned owl are also enemies, but probably do not take a heavy toll.

The mating moon rises in mid-summer and lasts about a month. Little is known about the courting habits of martens, but development of the young before birth requires a considerable length of time; the young do not appear until nine months after the mating season.

The den will be in a hollow tree or a deserted flicker's nest. This large woodpecker builds a roomy house. The dens will be lined with moss and grass. The young number from one to five. Their eyes will not open until they are six weeks old, but they will be active and demanding even though they cannot see. In about three months they will have equalled the size of their mother, and will leave in the fall to go their own way.

Female martens are smaller than the males, but they are more aggressive and savage, and they are sure to be more nervous and restless.

Anyone who watches a marten in a tree or in a cage will get an impression of tireless energy. They race up and down limbs, leap from branch to branch for hours without stopping. They

MARTEN   *Hugh A. Wilmar*

do the same when caged. Such activity calls for plenty of food so the marten spends a lot of time chasing squirrels, mice, and other small game. In areas where snowshoe rabbits abound, much time is spent chasing and catching them.

In a tree a marten will do endless acrobatic stunts. They seem to be constantly keeping in shape, practicing just as a circus acrobat practices. There is one odd thing about the way of life of a marten. Its range is that of the red squirrel but it does not invade the domain of the gray squirrel. This seems strange because the gray and the fox squirrel are more numerous on their range than are the red squirrels on their range. They are bigger than the reds, the martin could enter their dens, and they would make a more satisfying meal than the red squirrel.

Martens hunt both during the day and at night. Some woodfolk contend that the marten hunts only at night. That is because you seldom see this fellow. You have to follow the rules for observing wildlife strictly or you will miss him. Actually, the marten hunts more by day than at night; otherwise it would not be able to catch squirrels, chipmunks, and yellow-bellied whistlers.

Trappers say that the marten's hankering to know about everything, its desire to see, smell, and find out, is a serious failing which often leads to its downfall, but it is also a trait which indicates high intelligence. If a hunter has trouble in drawing a bead on a marten leaping from branch to branch all he has to do is whistle and the inquisitive marten will sit and peer down, thus furnishing a stationary target. If a marten is peering out of a hole in the trunk of a tree where its body would drop back and be lost if shot, the hunter simply walks around the tree and the inquisitive marten comes out in the open to see what is going on. They undoubtedly examine everything they come upon as does the raccoon.

In their restlessness they are like the otter, although if an otter tried to keep up with a marten it would soon become exhausted. However there is a kinship between them in many ways, as we shall see when we study otters.

Martens make fine and playful pets. But pine martens should be taken very young if you want them for pets. Taken young they become very much attached to those they know. A grown wild marten would rather bite than do anything else and few of them can be safely handled or even touched.

Naturalists and outdoor lovers have often been laughed at by people who have lived all of their lives close to the haunts where martens live in considerable numbers. There are no martens, they say, because they have never seen one. They have simply blundered through their woods and missed the elusive martens. Even if the marten is chasing a rabbit he manages to keep to cover and move without being seen. One trapper who had caught as many as eleven martens in one day had seen only three free and alive in the woods during his lifetime. Of course, he wasn't out marten watching; he was only interested in dead martens.

In parks where they are protected the marten will show himself, and even come into your camp to snatch any bit of food it can get hold of. It is so quick and agile that it may even get the pork-chop off your plate before you get seated.

Like the beaver the marten will eventually be protected, at least by closed seasons. This will be fine for those who love animals. The ladies could help if they would let Du Pont fabricate their elegant fur coats out of synthetic material and not demand murders as the price of a neck-piece.

These ladies have put a high price on this small hunter's head. With a pelt worth fifty dollars, life is a hazardous venture for a pine marten. Most of these furs now come from Alaska. The total value of the American and Canadian catch was over a half million dollars just a few years back. Thirty thousand martens died to decorate American women.

Maker of Tall Tales

One of my first books was *Carcajou*, a story about a wolverine. I searched diligently for information which I thought was reliable, going back to the reports made by the first men who saw this animal. Much of the material I could not believe, even though it was written by reputable observers. After twenty-five years and considerable intimate observation of this giant weasel, I am convinced I rejected some authentic material. My book was rejected by many big publishing houses, and the reason was always the same; no one could be expected to believe the things I was sure the wolverine had done. Finally The Caxton Printers, a small western publisher, brought the book out. It is still in print.

More tall tales have been written about this lonely, bad-tempered killer than any other that walks on four feet. It has inspired more fantastic stories than any other creature living in modern times. One old-time writer who had observed the wolverine stated as a fact that the beast, when it came upon the carcass of a big animal, would gorge itself, then squeeze its body between two trees growing close together, in this manner emptying itself so that it could gorge some more.

The feats of strength and the savagery of the wolverine do not need to be enlarged upon. The truth in his case is hard to believe. This twenty-five pound weasel has killed deer and moose, and has driven cougars and wolves and bears away from their own kills. No animal wants to tangle with him because he will die ripping and slashing rather than break off a fight.

Carcajou might well have been fathered by a bear and mothered by a skunk. He looks like a small bear and smells like a skunk. Even so, he has markings and many of the physical traits of a weasel. He has been called "skunk bear," "Indian Devil," "Glutton," and worse by trappers and others who have come in contact with him.

Many northern Indians believe that he is the reincarnation of a dead trapper who has to do penance for the many animals he killed during his lifetime. That is how he knows all of the trapper's tricks. There was a time when an Indian trapper would free a wolverine caught in his trap, fearing to kill it.

The flesh of the wolverine is so rank that it is never eaten by man except when he is faced with starvation. In such a case the motto is that of the pioneer mountain man: "Meat is meat." On the trapper's trail in the 1830's a starving man would gladly sit beside his campfire and devour a roast shank of wolverine.

Consider the strength and ferocity of a weasel weighing eight ounces and multiply it by fifty and you have a wolverine. Its gait is slow and bear-like, and it has very poor eyesight. Almost any animal can run away from it, but few can stay out in front once the wolverine has taken up its trail. Like the Canadian Mounties the wolverine never gives up once he has started to track down a victim. He makes up for lack of good vision and speed by strategy. Deep snow works for him by slowing down deer and other fleet-footed animals, as do tree limbs or rock ledges over a trail from which he can hurl himself down upon the back of an animal as big as an elk.

A wolverine will often halt and sit up, shading its eyes with a paw, as it stares at some object that has attracted its attention, but which it cannot see clearly. This bad vision is not a serious defect because the wolverine has a keen sense of smell and excellent hearing.

At one time the wolverine roamed most of the northern parts of the United States and Canada. Now it is very rare in the United States; the last one I heard about was killed in Idaho about fifteen years ago.

At the present time there are a few domesticated wolverines. There was a wolverine farm in Sweden, which is probably still there, and a Canadian had two wolverines that could be handled after a fashion. One of the pair recently died. These wolverines were used very effectively and realistically in a Walt Disney wildlife feature picture. They both displayed all of the meanness and savagery of wild wolverines when they came in contact with wolves and other animals, and they settled an argument which was being carried on in Seton's time: they proved that a wolverine can climb a tree in a very effective manner. However, a wolverine is not recommended as a pet. It is difficult to tame to a point where it would be safe to have around.

Not much is known about the courtship of this killer. It is agreed that it takes place in March or April and that the young arrive about three months later. The honeymoon is short, and the male soon goes his solitary way, though a few observers report that the pair stays together, and a few believe that they mate for life. I am inclined to believe that the courtship is brief. Seton stresses mating for life wherever there is any evidence of it between wild animals. It is a nice theory, and in some cases there is support for it, at least evidence that some animals do stay together for a number of seasons.

Quite a few wolverine dens have been found and examined. None was found in hollow trees; most were built in caves or under ledges. The mother does not seem to make much preparation as the nests are crude and poorly lined.

The young number from two to five, with an average litter numbering two or three. They have woolly coats, light brown or even white in color.

A wolverine mother with young is far more dangerous than a bear with cubs or a mother cougar with kittens. In one case an Indian boy was attacked by a mother wolverine. She rushed at him with bared fangs, her eyes blazing, and uttering sounds like the growling of a bear. The boy saved himself by hastily climbing a tree. In this nest there were four young ones about the size of muskrats. Seton reports that Bellalise, a half-breed Chippewa, told him that he shot an infuriated mother wolverine when she charged him furiously, screaming at him in a coughing manner. She had three cubs in her nest. In each case the intruder would have been badly mauled or even killed, if unarmed or unable to reach a tree.

The cubs stay with their mother until they are almost as large as she. They are apt to leave her late in the fall or early in the winter. This is the only time in their lives when they will be at all sociable. After the family breaks up, each goes his solitary way, a loner for the rest of his life.

The wolverine's food is mainly meat, but he will eat anything that pleases his sensitive nose or arouses his appetite. That is the only test he applies; it smells good, so he eats it. Here again, mice are high on the list. The big animals eaten are usually cripples or those made helpless by deep snow. Anyone who has seen a doe lying helpless in six feet of loose snow will understand. More than once I have skied up to a buck or a doe exhausted by trying to reach a wind-swept ridge where food was available.

The eating capacity of the wolverine has been grossly exaggerated. It undoubtedly is a glutton, but a wolverine obviously cannot devour a whole deer or mountain sheep at one meal. It may make a bed close to the kill and stay there until the carcass is all eaten, or it may cache the meat. It does not have to worry about foxes or coyotes stealing its cache; it smears the meat with a musk so vile that no other predator would touch it. It is prob-

WOLVERINE   *Tom McHugh*

able that the wolverine considers this a tasty sort of wild Worcestershire sauce.

Any carnivore who does not hibernate will eat hugely. In the summer, securing meat is not a big problem; the wolverine can pull down a fawn, or catch a jack rabbit, and every meadow swarms with mice, but when winter locks the slopes and ridges under deep snow, one meal may have to sustain a hunter for many days. Actually, as we study the eating habits of this big weasel, we find that kills of big game are made only when the wolverine is desperately hungry; its main diet is ground squirrels, mice, and lemmings.

But there are a number of well verified accounts of big game kills which show how fierce and savage this hunter is. As I have said, they must be considered rare instances, but they did happen. A Hudson's Bay trader was camped on the shore of a lake with a companion. They saw a caribou rush out of the woods with a black object on its back. It plunged into the lake they were camped by, and started swimming toward the far shore. They got into their canoe and gave chase, eager to secure camp meat. Overtaking the caribou, one of the men shot the animal on its back. They left it floating in the water while they pursued the caribou. When they reached the caribou it was swimming feebly, and the water around its neck and shoulders was bloody. They shot it and made a line fast around its neck to tow it to shore. On the way back they picked up the black animal. It was a very large wolverine.

A trained observer in the Canadian Geological Survey has described an incident he witnessed. He and the crew he was working with came upon a three-year-old bull moose lying helpless in deep snow. They shot it and discovered a large hole torn in its backbone. There was a great deal of moose hair scattered about. The tracks at the scene showed that the bull moose had had a savage fight with a wolverine. They even saw the wolverine but failed to get it. It is certain that the wolverine would have dined on moose meat for a long time, if they hadn't appeared and scared it away.

Everyone who has studied the wolverine admits that he is king. He demands and gets the trail when he meets a bear. No sensible wolf or cougar dares oppose him. The porcupine may leave a few quills in him as he slaps it aside, and may even bring disaster if the wolverine is starving. If he bolts down the quill-pig, hide and all, the quills may become arrows of death which will be a terrible, lingering demise. What he does when he meets a skunk has not been recorded, but as he produces a much ranker musk he may simply make a meal of the skunk.

The amazing strength of the wolverine has been well recorded. Samuel Hearne, the great Canadian explorer, tells of a Hudson's Bay woodpile which was upset by a wolverine seeking to get at supplies the men had concealed inside of it, knowing that if a wolverine came along he would break into the cabin while they were in town. This pile consisted of a winter's supply of logs and was more than seventy yards around and thirty feet high. The logs were big trees, mostly water-soaked driftwood.

When the men returned they were amazed to see that one or more wolverines had scattered the logs and had devoured all of the meat, cheese, geese, and venison. Bags of flour and oatmeal had been ripped open and their contents scattered over the snow.

The wolverine's courage is no less than its strength. One medium-sized wolverine took possession of a deer an Indian had shot. It stood on the carcass and defied the Indian until he shot it. On several occasions wolverines have chased a five-hundred-pound bear away from a carcass. California rangers reported watching a wolverine drive a cougar away from the carcass of a deer the cat had killed. Trappers all agree that this fellow is the toughest animal there is to kill. It can't be accomplished with a club alone; the finish has to be done with a knife.

Just how wise is this king? The answer is that he is diabolically wise as far as trappers are concerned. If a wolverine invades their cabin, they can expect him to carry off every piece of frozen meat, bacon, and ham in the larder and bury each piece in a separate spot in the snow after smearing each piece with rank musk. The trapper might follow the wolverine's track in the snow and recover the meat, but he could not eat it.

Once a wolverine finds a trapper's marten run he will pay nightly visits to the trap-line, destroying and eating every marten he finds trapped. He may even spring a trap and drag it a hundred yards, smear it with musk and bury it deep in a snow bank.

One wolverine discovered a gun-set that had been rigged to put an end to his depredations. A fish-line was attached to a tempting rabbit and led to the trigger of a shotgun loaded with buckshot. The wolverine studied the setup and cautiously cut the line and made off with the rabbit.

The urge to steal things and carry them off is strong in the wolverine. He will pack off things he cannot eat, and certainly has no use for: blankets, guns, axes, anything that strikes his fancy. In this he is like the trade rat, only he never leaves anything in exchange for what he takes.

When I wrote my book, *Carcajou*, I felt I couldn't make him a hero so I used him as the Nemesis to foil the villains. If I ever write another wolverine book I shall make him the hero. I have come to feel that there is something heroic about him.

Dolphins in Fur Coats

It was years after I left the Dakota hill country that I met and got acquainted with otters. Once I met them and knew them, I felt it was hardly right to classify them as members of the weasel tribe. These delightfully frivolous, fun-loving animals should not have to share the bad name of the weasel clan. I will quote what Ernest Thompson Seton said about them.

"But of all the beasts whose lives I have tried to tell there is one that stands forth, the Chevalier Bayard of the wilds, without fear and without reproach. That is the otter, the joyful, keen, and fearless otter; mild and loving to his own kind, and gentle to his neighbor of the stream; full of play and gladness in his life, full of courage in his stress; ideal in his home, steadfast in death, the noblest little soul that ever went four-footed through the woods."

That about sums up the otter, a fellow with a fine fur coat, perhaps four feet long and weighing about twenty-five pounds.

I have written many stories, a television script, and a book about otters. They intrigue me and I love them. The last story I did about them was for a Walt Disney Productions TV film. They make fine actors but they kept the cameramen in a tizzy because they never pause long enough for a pose or a reaction shot. Quite often when the scenes arrived at the studio and the film was developed there was no otter in the frame at all, just a grassy bank or a snow drift with otter tracks on it. The otter had decided to have a look at something in back of him and had flipped and gone in the opposite direction from the one the director expected and wanted.

I have often speculated on why this member of the weasel family managed to become so different from the bandits and bloodthirsty members of the tribe. Somewhere, far back in the past, the dark brown fellow decided to set a good example; perhaps he wanted to restore weasels to good grace in the eyes of the world. There is no denying that he is a weasel. He is long-bodied and formed like an oversized weasel, flat-headed, slender-bodied, with a tapering tail and short legs; all four feet are webbed. But the similarity ends there.

To know it, all you have to do is to watch a family of otters playing follow-the-leader in a pool. Around and around they go, traveling with amazing speed, each following the other. They are responsible for tales told by early explorers who saw them playing in a moonlit pond. The explorers reported seeing long sea-serpents in certain lakes and rivers of the middle west and east.

The intelligence of an animal may be measured by its curiosity. The otter has a very large bump of curiosity, exceeded only by that of the raccoon.

If you want to delight an otter, give him a silver dollar or a sardine can. He is likely to play catch with the dollar, tossing it from hand to hand for an hour before tossing it into the water and diving to recover it before it reaches the bottom of the pool. The sardine can will get the same treatment.

In the summer-time, otters make mud slides on the steep banks of a stream and scoot down them into the water. In winter-time they make snow slides and toboggan down them. When they aren't fishing, they are playing.

When playing in the water, the otters leap and duck and dive like dolphins. They are the fastest swimmers of all the land animals, and are credited with being able to catch the fleetest trout, even the flashy rainbow. Some observers doubt this and suggest that the otter chases the trout into hiding under a bank or rock and then catches it. It is probably true that otters catch more of the slower fish like suckers than they do the speedsters like the rainbow. But I have seen an otter surface with a rainbow in its jaws. Fish certainly do make up a large portion of their diet. They are seldom found far from a lake or stream.

Otters are sometimes guilty of taking more fish than they can eat. In this they are like human anglers. The difference is that otters do not hate fishermen though most fishermen hate otters. It is man's way to hate any creature that poaches on the domain he considers his private property. But mostly the otter goes fishing only when he is hungry. If fish are plentiful, however, he may not eat all of his catch.

The first naturalists who studied them were puzzled by the disappearance of otters during the coldest winter months. Some suggested that the otter hibernated. Quite a few trappers believed that they migrated to the sea, that the river otter and the sea otter were one and the same. Later studies cleared up the mystery. Otters winter along streams where they can be sure of getting fish. They can do very well under the ice even though they do have to have air to breathe. Dens in the banks, with runways opening under the ice, furnish air pockets for them. It has been discovered that an otter has another way of getting air while under the ice. Air breathed out at a depth rises in bubbles and as it does oxygen from the water is restored to it. The otter rises and breathes in the bubble trapped against the ice.

No water animal, even the beaver, ever leaves the water and exposes himself to sub-zero weather. The mink is careful to dry himself before venturing into freezing air, the otter does this in his bank den, where body heat from himself and his mate will warm the snug den.

But otters do like snow, and avoid it only during the bitterest weather. A family will slide downhill on the snow for hours. When they move over loose, deep snow they propel themselves toboggan-wise, or dive deep and come up yards away from the spot where they ducked under the surface. This trick serves them well if they are attacked by a coyote or big cat. They keep the enemy guessing. When they pop up the killer plunges toward the spot, but can't tell in what direction the elusive otter has gone when it again ducks under the snow. If the going is downhill the otter scoots along on its breast and belly, sending showers of snow into the air. On open ice they act like small boys, they run and then slide.

No animal is equal in all elements. The otter is the slowest of the weasel family on land and the swiftest in the water, but they do travel over-land in seeking new fishing water. In the spring an otter family is likely to take a long journey which will be a great circle tour that will bring them back to their home area. These are fun journeys with long stops at streams or ponds where the fishing is good and banks are steep enough to allow them to make mud slides. They may linger at a lake or pond for days when there is a moon to give them light for their games.

The social instincts of the otter are better developed than in any other member of the weasel tribe, except the sea otter. Two or three are seen together more often than one alone. They have a voice and seem to communicate with each other. They emit satisfied grunts, chirpy bird-like calls and shrill half-screams. The latter will carry as far as a mile.

Otters are accused of being cowardly. This is not true; the otter does not have a yellow streak, it never shuns a fight, and never surrenders. If trapped and unable to free a paw, it fights the trap savagely, and usually kills itself in a short time.

But the otter does not go around looking for a fight. If he meets a bristling dog, he will advance with his nose thrust out. If the dog allows the otter to touch his snout, the otter will treat the dog as a friend. But if the dog starts a fight, he will be worsted and badly chewed up. In my otter picture the script called for a series of scenes where two big, well trained hounds were supposed to attack a young otter in a pond. Both dogs and the otter were well protected from harm. The dogs eagerly leaped into the water to attack. Within a few minutes they were crawling up the bank, completely licked by one small, muzzled otter. It was impossible to get them out of their crates for a re-take. They cowered there until the otter was taken away.

One big otter has been known to invade a beaver pond and stand off a whole colony of beavers who are not weak antagonists when in the water, and when their home pond is being invaded. We can only speculate as to why this otter was so pugnacious. Many times a beaver pond will swarm with brook trout and this may give us a clue, the otter just went fishing and the beavers resented his intrusion.

I am a champion of otters, but they do cheat anglers out of a few trout, pike, and pickerel and undoubtedly a few bass. No one who loves nature is upset by this, and few who watch otters fail to be in sympathy with them and to admire them. Many nature lovers believe almost any wild animal is beautiful, but it is the otter that is most vividly remembered.

In selecting a den there is always one requirement which will not be ignored, the den must be close to a stream or pond so that there can be an under-water entrance. An outside escape opening may be made, but the main entrance is always through a tunnel under water. Thus the mother, when she approaches her den does not reveal its presence to prowling killers. Young otters are defenseless for some time, and mother likes her freedom to play and fish with father. The young spend quite a bit of time alone in the den.

Anyone who appreciates romance and affection, mother love and devotion, can find it in the home life of an otter family. Father shares the protection and the play time. He is not as close to the young while they are in the den, but he is always on guard out in the pond, and he hunts and fishes for the family.

Young otters are dependent on their mother for a longer period than most youngsters in the wild. Their eyes do not open for thirty days and they do not enter the water until they are at least two months old. Though they will grow up to be the greatest of swimmers, they have to learn to swim. In this they are taught as carefully as any four-year-old child is taught by loving parents. Father helps mother with the lessons.

Learning to swim is a slow process with the young otters. They are actually afraid of the water and have to be tricked into entering it. For a few days their mother lets them play on the bank. This is their first outing away from the den. Here we probably discover the reason for the outside exit; in order to leave the den the babies do not have to enter the water. They find many things to examine. They cry loudly when the mother leaves them to take a swim or catch a fish, but she never goes far. She does not leave them alone for long, because this is a time when any predator that happened along would snap them up. It is a critical time in the life of any wild baby.

When the mother returns to the bank she will let one or both of them climb on her back, and she will take them for a ride along the shore. The next step is for her to enter the water with one of them on her back. The baby will cling to her and wail as she swims around. If there are two youngsters the father may take the other one for a ride. Finally the mother dives and leaves the little otter floundering and struggling. She surfaces at once and lets the youngster climb on her back. This is repeated until the youngsters discover that they can stay afloat and paddle on their own. After that they are soon swimming and have come to like the water. She and father keep working with them, tempting them to dive noiselessly, to creep along on the bottom when stalking a fish, to stir up mud with their webbed feet, and to thrust their heads into the mud to catch eels, which are the tastiest items on an otter's list of foods.

Learning to swim and hunt takes time, but after they have learned, the youngsters stay with mother and father until she decides to raise another family. or they feel the urge to have families of their own. If you see three or four otters together it is not necessarily correct to suppose that this is mother, father, and two youngsters; the group may be just mother and her young.

Among almost all wild animals the young play and wrestle or stage sham battles, but after they grow up they cease to play at all or do so only on rare occasions. Otters continue to play, however, even when old. This seems to have nothing to do with instincts of feeding, fighting or multiplying; it is done simply for amusement.

Running an otter down with a half dozen big hound dogs is considered sport by some men. On land a little otter has no chance at all against a pack of dogs. If deep water can be reached it will be more than a match for a pack of dogs. It is difficult to understand what satisfaction men can get out of watching a pack of dogs destroy a beautiful creature like an otter. In a bull fight the bull has at least a chance to kill some of his tormentors and sometimes does. Perhaps it is because the otter always displays courage when faced with overwhelming odds, and the fact that he dies fighting.

Otters kept in captivity as pets always show affection for each other and display none of the jealousy common to most other wild animals kept as pets. There is a case on record where an otter has mourned for weeks over the loss of a companion or mate. No human consolation will help, nor will the attempts of other otters to give sympathy. Manley Hardy insists that otters will bury one of their group that has been accidentally killed, by covering the body with sticks and leaves.

We have long been told that wild animals are dumb brutes. But if we take the trouble to know them we will be forced to change our thinking about them. There are traits in all of them that are very close to the motivations and drives which govern and direct our own lives.

Down to the Sea

It is interesting to speculate that hundreds or thousands of years ago a pair of weasels decided to get as far away as possible from their bloodthirsty kin, and their progeny became sea otters. A pair of river otters may have set out to find a distant island where they would never meet any others of the weasel clan. Or they may have drifted down a river to the ocean and decided to stay there. When they reached the Pacific Ocean they headed north along the coast until they came to islands of their liking where they stayed.

The robe of the sea otter is the most beautiful fur the world has ever seen. The undercoat is unusually fine, soft and dense, about three quarters of an inch long and overlain by long guard hairs. Close to the roots, the hair is white or silvery. The fur is always prime. This robe is so loose it could serve for an animal twice the size of the sea otter.

The discovery by Russians of this fabulous fur brought ships and hunters to the islands and the shores of Alaska. During the first year after the discovery it is said that five thousand sea otters were killed. The method was simple. The hunters just walked ashore and clubbed the trusting animals to death. The following year they could secure only a thousand skins.

Hunters swarmed over every reef and island. Within five years hardly a single otter could be found in the north, and the quest was pushed south along the Pacific coast. The quest took the Russians as far south as California where they established headquarters on the Russian River. The Spanish, who claimed the territory, tried to drive them out, but were unsuccessful. It was the otters themselves and the pocket gophers that made them leave. They destroyed all of the otters, and the pocket gophers destroyed the Russian crops. They finally gave up and left.

The way of life of the sea otter changed as it fought to survive. From a land-living, gentle, and trusting creature, it changed to a sea animal, shunning the land, living its life in the offshore kelp beds, even bearing its young in a bed of coarse sea weeds. Now rigidly protected, the sea otter is making a comeback and may be seen along the Pacific coast from California to Alaska.

Sea otters like company and if you spot one you are apt to see a number of them. They are graceful swimmers and divers but they spend much time just floating on their backs with forepaws clasped over their breasts.

The sea otter's food is found on the floor of the ocean, and he may dive as deep as a hundred feet to get it. Down he goes with strings of silver bubbles marking his course. In the murky depths he gropes about seeking a squid or a sea-urchin or an abalone. He need not hurry because he can stay under water as much as five minutes.

No one knows how an otter can pry an abalone loose from a rock. Fishermen use a heavy iron bar to do it. There is one case on record where a Chinese tried to pull an abalone off a rock with his hands at low tide. The powerful muscle of the abalone closed on his finger and he was unable to jerk loose. When the tide came in he was drowned.

The otter lies on his back and uses his breast as a table when he dines. He smashes the shell of his catch and picks out the meat with his forepaws. One observer tells of seeing a gull swoop down and peck the otter on a very sensitive part of its body making it

SEA LION HAREM   *Harry W. May (Copyright 1948, Fouke Fur Co.)*

spill the squid it was eating. The gull snatched up the squid and flew away.

Sea otters pair and stay together, probably for life. The love of a mother for her baby is almost human. She fondles it and will mourn for weeks if it dies. When she dives for food she will anchor it to a mass of kelp with a tendril. She will spend hours tumbling it into deep water and teaching it to swim. She will croon to it and sing as she floats on her back with the baby cradled on her furry breast.

Sea otters resemble porpoises when they frolic in a band. Away they go on a fast race, diving, leaping into the air, turning somersaults, backs up, bellies up, it does not matter. They play mostly in rough weather even in a heavy storm. In calm weather only the youngsters frolic.

The big, black eyes of the otter are keen, their sense of smell is the best of any of the sea animals. The otter has need of good eyesight, smell, and hearing. China sharks have to be spotted in time to allow the otter to reach a kelp bed. The same is true of the killer whale who is the otter's most dangerous enemy now that man no longer hunts it. When the sea otter spots tall, black fins cutting through the water, it darts into a kelp bed and lies there. The killers do not like to get entangled in the kelp. There is one other trick the otter can use. If far from a kelp bed he may lie like a drifting log, letting the stupid whale pass without noticing him.

The savage storms of the north are another enemy. The otters have to stay awake and battle seething currents to keep from being dashed on the shore and smashed on the rocks.

The Russians were the first to enact laws to protect the sea otter. Later a treaty was signed between Great Britain, Russia, Japan, and the United States setting up rigid protection. This was done in 1911 and it is one treaty Russia has lived up to. The Russians have always cooperated in enforcing this treaty.

The restoration of the sea otter is a shining example of what man can do to preserve the beauty of nature and to save nature's children for future generations.

Every summer hordes of other sea dwellers head north from coves and bays along the Pacific coast. Most of them have a common destination, two mist-shrouded islands, St. George and St. Paul of the Pribilof group in the Bering sea.

It is a strange and interesting phenomenon, perhaps millions of animals all headed for a rendezvous on two small islands. They swim swiftly past hundreds of inviting islands and drive on to the north.

Fairly warm ocean currents flow from the south and these currents cause the islands to be shrouded in mist. Fur seals live most of their lives at sea. The short northern summer is the exception, they spend all of it on the two rocky islands. The bulls do not even leave the islands to fish, they eat nothing during the summer. The cows and the pups put out to sea for short fishing trips, but not the bulls.

The robe of the fur seal has long been a staple item in the fur trade. Today the take is several million dollars a year. When the Russians could no longer find sea otters they started slaughtering fur seals. Why the fur seal herds were not reduced to the same near-extinction as the sea otter has never been explained, but survive they did.

The killing of fur seals on the high sea is now prohibited by treaty and St. George and St. Paul have been turned into gigantic fur farms. The killing is done on a regulated basis. In 1941 Japan abrogated the treaty, claiming that the seals were depleting her supply of fish. Now twenty percent of the skins go to Canada and eighty percent to the United States.

The fur is thick and silky with black guard hairs. Three-year-old animals are usually selected for killing. The older bulls are usually scarred from fighting which makes their skins worthless.

The big males arrive at the islands first and haul themselves out on the rocky shore. They will weigh up to five hundred pounds. When they arrive they are so fat that the skin around their neck and shoulders seems swollen. When they move their whole body shakes. The bull's head appears small when compared to the immensely thick neck and shoulders.

A bull will be fully grown at the age of seven years. They find that the foggy, humid summer has started when they arrive. This is seal weather. Each bull selects a small plot of ground and guards it against all comers.

The cows arrive about three weeks after the bulls. They only weigh a fraction as much as the bulls. When the cows start landing, the old beach masters are kept busy hauling them out of the water and herding them to the eight-foot-square area of rock that will serve as a harem.

As the space along shore becomes limited the bulls have to fight off late-comers, as well as rivals who try to steal cows from

SEA LION COW AND BULL   *Harry W. May (Copyright 1948, Fouke Fur Co.)*

SEAL PUPS   *Harry W. May (Copyright 1948, Fouke Fur Co.)*

their harems. These fights go on morning, noon, and night and fill the air with roars and bellows.

These battles are mainly fought with the mouth. The opponents seize each other with their teeth. Their grip is so powerful that nothing but the full strength of a bull can shake it off. That effort results in ugly wounds, deep gutters cut in skin and blubber.

The bulls who have managed to hold onto their plots will not leave them for a single moment. They live off their stored fat from June to August. A bull will usually have ten or more cows in his harem.

The cows time their arrival perfectly. They do not come ashore from any desire to meet their uncouth lords and masters but to give birth to their pups, which are often born a few hours after they land, seldom longer than a couple of days elapses.

Except for the pups, the fur seal seems to get little rest, awake or sleeping. The period of sleep for a bull on a rookery is seldom more than five minutes. The cows sleep but are constantly jerking and shuddering as though having bad dreams.

The pup at birth and for the first three months wears a black coat of fur. It will weigh from three to four pounds and be about a foot long. The mother shows no affection for her pup and the bulls are indifferent toward them. They will trample a pup to death if it gets in their way while they are battling an invading bull. The pups look alike and with the rookery literally covered with them it would seem impossible for a mother to find her own pup when she returns from fishing. But she always does and will accept no other. Thousands of pups will be piping loudly, they keep this up most of the time. The cow will pick her pup's voice from among the chorus.

The pups have to learn to swim. They get no help from their mothers, they have to do it by trial and error. But they are born with a liking for the sea and are drawn to it.

By the middle of July the bulls are so enfeebled by fighting, fasting, and the excitement of bestowing favors on their many wives that they relax their strict supervision over the harem and the cows do as they please.

About the first week in August the old bulls start dragging their weakened bodies down to the water. They plunge in and start swimming south. They will go only as far as they have to in order to find shoals of fish.

The rookery now becomes a confused mass of young bulls, cows, and pups. The young bulls seek the favors of young cows who have attained maturity late in the summer. A great many of the three-year-old bulls will have made the slow trip over the hills to the slaughter grounds.

Women will go on wearing fur coats. Thousands of seals will surrender their robes, but thousands of little bulls will be saved because they are needed to keep the supply of gold from drying up. Instead of nature maintaining a balance, in the case of the fur seal, it is man.

The sea lion is a one-ton member of the seal family, a striking beast. Its bulk and strength can be appreciated when its measurements are noted. It has a length of from ten to twelve feet, a girth of nine or ten feet around the shoulders. Its teeth are long, sharp, broad-based canines, which gleam like sabers when it pulls back its lips.

Perfectly equipped to be a killer, it attacks only its own kind. The battles between the bulls at mating time are as savage as those between bull fur seals, and the scars are as deep.

Bull sea lions do not hold their harems under as strict supervision as the bull fur seals do, but they will fight an intruder to the death in defense of the cows. This does not apply to man. Sea lions exhibit much fear if a man approaches them.

The cow sea lion is less than half the size of a bull. She will not defend her pup against a man. And she shows little interest in her offspring, beyond allowing it to suckle.

As a swimmer, the sea lion has few equals. It swims mostly under water, thrusting its muzzle above the surface only long enough to suck in a lot of air, which it needs to carry it along under water for as much as ten minutes. If alarmed it fairly flies along at a depth of two or three feet.

When the tall black fins of a pack of killer whales appear in a cove, the sea lions are driven to a frenzy. If they are sunning themselves on shore, they plunge into the water and swim wildly about. The result is a terrible slaughter. They desert the safety of the rock, perhaps because they consider deep water the only secure place for them. Against any enemy but the killer whale this would be true.

When arctic storms come, the sea lions head south and travel down the coast as far as Southern California. But when spring comes they want to be back on the misty islands in the north. Many of them summer near the fur seal rookeries.

The seals that you see in circuses and zoos belong to this tribe but are much smaller. No one has tried training a sea lion to do tricks, so far as I know. But if you pause on a rocky shore where there are sea lions, they'll put on a real show for you, a water ballet you will remember.

Some
Desert Dwellers

When the first westward-trekking trappers tried to reach the Pacific coast looking for beaver water, they found themselves blocked by a towering granite barrier which extends from Canada to Mexico. This barrier was named the Cascade Range and the Sierra Nevada range of mountains. They spent weeks climbing to the crest of the latter range. Once there they found themselves looking down into a vast chasm which is now Yosemite National Park. They learned what the Indians had known for centuries, that neither man nor beast could descend the face of those sheer cliffs over which great waterfalls thundered. They perhaps failed to notice that those roaring cascades and falls poured into a river that flowed west toward the Pacific ocean. But they found ways of descending after a struggle along the crest and reached lush and fertile valleys below. Moisture-laden winds from the Pacific, however, are stopped when they reach the barrier of the high Sierras.

For centuries rain-laden clouds have been pouring life-giving moisture on the western slopes of the range and upon the great valleys, while no rain, except scant showers or an occasional cloudburst, falls on the eastern slopes, or upon the vast area east of the barrier. Thus was created one of the world's biggest deserts, the Great American Desert.

The highest point in the United States outside Alaska is towering Mt. Whitney, its peak rising nearly fifteen thousand feet above sea level. In the very shadow of this mountain lies Death Valley, the lowest point on the American Continent and the hottest and bitterest of deserts. Other areas scattered over the great plateau have names: Mojave Desert in California, House Rock Valley in Arizona, Valley of the Monuments in New Mexico, the Painted Desert of Arizona, and many others.

The silent dunes and sun-baked hills appear to have come down through the ages unchanged, but this is not true. Nature leaves nothing unchanged; there are forces constantly at work altering the face of the desert, breaking down its cliff walls, carving out caves, grinding rocks into sand which drifts with the desert winds, building great dunes. Millions of years from now those relentless forces may have removed the High Sierra barrier and changed the desert into a verdant garden where millions of people will live.

One might conclude that no wildlife could be found on the desert, but that is not true. It is true that no living creature can survive there unless it has adapted itself to a way of life suited to the waterless terrain which is constantly baked by the blistering rays of the sun and lashed by sandstorms.

Nor would you expect to find plant life, but the plant life is one of the striking features of the desert. Plants and trees there do not shed their leaves in the fall, they shed them during extended periods of drought, and replace them when a little rain falls. It is the plant life on the desert which makes it possible for animals to exist there.

The face of the desert changes when an occasional cloudburst sends a flash-flood plunging down a slope, creating new arroyos and canyons, a wall of water that sweeps everything before it, grinding rocks to sand, moving tons of yellow earth. As it moves down a slope, it grows in force and size. In this vast wasteland there is no place for a lost river to go, it just fans out when it reaches the desert floor and deposits its debris over the lowlands.

But it brings needed moisture. The tons of water sink into the ground where it can be sucked up by the thirsty roots of the desert plants.

Many of the desert plants have no leaves at all. Water evaporates from leaves, and the desert plants cannot afford to lose any precious water. The cactus plants are simply small or large storage tanks covered with thick, green skins which take the place of leaves in changing mineral matter into plant food. Naturally in so dry a region these water-filled cactus plants attract animals which are thirsty. To protect them, nature provided cactus with a covering of spines which have needle sharp points. Few animals dare try to steal the water stored in a prickly pear or a barrel cactus or a giant saguaro. A thirsty traveler armed with a hatchet can get himself a drink, but not many animals try it.

The desert has life and it has a voice. The loudest voice can be heard at dusk and at dawn; it is the glee-filled song of the coyote, the song-dog of the dawn. It takes only a couple of coyotes to fill the air with sound. Insects sing and so do some of the mice.

The best place to look for signs of life on the desert is a sand dune or a sandy stretch between a catclaw bush and a cactus plant. Here you will find tracks which will tell you what creature has passed that way during the night or perhaps only an hour before. Tracks are soon obliterated by drifting sand, so if you find any they are sure to be new.

The kangaroo rat leaps along on big hind feet and leaves a deep imprint with claw marks. The pocket mouse leaves a blurred trail that turns and twists, the coati leaves a deep print with toe marks, the desert tortoise leaves a three-toed track with its forefeet and a five-toed track with its hind feet. The coyote and the desert fox leave dog-like tracks, the fox's track being similar to the coyote's except much smaller with the toe marks less prominent. Rabbits leave two sets of pad marks placed close together, side by side. Rabbit tracks will tell you whether the rabbit was in a hurry or just out for a leisurely stroll. An antelope jack rabbit, if he is in a hurry may move in six or eight-foot leaps. You

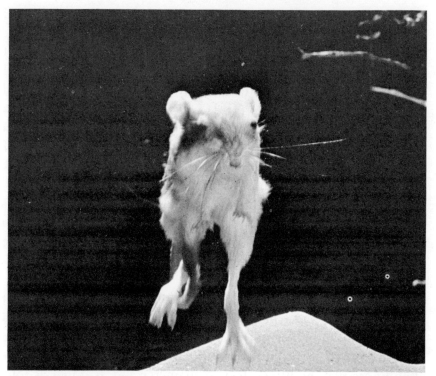

KANGAROO RAT   *N. Paul Kenworthy, Jr.*

can learn a lot about a bobcat or a cougar by studying their tracks
around a thicket, or a bed of prickly pear cactus. Belly marks
where the cougar has flattened himself to watch his prey, deep
impressions which seem to vanish, indicate that the cougar has
leaped. You may have to search twenty or thirty feet away to
find where he landed. Bobcat tracks are bunched, and you will
find stops where he sat down to sniff and listen. The desert lizards
and the chuckwallas leave claw marks and tail trails. The sidewinder rattler leaves a distinctive trail like the rungs of a ladder,
one long mark slanting above the other. Trying to read the story
told by tracks can be fascinating; it may be the story of tragedy or
of an heroic escape from death.

There is one fascinating fellow who is seldom seen because
he shuns the daylight, and even stays in his nest if the moonlight
is bright. Tracks will tell you a lot about him and you can visit

his castle. The kangaroo rat is not a rat, and he is not a kangaroo; he is close kin to the pocket mouse.

Although he is elusive and shy, you may catch a glimpse of him. The best way to do it is to follow a dim dirt road or a trail which leads through a joshua tree grove. Kangaroo rats are found over a large part of the desert. If you are lucky you will see two ruby red lights winking at you from the side of the road, then a gnome-like little creature will flash away in one long leap. If there is light enough, you will see that this little fellow does look like a kangaroo with a big tuft of hair at the end of a long tail. His forefeet are very small and held close to his chest as he leaps along. His hind legs are big and strong. Balancing himself with his tail he bounds along on his hind legs, never touching the ground with his forepaws; they are used as hands to pick seeds and berries.

The kangaroo rat's house is really his castle. He inherits it and adds to it, and when he is ready, he goes forth and finds a mate whom he brings to the castle to live with him. The castle may have two or three levels, one of them underground. This fine house may be fifteen feet in diameter and as much as four feet high. There will be from three to a dozen small doorways, each three to four inches wide and high.

If you kneel beside the castle and tap on a wall near a door you may hear the owner inside thumping on a floor. These sounds are made by rapping the big hind feet on the hard floor. They are not welcome signals inviting you to come in and make yourself at home. They mean "Git! Go away!"

The large castles are the work of generations of kangaroo rats who have lived there over a period of years. Most of the earth in the mound comes from tunnels and rooms excavated. As the castle grows, new levels many be added with hallways and rooms. The hallways and galleries form a labyrinth with ramps leading up and down from one level to another. The sizes of the hallways vary with the sizes of the owners. There are small and big kangaroo rats. Food caches are made along the hallways; these are thimble-sized pockets in the walls, placed in the driest part of the castle.

The kangaroo rat's bedroom is located on the bottom level. The bed will be about four inches wide and have a mattress of soft grass or thistledown. When the mate arrives this will be used as a nursery and papa will have to sleep elsewhere, which is no problem as there are dozens of empty rooms.

A kangaroo rat keeps his body spotless, but he is not very careful about droppings or about hulls from seeds or bits of discarded grass. His floors are always littered. If the litter gets too deep, he just kicks it out through a convenient door. He takes frequent dust baths and spends a lot of time grooming his fur.

If you find a castle, and that should not be difficult when you know where to look, it may be abandoned. An owl or a sidewinder may have caught the owner and eaten him. In that case the castle may be the home of a pocket mouse or a grasshopper mouse, a ground squirrel, a wood rat, a pair of brush rabbits, even a Gila monster. Even when the owner is living in the castle, there are bound to be centipedes, scorpions, beetles, spiders and other insects who just move in. There is plenty of room for all. The unwelcome visitors are the other small animals. They will be met with smashing blows from the kangaroo rat's powerful hind legs with their clawed feet.

Ceilings and doors are high because the kangaroo rat hops in an upright manner and needs head room. When the dweller feels it is time to go seed-hunting, he approaches a door and halts to thump loudly on the floor before venturing outside. If there is an enemy lurking outside, this may cause it to betray its presence. The little rat has very sensitive ears and will hear the slightest sound. Once outside he stays close to the castle for a while. At the slightest sound or movement in the shadows, he flashes into his castle and will stay there until he is sure the prowler has passed on.

All kangaroo rats are not thrifty. Some of the small members of the species store nothing at all. but the big members work hard and fill many bins with food. As much as a hundred quarts of seeds and cut grass have been found in a single castle. The various kinds of seeds and lengths of cut grass are stored separately. Possibly the kinds of seeds the harvester likes best are harvested first and thus stored in bins by themselves. Of course it is possible that the kangaroo rat knows the difference between the items and may not wish to dig through a mixed pile to find a choice morsel. Grass seeds are the most important part of the food list and are the easiest harvested and stored. Seeds of brome grass, gramma, and fescue are popular; berries are also stored.

Kangaroo rats have a sort of community life. If you see narrow, well-beaten trails leading away from a castle and follow one of them, it is almost sure to lead you to a neighbor's castle. However, two grown members of the tribe never live together, except during the mating season.

Any small kangaroo rat who tries to slip into the castle and steal a meal will be stamped to death by the owner if caught. The same fate will befall any inquisitive ground squirrel. The owner will even face the savage grasshopper mouse, a deadly killer of other mice.

A kangaroo rat goes everywhere in his big house by taking six-inch hops. When outside and in a hurry the leaps are much longer.

The kangaroo rat has many enemies. Hawks are not a problem because they do not hunt at night and go to roost early in the evening, but owls, big and small, hunt at a time when the little seed-gatherer is venturing forth. The diamondback rattler, the sidewinder and the king snake will kill any kangaroo rat they can catch, and the rattlers do not hunt by sight, but by detecting body heat. It is said that if a kangaroo rat cannot leap away fast enough he will kick sand into the eyes and mouth of the snake and sometimes escape. In a locality where there are badgers they will break into a castle and devour the owner unless he manages to escape through one of his many doors. Even this may not save him if a coyote has attached himself to the badger and is loitering outside waiting for a rat to attempt an escape.

The next time you are out on the desert don't pass up what looks like just a big mound of dirt; take a close look. You may have discovered a king's castle and get to meet an interesting character.

They Crawl

There is one set of desert tracks worth following if they are fairly fresh and but little wind-blown. Tracks on the lee side of a cactus or bush may seem fresh. The test will come when they lead out into the open across stretches of sand. The tracks I am speaking of are those of a desert tortoise. A tortoise plods along slowly, using only the claws of his forefeet but setting the hind feet down solidly. You will note as you move along that the tortoise turns aside often to nibble on a succulent plant, and that it does not seem to have any definite destination in mind, doubling back, circling, just wandering.

Like the barrel cactus the tortoise stores up water against long dry spells. A tortoise could live out his whole life without taking a drink of water. He may drink when there is a shower or a flash flood but he does not have to. The green foliage he eats is from succulent plants and is water-filled. He has two storage tanks concealed under his shell where his drinking water is stored for use when he is thirsty.

The desert tortoise seldom exceeds nine inches from the front to the back of his high-domed shell. His solid and deliberate way of walking gives him much dignity. He plods along nodding his head as though expressing satisfaction with the terrific heat and the general goodness of his world. Plod, plod, with an occasional pause now and then so that he can snip off a juicy stem.

The tortoise is completely at home in the hot desert, even if he wanders down into Death Valley when the temperature is one hundred and thirty degrees above zero. When he first leaves his den, he will move slowly and not go far. He is warming up, waiting for the blistering sun to warm up his shell. Once he feels the heat he will quicken his pace and become more alert.

After a while when the heat is so great that even the giant saguaros seem to droop and heat waves play like flames along the tops of the dunes, a tortoise may pause and rest for a while in a patch of shade.

The desert tortoise is almost the color of the sand and clay he walks upon. Circular whorls on his shell allow him to blend into the pattern of the desert's surface. The first desert tortoise I met startled me. I never expected to find one of the turtle tribe so far from water. I had believed that they lived in or near ponds and sat on mossy logs or on grassy banks or swam about submerged with just their heads sticking out of the water. I was very familiar with that kind of turtle.

There seem to be very few times when a tortoise finds anything exciting to do. Once every season he starts out to find a mate. This is a hit-or-miss venture, dependent upon accident, perhaps. But one should never underestimate nature's ways of making sure that a species reproduces. If he does find a female, a period of romance brightens his life. This will be a short break in the drabness of his usual way of life, and he will soon be plodding along alone again.

He may meet another romance-seeking male tortoise, or he may even try to take a lady away from her admirer. Like all wild males in a mating mood, the sight of a rival will rouse him to anger, and a battle will follow. Both knights are so heavily armor-

TORTOISE   *Dick Smith*

plated that biting and scratching can do no harm. Feet and head
can be quickly retracted; neither can get up enough speed to
butt the other very hard. But there is a way to inflict decisive
damage and even cause the death of a rival.

Every tortoise has a hard rim projecting forward from his
lower shell. Each makes a determined effort to hook that rim
under the edge of his rival's shell and flip him over on his back.
Face to face they circle slowly, trying to get into position. They
meet with a slight jar, and each strains with his strong back legs.
The tortoise having the firmer footing has the advantage. If
either slips or loses his footing the other heaves. Our tortoise
may step on a loose stone and be thrown off balance. A second
later he finds himself on his back.

He waves his feet helplessly, trying to get his claws fastened
upon a rock or the limb of a bush, but never able to plant a foot

on solid ground. If there is a female watching the fight, the victor marches off with her.

The overturned tortoise is in a desperate plight. The whole weight of his internal organs is now pressing down upon his lungs, threatening to smother him. But he has a trick which may have saved him before. He starts rocking back and forth desperately, reaching out and trying to get a claw on a rock or a branch, or a grip on firm ground.

If our tortoise can get a claw hooked onto a branch or a rock ledge, he can right himself. If he has been overturned on smooth sand he will slowly smother to death.

If he is able to right himself, he will go plodding on his way, probably forgetting the whole episode as soon as he recovers his breath. With wild creatures, the shadow of death passes quickly after the threat is gone. When a ground squirrel is pursued by a coyote fear gives him speed, but if he is able to dart into a rock slide or into his den, the fear vanishes as soon as the coyote is out of sight; it is replaced by caution and wariness.

The desert lizards live where survival is a problem. Each has developed its own way of meeting the problem, otherwise they would long since have vanished from the desert. The chuckwallas are big, clumsy lizards with a color pattern which blends with the desert. If they freeze and remain unmoving they are difficult even for a coyote to spot, but they have to eat and that requires moving about. On the desert, food is not plentiful so they must cover quite a bit of ground. Unlike the Gila monster, the chuckwalla is not armed with poison fangs. The Gila monster has the same defense as a rattler. Being so protected it goes about openly flaunting a gay circus-colored coat of black and orange. It is easily noticed, but no bobcat or coyote would think of attacking it because of its poison fangs. It seems unfair that nature should equip the Gila monster with so perfect a defense while the chuckwalla has only a drab camouflage coat to protect a fat body which tempts all of the predators into persistently hunting it.

But the chuckwallas have worked out a scheme for staying alive. They forage close to ledges and rocky formations. If a coyote appears the chuckwalla will freeze and remain motionless on a rock. But if the coyote should discover the big lizard by scent or sight and start to attack, the chuckwalla scrambles into a narrow crevice where he inflates his body with air, and wedges himself so tightly that the coyote cannot pull him from his hiding place.

You can easily recognize a chuckwalla if you see one. He is a large lizard built like a miniature dinosaur. He looks fierce, but that is bluff; his safety depends upon flight and his ability to make himself almost invisible.

Most of the small lizards depend upon protective coloring and speed for safety. You will notice that they duck and dart swiftly, but at intervals they pause and remain very still, blending with a leaf or a rock. They are careless in their movements, liking to dart about in the open. Bobcats, foxes, coyotes and hawks catch many of them. Mother lizard goes on blissfully producing big families unaware that most of her young are gobbled up by meat eaters.

In arid and semiarid regions where sage, mesquite, cactus and other spiny plants grow, where the terrain is rocky and there are plenty of cracks and crevasses to hide in, you will find a small round fellow, perhaps a little bigger around than a silver dollar. He has small bright eyes and his grayish skin is covered with spines, even his spike tail has spines on it, making him an unappetizing tid-bit for predators.

The instant you see him darting for cover under a rock, you will know he is a lizard. In most places he is known as a horned toad but most of the boys who know him call him horny toad. And you can be sure boys living on his domain will know him. There will be few among them who have not had one or more horny toads as pets. I doubt if this has changed much over the years. I caught horny toads as a boy and my son caught them, my

HORNED TOAD   *Dick Smith*

grandchildren would catch them if they lived where there were
any horny toads.

I never knew one of the spiny little fellows to show any affection in the way a dog or a cat or most other animals will when
kept as pets, but they do not mind riding on a boy's shoulder or
in his pocket, and they seem to enjoy being stroked with a finger.
However, they will wander off and not come back if turned loose.
That's the way I always lost the horny toads I caught and kept
as pets.

Catching this small lizard is not difficult as he will duck into
the first crack he comes to or under the first rock. He will not bite
and his claws do no damage. In a very short time he will get used
to being handled. If he does not take to cover, however, he will
give any boy a merry chase. He can move fast and duck and
change direction with the agility of the swiftest of lizards.

The horned toad is one of the most charming of nature's creatures and one you are almost sure to see if you are hiking on his range. He is out during the day and likes sunshine. He darts about looking for insects or sits sunning himself on a rock.

Life on the desert—and everywhere else where wild creatures live—is a constant struggle to survive, and to do that they must find food, raise families and elude their enemies. None of them seems aware of the grimness of the struggle, except when danger threatens. A few are so well protected that they are never threatened. Some, like the mice, are so prolific that, although millions are devoured, there is always a horde that survives.

There was a time, before the white man arrived on this continent, when the big predators, the cats, the bears and the wolves had little to worry about except securing food. Today they walk in fear and have changed the whole pattern of their lives; some, like the gray wolf and the grizzly hardly exist except in the remote regions in the far north, having been nearly exterminated south of the Canadian border. What wildlife we have left, has survived because it has been able to adapt itself or because it lives in areas man has deemed unworthy of his notice, like most of the Great American Desert.

The desert snakes are all flesh eaters. The list of their prey includes birds and small animals, some of them so large it would seem impossible for the snake to swallow them, and swallow them he must because he cannot chew them up or tear them apart and eat them by the piece.

The snakes you are apt to see on the desert are the diamond-back rattler, the sidewinder and the king snake. The rattlers are endowed with poison-injecting fangs; the king snake is a big, harmless fellow; he is a friend to man, in that he destroys rodents. A belief has persisted in the west that a king snake will kill a rattler. I have no proof of this but have heard the story since I was a boy.

Snakes help to maintain a balance in nature; thus, they are a part of our wildlife pattern and should not be destroyed except when necessary. They devour thousands of mice and this keeps the mouse population from taking over all of the outdoors. This threat can be understood when we learn that a meadow mouse can produce seventeen litters of from five to thirteen babies every season, and that the female members of these litters will start having babies of their own when four weeks old. Three weeks later their female babies will be born.

The diamondback rattler and the sidewinder are deadly trackers. They have two scent sacs above their mouths, so sensitive that they can detect the faintest trace of an animal's body warmth and follow the invisible trail. They do not depend upon sight or sound at all.

Down through the ages most people have hated and feared snakes. The mischievous minority makes itself unpleasantly notorious, and thus discredits a whole class. Even the rattler strikes at man only in self-defense when he feels he is being threatened. Snakes do not make responsive pets but I have often carried grass or garter snakes around in my shirt pocket. I soon discovered that having a snake in my pocket did not make me popular except with my boy pals; the toad- and frog-packers envied me. Later, when I was teaching a biology class in the Cedaredge High School in Colorado, I brought a small water snake to class to give a live demonstration of the operation of a snake's jaws. Half of the class was nervous, but I gave my demonstration, and when I finished it I tucked the snake into my shirt pocket, intending to free it after school. I forgot about the snake and went into a barber shop to get a shave. The barber was a lady. I lay back and she adjusted the cloth around my neck and started lathering my face. At that moment the snake poked its head out. The lady barber became hysterical. With my face half-lathered, I had to rustle a fruit jar from a back room and deposit the snake on the sidewalk. I shuddered as I thought of what could have happened had she been shaving my throat when the snake popped his head up. Some people hate snakes so much that they will kill a worm because it reminds them of a snake.

But the snake is an interesting character. The way they are put together is different from the body structure of other wild creatures. The development of poison fangs in snakes came about slowly. In the diamondback they are a marvel of efficiency, and an example of how nature plans a perfect piece of machinery to do a certain job.

A portion of the salivary gland, which lies behind the eye, was transformed into a poison gland. From this gland a tube extends to the eye teeth on each side of the jaw, these being the front teeth. There is a groove in these fangs which extends to the tip of the fang. Around the gland there is a powerful muscle, which when contracted shuts the jaw and forces the venom along the tube. Nothing is overlooked to assure that the venom reaches the already inflicted wound. The waste of venom every time the snake shuts his mouth is taken care of. A strong muscle at the end of the duct has to be relaxed before any poison can escape. This muscle allows the diamondback and the sidewinder to swallow their prey without losing poison.

The Hopi Indians have a snake dance they perform to bring rain. For weeks the Hopi men comb the desert for rattlers. They work in pairs because no one, not even a Hopi, can be sure which way a snake is going by looking at its track, so one goes one way and the other goes the other way. In the dance they reach into a canvas-covered box and pull out handfuls of snakes. The snakes writhe around their arms and necks. The dancers will be bitten but suffer no ill effects. I personally checked some of the snakes and their fangs had not been removed. The chief of the Snake Clan assured me that the snakes were not tampered with. No one in the tribe except a member of the Snake Clan is permitted to enter the dance. The clan has its own kiva and from boyhood the members spend much time preparing for the dances. Their secret

RATTLESNAKE   *Dick Smith*

is well guarded but it seems certain that they have learned a way
to become immune to snake venom.

A snake's entire body has been designed to fit its way of life.
The construction of the head is one of the most interesting things
about a snake. A snake has no chin and no front teeth on the
lower jaw. They have upper and lower teeth on the sides of the
jaw. The jaws are not hinged at the back. A snake can take its
head almost apart when swallowing. Its teeth all slope inward.
The snake literally opens its head with the jaws staying on the
same plane. It opens its mouth as wide as necessary to swallow its
prey. Once a sidewinder has fastened its fang upon a bird or
animal it cannot spit out its prey if it wants to. The struggles of
the victim help the snake in swallowing. The in-sloping teeth
leave no way to go but down the sidewinder's throat. And the
body can expand to fit any size of meal. There are hazards in this

way of swallowing. I have described previously what often happens when a rattler tries to swallow a weasel.

Aside from man, the rattler's most dangerous enemy on the desert is the road runner, a long-legged member of the cuckoo family, although in areas where peccaries are found no snake is safe if discovered by these wild pigs. The road runner is a typical desert bird. It resembles a game cock in its rangy build and size, except for the long sharp beak. Like many desert creatures it drinks no water, and it prefers to run rather than fly.

The road runner is a tough bird, building its nest in a spiny cholla, thorny catclaw or mesquite bush the same as the cactus wren. The road runner's speed is dazzling, its long legs seem to flash over the ground. This bird is also somewhat of a prankster, it will dart in on a ground squirrel, peck the squirrel and dash away. But when a road runner sees a rattler, he moves with the intent of dining upon snake meat.

The battle which follows may last a while, but it always ends up with the snake dead and a meal for the road runner. The bird leaps around the coiled rattler, darting its sharp beak out, striking at the rattler's eyes, feinting the rattler into striking so that it can get at the back of the head. When the snake is weakened and possibly blinded, the road runner moves in for the kill.

Another dangerous enemy is the red-tailed hawk. This hunter sees everything that moves on the desert as it rides the updrafts from the desert on almost motionless wings. If it spots a diamondback gliding from bush to bush it dives down in a whistling descent, wings pulled in, talons extended. Just before it reaches the snake it fans out its tail and extends beating wings. The rattler may have time to coil and strike but its fangs have little effect because of the dense feathers. The power of a hawk's grip is amazing. It does not strike with its hooked beak; it is the talons that are deadly. They will quickly crush the life out of the rattler.

When hiking on the desert you should add a snake bite kit to your first aid supplies. With proper equipment and written instructions to follow, there is little danger of critical effects from snake bite. Head and neck bites can be fatal, but the chance of receiving one is remote. But you might get bitten on the arm or leg if you sit down close to a bush where a snake is resting. I have several times sat down on a grassy hummock or inviting ledge and found that I had a coiled rattler for a companion. Feeling I had invaded his privacy I always excused myself fast. In no case did I kill the rattler. Don't depend upon the rattler giving you a warning buzz before he strikes. He may strike first and rattle afterward. The best thing to do is to look into any bunch of grass you plan to sit down upon and under any bush you may wish to use as a spot of shade.

You are not a good woodsman or nature lover if you kill every snake you meet. Most of them are harmless. graceful creatures who ask only to be let go their own way in peace.

More Desert Dwellers

One would not expect to find toads on the desert. We usually think of them as living in moist places, near ponds or in a garden. I have never been able to understand how they could multiply, as they need water for the hatching of their eggs and for the first stage of toad development. But there are toads on the desert and they get along very well. Most of them dig in and bury themselves during drouth spells, but if a toad can find a desert waterhole he will have a more active life. Toads do not go hunting for food as do most wild creatures. They do not dash about like mice and ground squirrels. A toad just sits and waits for his dinner to come to him.

Any full-grown toad looks old and venerable, an ancient one sitting looking out upon his world. A toad seated by a waterhole sees a lot of desert life. He is interested mostly in the things he can eat. He will flick out his long tongue and lap up an orange-colored centipede or a black millipede sliding along on its thousand feet. Most insect hunters won't eat a millipede. It can roll itself up into a hard ball and when attacked it gives off an offensive stench. This does not bother the toad; he may not be able to smell, or a millipede may have a flavor he likes.

Few insects, if any at all, will avoid a toad. They cannot distinguish between the motionless toad and the rocks and bumps around him. All he has to do is wait until the bug or beetle gets within range of his sticky tongue. The toad, himself, is not a very good judge of what it is safe to spear with his tongue. If a tiger beetle comes along he looks like ordinary fare to the toad, but he is a savage killer who will charge upon a grasshopper four times his size and seize it with his powerful pincers. This fierce hunter offers no problem to the toad, he crushes the hard shell and eats the beetle.

The hairy-legged tarantula cheats the toad out of many tasty bits of food. This huge spider is a very persistent hunter and as insects are attracted to a waterhole the toad may have a number of them as competition. The tarantula is one crawler the toad does not relish.

A tarantula spends most of his time hunting for insects, but at times he will hunt for the den of a female tarantula, which will be a burrow dug into the ground where the soil is loose. She digs it with her sharp nippers and kicks the clods out of the hole with her feet. She will coat it with a mixture of mud and saliva and then line it with spun silk. She will have an elegant bedroom where she spends much of her time.

The courting tarantula will approach the bower and rap on the ground close to its opening. When the lady hears the knock, she will come to the door. The male will seize her and she will appear to faint. Then he will drag her away. This little drama may not interest the toad but he will see it because he watches all of the crawling things around him.

On the desert, be sure and watch for a black-bodied wasp. If you see one it may well be worth your time to follow her as she darts about, walking more than flying. It is clear that she is searching for something. I have followed these slim-waisted wasps for hours. She may find a caterpillar but on the desert she is more apt to come upon a hairy-legged tarantula, a spider many times as big as she is and a creature equipped with deadly poison fangs. But she will attack the big spider. This happens so often that this wasp is often called a "tarantula hawk." She is driven by a powerful urge to provide for her unhatched young, and a tarantula will fill her needs perfectly.

To the tarantula the wasp is just another insect to be eaten. To the wasp the tarantula will furnish enough food to provide for her young until they are able to hunt for themselves. She darts about, wings flicking rapidly, seeking a chance to sink her stinger into the hairy body where it will paralyze the spider.

She risks death in order to get close enough to use her stinger. Victory may not always be with her, she may end up as a meal for the tarantula, but more often than not she is able to render the big spider helpless. If she does she will drag the helpless spider to a hole she has dug in the ground. When she reaches the hole she will drag the tarantula into it and lay her eggs on the body. The paralyzed spider will stay alive until the eggs hatch. The mother wasp has provided fresh meat for her young, which she will never see.

Our toad may watch a scorpion dance. A scorpion will unearth a mate from a small dune and join claws with her in a bride and groom dance that will end in a honeymoon. A time of romance comes to every living dweller of the desert.

There is one beetle, the longhorn beetle, that will get the best of the toad. The toad does not seem to know one beetle from another. When he licks up a longhorn he gets a surprise. The longhorn will fasten his powerful pincer jaws on the toad's tongue. The toad will hastily spit out the beetle. If it circles around and comes close the toad will snap it up with the same results as before.

When you see a giant saguaro cactus towering thirty or more feet above the desert, do not pass it by without a good look at it. Its top spines may be the home of a swift-flying red-tailed hawk.

SCREECH OWL   *Dick Smith*

Also you may discover a tiny elf owl peeping out of a hole it has pecked in one of the fluted columns of the saguaro. He will have a tiny round head and the big eyes and hooked beak which identify him as an owl. This little owl spends a lot of time seated in his doorway looking out over the desert.

You may even find a pair of woodpeckers living in a hole they have drilled in the trunk of the saguaro. They will be worth watching. Their domestic life is not unlike that of many married couples. They may appear to be the picture of domestic bliss as they make gestures at each other outside the opening, or a real quarrel may start inside the nest. The male is the one who will be ousted. He will fly to another cactus where he has a retreat. I think this is accepted practice with woodpeckers. I watched a pair for a number of seasons. Their main residence was a big hole in the top of a power pole across the street from our house in Los Gatos, California. The cross-arm made a fine patio and they used it, chasing each other playfully back and forth along it, going around and around the pole. But there were times when they had rousing arguments. When this happened papa made off to a hole he had made in the next pole down the street. I am certain it was his private retreat because I never saw the female go near it.

If the woodpeckers are in the air catching insects and the red-tailed hawk launches forth from his skyscraper home, the woodpeckers will attack him furiously. But he is used to that; almost any bird, even a cactus wren, will chase him. He ducks and dips and side-slips to save the feathers in his tail. It seems odd that a killer like the red-tail, who will strike down a fleeing bird or an animal on the ground would let a small bird bully him if that bird attacks.

The bobcat is one animal who is not afraid of the spines of a saguaro. He sometimes climbs to the top of one. The view is fine, almost as good as that enjoyed by the eagle and the hawk. Also he may use the big cactus as a refuge if a herd of peccaries go after him.

The desert has a brooding somber beauty at all times, but there are seasons when it really flames with color. Spring is when the desert plants bloom, then you see the flaming beauty of devil's finger, and the ivory colored blossoms of the night-blooming cereus, the deep pink flowers of the beaver-tail cactus, the big pastel colored blossoms of the prickly pear, the masses of white flowers produced by the saguaro. There are many others like the California poppy and the blue lupine that spread acres of color over the slopes.

But the cactus family, typical of the desert, surpass all of the others in the size and beauty of their blossoms. No matter when you visit the desert, you will be treated to scenes of beauty.

When I am out on the desert in the evening, I like to climb to the top of a dune and enjoy the sunset. Nowhere have I ever seen such a display of color from deep purple in canyons and arroyos to reds and pinks and every other shade. Even the air below on the desert is filled with color. In New Mexico I have often sat and looked at Shiprock as the glow of the sunset enveloped it. It looks like a great sailing ship moving through a sea of gold.

Mice
Including a Gopher

Pocket mice are found throughout the west and come in two sizes; the big mouse is nine inches long, including a long tail and weighs an ounce; the Pacific pocket mouse is the smallest rodent in North America. It weighs one third of an ounce and, counting a long, bushy tail, is four inches in length.

A pocket mouse never overeats, it stores away most of what it gathers. When it is harvesting seeds its tiny white hands flash so fast that all you can see is a blur of white color. Each hand moves back and forth as it stuffs seeds or berries into its cheeks. By stretching the pouches the mouse may be able to tuck away a dozen mesquite beans. One tiny Pacific pocket mouse was timed while gathering mustard seed. She gathered and stored three thousand mustard seeds in an hour.

A tame pocket mouse may live to be five years old, the wild ones seldom celebrate their first birthday. The death rate is enormous among pocket mice. They have to forage in the open because of the food they eat. In the west, spotted skunks kill thousands of them. Hawks, snakes and even the big predators kill thousands more. Why the big killers bother with a morsel weighing a third of an ounce is hard to understand. It would require hundreds of these mice to fill a corner of a cougar's stomach, but the cougar hunts pocket mice big and small diligently.

The place to look for them is in dry, semi-arid areas. They shun mountain regions unless they are very dry. Much of the Great American Desert is ideal for them; here they have the parched eastern slopes of the mountains and a vast expanse of dry desert. Areas where catclaw, cactus and mesquite thrive are ideal for them.

The coloring of pocket mice varies with the type of terrain they inhabit. In New Mexico it varies from light gray to black. The light variety lives in a terrain where the soil is almost all white gypsum, the blacks live in areas where the ground is covered with black lava rock. The coloring is probably brought about by natural selection. Predators caught those mice they could see easily, leaving those that blended with their background to mate and produce young. Over the years the survivors lightened or darkened.

Pocket mice are gentle and inoffensive. If they are caught and handled gently they will not bite and soon lose their fear. It is not safe to handle other wild mice without leather gloves, but it can be done with the pocket mouse. They make fine pets and will live happily in a small cage, which need not be more than eighteen inches square. But pocket mice are not gentle with other mice. Small as they are, they will attack a bigger mouse.

The mating time is irregular with this mouse. In the south the female may have two litters a season. The size of the litter varies from two to eight. The young develop fast, and quickly learn to forage for themselves. With such a short span of life ahead of them there is an urgent need to get to living quickly.

An adult pocket mouse will dig tunnels and excavate rooms. In some places the burrow will be less than a foot deep, in other places as much as six feet. There may be a network of tunnels which offer protection from snakes. The pygmy weasel as well as the snake can enter their tunnels.

The pocket mouse eats all kinds of seeds. It needs no water which makes it an ideal desert dweller. Water from green plants furnishes all of the moisture it requires. Even on over-grazed range, cropped close by sheep, the pocket mouse prospers, and survives severe drouths.

Being a miser, the pocket mouse will accumulate a big store of food which it is not likely to live long enough to eat. But that will not make it overeat or stop scurrying back and forth between field and storeroom with its cheeks stuffed with seeds. Of course, there is a need for a supply of food to carry it through a dry spell and through cold weather. When the weather is bad, the mouse stays in its den.

To observe the pocket mouse all you have to do is sit in the shade of a bush not far from its burrow and wait. The owner may duck inside the burrow when he sees you approach, but he won't stay underground long. Once you are seated and do not move you become a rock or a stump, and he will go about his business unworried.

There is one meat-eating killer in the mouse tribe. This little terror of the night weighs only four-fifths of an ounce, but it is as savage and bloodthirsty as any weasel. It is the grasshopper mouse.

The grasshopper mouse is a chunky little fellow with stubby legs and a white vest. If you see one come out of his den in the evening or on a moonlit night, you might think he was just another seed-gatherer who would not harm his neighbors.

But the chubby mouse with the white vest is not a seed-eater, nor does he store any kind of food. Nine-tenths of his food comes from living creatures he can master, and that includes kangaroo rats, large and small.

A grasshopper mouse will eat flesh equal to its own weight if it can get that much, and most of the time it is able to fill its stomach.

Before taking off on a hunt the killer will open his mouth and utter a shrill whistle. Then he is off, trotting around thorn bushes and cactus, climbing little knolls where seed-bearing grasses grow, a spot where the hunter may find a kangaroo rat or a pocket mouse.

The grasshopper mouse lacks the patience of a coyote or a cougar. If he scents prey, he rushes in savagely. This impatience must cause him to miss a good many kills. Alerted, a jumping mouse will be gone in one long leap, and a kangaroo rat will dart away faster than the killer can run. But if the sudden rush surprises the intended victim and the killer gets his claws fastened into the neck of his prey, he will make a kill with his sharp lower incisors in a matter of seconds.

In a few minutes there will be nothing left of the victim but a few scraps of skin and some hair, and the killer will be busy cleaning his white vest with his tongue and forepaws.

The grasshopper mouse kills, in addition to other mice, a great many grasshoppers and other insects. Much of its fare consists of beetles but it will kill and eat any scorpion it finds. During the summer much of its diet consists of insects, but during the winter it depends upon a diet of other mice.

Living as it does, hand-to-mouth, this mouse has periods when it goes hungry and other times when it can gorge itself. Like most of the meat-eaters, it has a huge capacity, and can consume an incredible amount of flesh and blood, considering its size.

Like all hunters this mouse has a keen sense of smell and hearing. It is an expert trailer and once on a warm scent it will not lose the trail.

The grasshopper mouse can dig burrows but prefers to take over the den of a ground squirrel or another mouse if it can overcome the owner, which it usually does. The den it finds may be deserted because of the high mortality rate among desert dwellers.

The young are born in the spring and within four weeks are on their own. Young and adults do not escape the usual enemies of the mouse tribe; they are snapped up by the big killers on the ground, and taken by the killers of the air. Their night-prowling habits give them much protection, however.

Although a savage killer, this mouse has to be listed as a friend to man because it kills many pests, including mice which eat farm crops. It also helps maintain nature's balance of wild population.

There is one mouse you will find wherever any mammal can live, from the depth of Death Valley to the last stunted bushes at timberline, and eastward over a large range. The weather can't be too hot or too cold for a white-footed mouse.

If you spot a mottled black and white face, with a patch of black between two bright little eyes, peeping out at you from a clump of grass, you have spotted a white-footed mouse.

These mice build their nests any place. They are at home in a swamp or on the driest desert. They will also move in and live in a house with people. When they do, they are retiring and clean, never prying and dirty like the house mouse. A white-footed mouse spends a lot of time cleaning and brushing its brown and white coat of fur. But when it comes to its outdoor nest, it ceases to be cleanly. It eats in bed, dropping bits of food about, using the nest as a toilet so that it smells very bad. In fact a white-footed mouse has to have more than one nest. It will not be able to tolerate the bad smells for more than ten days or two weeks.

A white-footed mouse can sing a buzzing sort of tune which can be heard at a distance of fifteen yards. The desert species are gentle and so are those found on the west coast. They have an interesting ritual they perform when courting. First the female fights off the male, but this does not last long. When she stops snapping and biting, he becomes coy and she has to coax him. After much wooing she gets him into her nest and a honeymoon of a couple of days starts. Suddenly the lady becomes bored and drives the bridegroom out of the nest.

The mother mouse builds a nest lined with the softest material she can find. She fluffs this out with her teeth and paws. In contrast to a house built just to live in, the nursery will be kept fairly clean. A wad of shredded grass closes the entrance-hole keeping the house snug and warm.

From the romance period to birth, twenty-five days elapse. The white-footed mouse may leave her brood an hour after they are born and go out to seek a mate, or she may wait a couple of weeks. This eagerness to have families might cover the land with mice if they did not fall easy prey to the killers, ranging from the hawks and grasshopper mice to the big cats.

There may be as many as nine mice in a litter. When they are first born they are pink and wrinkled, and so transparent that the milk in their stomachs can be seen. They are born furless, except for their whiskers, and are deaf and blind for the first two weeks. It is easy to see why the mother has to build a warm nest for them. She covers them as a mother hen covers her chicks when she is in the nest. When she leaves to forage, she carefully plugs the nest-opening so that they will not be chilled by draughts.

When they are a week old they can take a firm grip on their mother's nipples and she can carry them dangling from her breasts if she has to move them. Any threat of danger will make her seek another nest. A snake may discover the nest or a spotted skunk may start sniffing about it. As she will have at least five or six babies this will make quite a load.

If the mother has mated as soon as they were born, the youngsters will have only three or four weeks to develop to the point where they will have to take care of themselves. But the mother does not drive them out of the house when the new brood is due, she leaves them there and builds a new nest.

White-footed mice are subject to many of the ills that plague mankind, including cancer. Researchers take advantage of this and use hundreds of these mice in experiments. One of the ailments these mice suffer from is epilepsy. When excited, the mouse may have a fit, writhing, staggering about and falling down. The mouse may die from the attack.

Illness, predators big and small, keep the white-footed mouse population from exploding, but once in a while it does explode and the woods and meadows seem filled with mice.

It would be impossible to list all of the things a white-footed mouse eats. They eat all kinds of seed, nuts, berries and fruits which grow where they live. They become pests when they move into harvested and shocked grain fields where they build nests in the shocks. Here they find shelter as well as an abundant supply of food. The huge wheat fields of the west do not suffer because the grain is harvested by a combine and is not shocked.

This mouse stores a great deal of food. The carcass of a deer may serve as food for a whole winter if coyotes or bears do not find it. If it is buried under the snow the mice can set up house-keeping inside the carcass and not be disturbed.

The life of a white-footed mouse may not seem to be very attractive, but who can say that during its short span this small creature does not experience the joys and rewards of being alive.

Anyone who has spent a night in an abandoned cabin in the woods has probably seen and heard a wood rat. This is a fellow that every miner and every woodsman knows. The western wood rat is often called a "pack rat" or a "trade rat." It is one of the few wild animals that stores away things it can't eat or use.

If a pack rat gets into your cabin, he is sure to carry away any-thing which strikes his fancy and which he is able to lug away. He seems to feel that he is making a fair trade with you if he leaves a stone or a cactus bud when he carries off your watch, your knife or the loose change you may have left carelessly on a bench or table. The most reasonable explanation for this is that when the pack rat sees your watch it appeals to him more than the rock or the cactus bud, so he drops what he is carrying and takes your watch.

Many old timers in the west felt the pack rat was an honest fellow because he always left something in exchange for what he took. Also the evidence of the rat's having been there prevents accusations of theft between partners, which have happened when the pack rat left nothing. There is not much in a cabin a pack rat won't carry away if he is able to move it. There is a case on record in which a miner carelessly left his false teeth on the floor beside

PACK RAT   *Dick Smith*

his bunk and awakened the next morning to find the teeth gone, and himself facing a diet of soup and mush.

The pack rat is a furry creature. He bears no resemblance to the house rat or wharf rat in looks or habits. He prefers to do his prowling at night. If he gets into a cabin, he thumps about making no attempt to move silently. I have often been awakened by a pack rat exploring the cabin cupboard, or refuse box. When occupying a mountain cabin I always make everything secure before rolling into my bunk. One annoying thing a pack rat will do when he visits a cabin is to run along the roof beam and rap his feet loudly.

I have several times passed up the shelter of an abandoned log cabin because it had been taken over by wood rats. The prospect of listening to the rattling of pots and pans and other utensils was one reason; the other reason was the strong rat smell. I once almost burned down a cabin by lighting a fire in its mud fireplace without first looking up the chimney which was filled with a mass of sticks, cactus spines and grass, put there by a pack rat. Luckily I had brought a bucket of water from a nearby spring and was able to douse the fire before the dry nest started to blaze.

The fact is that the wood rat has made a lot of people dislike him; they simply hate rats as a lot of people hate snakes. There is no basis in reason for this dislike. The wood rat is a soft-furred animal with long hair on its ears and a brush-tufted tail. The house rat is short-haired and has a long scaly tail. The little trader does not live in droves and he stays away from cities and towns. He is no sewer-living animal, but is a child of the outdoors, who prefers the wide open spaces where he can build a castle to live and store his treasures in. Everyone who has contacted this little fellow finds him attractive and likeable. The exception might be someone who has lost a wrist watch or ring or some other valuable article which a pack rat has carried away. If you have suffered such a loss and suspect a wood rat, start searching for his castle. He does not bury his treasures; he keeps them in his big nest which cannot be hidden from sight, in most cases.

When camping out, I always make a practice of putting all food and any other thing a pack rat could carry away into a securely fastened grub box or the trunk compartment of my car. I am protecting my possessions against not only the pack rat but against a wandering black bear or a nosy raccoon. I learned my lesson the hard way, by having at least four trade rats visit my camp one night and make off with all of my knives, forks and spoons which I had left on the camp table in the usual spoon holder, a tomato can. The sugar can was licked clean, and the salt cellar was also missing. The traders passed up the pepper shaker, probably having gotten a strong whiff of pepper when they examined it.

Some of the wood rats' nests I have examined were on the ground, a few in trees, but most of them were in caves or crannies on a cliff face. Abandoned cabins have to be added to the list of nest-sites, but there are not many the trader can find.

The builder of these big nests is not choosy about the materials he uses; anything at hand will do. He just starts accumulating a pile of sticks, grass, cactus joints, catclaw, mesquite and cholla. One would think that he would avoid prickly pear joints, and cushion and barrel cactus, all covered with bristling, needle sharp spines, but he does not; half of his nest-pile will be cactus. It is impossible to dig into a pack rat's nest with your bare hands. It may be that the cactus spines offer some protection against predators.

The castle may cover four square feet or more and be two or three feet high. The shape will be governed by the size and shape of the cave or crevice it is built in. If built on open ground, it will be round or oval. The nest proper will be at the top, with a number of passages leading up through the pile to it. The sleeping quarters will be a round mass about ten inches in diameter made of fine shredded grass and bark. A small entry-way leads into the nest from the side. The actual cup will be about four inches in diameter. Here the pack rat spends the day.

A lot of other creatures take advantage of this bristling house; crickets, tarantulas, beetles, scorpions, snakes, salamanders, lizards, tree frogs, white-footed mice, shrews and rabbits, and even brooding quail. It offers a sanctuary of sorts to many small desert dwellers.

Big houses are built by wood rats in the prime of life, active fellows who do not mind hard work. In his old age the trader will settle for a small house, poorly built.

Of course, all of the trader's treasures will be hidden away in the pile where he can easily find them. He will keep adding to his store of curios, bringing home something almost every night. Cactus buds, bits of stick, and similar materials become a part of the nest, but the bright pebbles and bits of bone and the things filched from cabins and camps remain treasures the trader can admire.

A short time ago I worked on a Disney nature film. I put a pack rat into the story. He had a fine house on a ledge in a cave.

A cougar, seeking a place where her cubs could be born, found the cave and took it over as a nursery. Looking around for materials with which to make a nest, she spied the house and pulled it down, kicking aside the cactus joints.

The pack rat escaped to a high ledge where he sat rapping his feet in anger. All of his treasures were scattered over the floor of the cave. One small, white stone was his most prized possession. He sat moving his head back and forth as he watched the black tip of the cougar's tail roll the white stone back and forth.

The production boys were dubious about trying to make a pack rat into an actor. Several pack rats were caught for the studio by the Utah Fish and Game Department. They turned out to be both fine actors and easy to handle. In fact they were perfect "hams." The scene where the trader moved his head back and forth as he watched the white stone was easy to make. One of the boys simply held a peanut to one side of the trader's head. He turned his head and expressed eager interest. The peanut was shifted to the other side, and he turned his head that way. He had learned to like peanuts. The film editor just cut back and forth, first to the rolling rock, then back to the trader's head as it moved. The result was perfect, and it was exactly what a pack rat would do.

Scientists have described twenty-eight species of wood rats but the differences are things that would concern only a scientist, and need not bother anyone who is just out to watch these dwellers of the desert, plain, and mountain. They all have temperaments very much alike. Living on the desert will force some adjustment on a wood rat; the same is true of living in the woods.

In courting, the male is master of the situation. The date of the mating moon can be predicted in areas where the seasons change. In California and the deep southwest this may not hold true. But we do know that when the urge to mate comes to the trader, he will become very restless, and will go on rambling tours through the forest or out across the desert which will take him far beyond the borders of his normal range. During the mating season both males and females produce a strong-smelling musk. They both leave scent messages as they wander about.

When a male does find a female, he will discover that she is far from a coy maiden. When he approaches her, she will greet him with thumping hind feet and bared teeth. If he boldly moves in to offer his favors she will rain blows upon him. But the urge of the mating moon cannot be denied, and the male is persistent. In the end she always accepts him with affection.

The average number of young is two. The babies will weigh about a third of an ounce. When they get hold of a nipple they hang on and cannot be pulled off. If the mother wants to free herself she has to nip them on the backs of their necks to make them let go. A twinge of pain will cause them to open their mouths to cry.

When three weeks old, the babies open their eyes and see the world for the first time. The opening of the eyes marks the first time they have taken any interest in the nest. Within a month or six weeks they will strike out into the woods on their own.

All of nature's babies face the most critical time of their lives while they are very young. A fawn hidden in a thicket is helpless, baby mice and rats are helpless while in the nest and very vulnerable when they first leave it. If the young wood rats can survive until they have grown strong and active, they can look forward to being able to cope with most of the hazards and dangers all small creatures of the wild face.

Jumping mice can be found from the Arctic Circle to south-central California, Missouri and North Carolina. They are the world's champion jumpers for their size. Weighing less than an ounce, they can jump ten or twelve feet at one leap. If a kangaroo could put as much power back of a leap, with its two hundred pounds of weight, much of which is sinew and muscle, it could span four miles at one jump.

The very long leaps of this mouse are made to escape enemies. When terrified by a weasel or a skunk, they take off and sail

JUMPING MOUSE   *Dick Smith*

through the air. Ordinary jumps when foraging or playing are seldom over four feet. Here again we have an example of one of the many ways wild creatures have of protecting themselves from their enemies. Even a weasel can't keep up with a jumping mouse.

The yellowish-brown marking of this mouse lets it blend with its surroundings so completely that even the keenest hunter will miss it unless approaching down-wind from it. Its very long tail serves to balance it while it sails through the air. Like the kangaroo rat, the jumping mouse has powerful hind legs and small, hand-like forepaws. Its upright posture is much like that of the kangaroo rat.

Jumping mice are extremely clean, elegant little creatures with a pleasant voice which is deep-toned and unlike the voices of other mice.

There are grassland and woodland jumping mice, but to the

ordinary observer they both look the same and act the same. The main difference between them is the way they live, each adapting to its environment.

The best place to look for the nest of a jumping mouse is in a shelter of overhanging grass, or in a hollow tree or a crack in a rock. The summer nest will be a ball of finely-woven grass, conical in shape. Its outside diameter will be no more than four inches and there will be a small opening on one side. Room space inside will not exceed two inches. The inside will be lined with feathers or moss and soft grass. Sometimes the nest will be suspended several inches above the ground, hardly enough to give any protection against snakes or weasels. Here the jumping mouse lives alone. The woodland jumpers also often build underground.

The winter residence will be built underground for warmth, and if you examine it you will find it snugly lined with grass and moss. This is the nest where the jumping mouse will sleep through the winter. They will retire in the far north in late summer, in the south, late in the fall.

If you see a jumping mouse that is so fat and sluggish that it is unable to make a soaring leap if you startle it, you will know that it is about ready to retire for its long sleep. It will have increased its weight by a third, all of it layers of fat. At this time they become easy prey for the killers.

The jumpers go to sleep and stay asleep until spring arrives. When the time for them to wake up comes, they do it in spite of the weather. They do not seem to mind if spring is late in coming.

The family life and raising of young are much the same as with other mice. A brief romance, babies to be cared for for a few weeks, mostly during June and July.

Jumping mice get along together on their selected range, but they never live together except at mating time. There is no community life among them. They go their solitary way, leaping through space, singing their oddly melodious song when they feel happy, content in their small world.

POCKET GOPHER   *National Park Service*

Not even man can equal the prowess of a pocket gopher in digging tunnels. Man with all his power tools is slow compared to the gopher. In ordinary ground it can dig three hundred feet of tunnel in one night.

The pocket gopher is constantly at war with farmers, orchardists and gardeners. It is one wild creature they have never been able to master. Prairie dogs can be killed by pouring heavier than air gas down their burrows. A whole town can be destroyed in a day; rats can be eliminated by a determined extermination program. About the best we can manage with the gopher is to try to keep even with him. Garden supply stores have shelves lined with poisons and potions calculated to destroy gophers. The makers of these potions have learned that it is not safe to guarantee the customer his money back if they do not eliminate his gophers. Traps have been designed especially for pocket gophers; bombs are on the market which an unwary gopher can trigger and get blown up, fumes from the exhaust pipes of tractors and trucks have been piped into their burrows, deadly pumps have been designed which force cyanide gas into their runways, the same lethal gas as is used in the gas chamber at San Quentin Penitentiary.

I learned about pocket gophers when we moved to a ranch on a slope of the Santa Cruz mountains in California.

We had seventeen acres of orchard, and a yard in which there were a hundred varieties of roses. As a champion of the right of every animal to live and work out his personal destiny, I was reluctant to start exterminating the gophers on our ranch. But I soon realized that if I wanted to have any fruit trees or roses left I'd have to fight those gophers. I sadly announced to my wife that I hated to exterminate the gophers, but had decided they were doomed. Only that morning I had discovered that one or more gophers had devoured the roots of her favorite climbing rose which covered the side of the house. It hung there withered and dead. The battle which followed was a bitter one. I used all of the weapons available, even to buying a cyanide gun, a gadget I was deathly afraid of. I trapped, gassed, put out tempting baits of strychnine-poisoned carrots. In the end I settled for a truce. If I could reduce their numbers enough so that my orchard and my rose garden had a fighting chance to survive, I was lucky.

I decided I could either spend my time fighting gophers and other pests or I could forget the fight and settle down to writing the books I had to write to support the family and the ranch.

This gopher gets his name from the fur-lined pouches on each side of his head and shoulders. They are true pouches and not big cheeks outside the jaw bones as is the case with the chipmunk.

You will know when a pocket gopher has taken up residence in your yard or garden by the mounds of fresh dirt he pushes out of the tunnel he is digging. During the day you may see a furry brown head poke out of a hole and have two beady eyes stare at you. When young, a pocket gopher may wander about above ground. But during his lifetime a pocket gopher spends most of his time in a lightless tunnel underground.

East or west there is little difference between pocket gophers. It takes an expert on rodent teeth to tell them apart.

In warmer climates the tunnels are shallower than in places where frost penetrates deep. The tunnels will be in tiers. The upper tunnels are used for foraging. At the ends and along the sides of spur tunnels, rooms will be scooped out for storage, and for bedrooms or nursery rooms.

A gopher just starts digging knowing that he will find plenty of roots as he goes along. If he comes upon an extra tasty plant root, he may burrow upward and pull the whole plant into the ground. If you are out in your garden on a windless day and notice a tomato plant sawing and jerking you can rush to its rescue and start stamping on the ground, or you can stand and watch your tomato plant sink into the ground. You may as well watch because the gopher has already eaten the root off the plant.

If you get a shovel and start digging you may find your tomato plant in a small room a foot or so underground along with some of your carrots and beets, but don't try to dig the gopher out, you'd never catch up with him.

The pocket gopher spends most of his time in the dark. He does not need light to show him his way. If he is moving ahead he can depend upon his whiskers to keep from bumping into the sides of the tunnel or cracking his head on a rock cave-in. If he is backing up, the nerve endings on his tail serve the same purpose. A man by the name of Macabee in Los Gatos, California developed a trap which takes advantage of this feeler system. The jaws of the trap open like ice-tongs. The gopher feels his way between the tongs and pokes his nose against a sensitive trigger. The tongs snap shut on him. The Macabee trap is the best pocket gopher trap made and the most vicious.

When two gophers meet in a tunnel they fight furiously. With their chisel teeth they try to get a grip on each other's snouts. If the loser fails to get away, he will be killed. Gophers do not tolerate visitors who seek to use their tunnels.

When the mating urge grips a male pocket gopher he gets

restless and excited, even reckless. He seems to know that the mating moon will wane in a couple of weeks. For months he has lived a solitary life, fighting any gopher who dares call on him, but now he goes above ground, usually at night, but sometimes during the day, and strikes off across country. Nobody knows how he locates the females hidden deep underground, but he does. After a short period of romance, he deserts his mate and strikes off for home. The mating moon rises in November in the south and much later in the north.

When the time comes for the young to be born, the mother retires to a well-stocked room. Here one or two babies are born, rarely three. They will be blind for five weeks and have to depend upon food brought to them by their mother. They probably eat much of the green fodder she has stored in the nursery. After their eyes are open, they go their solitary ways. All pocket gophers are driven by an urge to dig, and they keep at it steadily throughout their lives. They have one advantage over other small foragers who live above ground, they have very few enemies who can destroy them. The badger has almost vanished. In localities where there are badgers, it is doubtful if the big hunter can dig fast enough to overtake a pocket gopher. He can get at the nest with the young in it, however. Other wildlife may vanish, but it is likely that we will always have pocket gophers.

The Whistlers

There are three American members of the woodchuck family, the yellow-bellied marmot, the hoary marmot and the wood-chuck. The yellow-bellied and the hoary marmots are found in the west. The woodchuck comes only as far west as Montana, its range is the northeastern part of the continent, north to Nova Scotia. The woodchuck looks wise but actually it has just about enough brains to keep alive. Its only claim to fame is that on February 2 it is supposed to come out of hibernation and look around. If the sun is shining and it sees its shadow it is supposed to return to its den for another six weeks and terrible blizzards will rage. If the sky is overcast it stays out and spring weather is assured. In colonial times people had a lot of faith in "ground-hog day." Some people today may have faith in the woodchuck as a weather prophet. Actually he is a stupid fellow. The mar-mots are much more interesting.

All woodchucks whistle but the hoary marmot, sometimes called whistle pig, is champion. Both kinds of western marmots have coats with frosted white-tipped hairs. Look for the whistle pig in the mountains at or near timberline; the yellow-belly lives at a lower altitude. They prefer meadows or parks close to cliffs or rock slides. Because of this they are often called "rock chucks." The yellow-bellies are smaller than the hoary variety and have a less shrill whistle, but a good one; it is not a blast like that of their bigger cousin.

The first time that you hear a whistler you may think that one of your hiking companions is trying to signal to you. It may be that a sentinel perched on a rock has sighted you and is sounding a warning to the clan. If you start looking for the source of the whistle, the sentinel will sound off again and a dozen or more chucks will join in as they dash toward refuge in a rock pile. It will be a racket you won't forget.

If you hide well in a spot from which you can watch a small meadow below a rock-slide you may be treated to a fine show. Rock chucks will be scattered over the meadow feeding, and there will be a sprinkling of ground squirrels and chipmunks dashing about looking for seeds. A pair of blue grouse may join the party and birds will be chirping and singing.

A golden eagle or a red-tailed hawk may sweep out from the high rim above and come down upon the meadow in a screaming two hundred mile per hour dive. Instantly the old sentinel will sound a warning. Squirrels, chips and mice scamper for cover along with the rock chucks, who will be whistling defiantly as they run. By the time the eagle dives at grasstop height over the meadow, it will be deserted and silent except for the humming of insects. Everyone who has a den is underground; the rabbits have taken to cover in a thicket.

Rock chucks need a safe haven. They tempt all of the large hunters. They feed in the open on the ground and in the daytime. Up to twenty pounds of fat rock chuck is bound to tempt a predator. Their whistling lets any killer know the location of the colony. They have to be watchful for killers every minute they are outside their rocky dens. Even a mink or a weasel will try for a baby chuck.

The sight of a dozen fat marmots feeding in an open meadow, working through tall grass, just can't be resisted. But the hunter will have to use everything he has in his bag of tricks if he is to catch one. He has to approach unseen to a point where he can cut

MARMOT   *Hugh A. Wilmar*

off a rock chuck when the rush for the slide starts. Brush cover around the meadow will not be close enough for an ambush. There would be no rock chucks left if there were. A bobcat may be able to creep through the tall grass unseen, but a cougar or a bear will be spotted immediately. The bear will be the most frustrated of all. He is so big that the sentinel spots him at once and sounds a warning, which is joined by all of the whistlers as they bound away. With an angry roar the bear will dash across the meadow. But the chucks have a good lead and will tumble into their rocky dens before the bear can catch up with even the slowest straggler. As soon as they are underground defiant chuckles will float up from inside the rock pile.

I once found a rock slide where a black bear had left many tracks and plenty of evidence that he had tried his best to hurl aside the rocks and get at the chucks hidden away. It was easy to imagine what had happened. It takes a lot to stir up a lazy black bear enough so that he would attack a granite rock slide. I have been told there are cases where a bear actually was able to claw aside the rocks and get at some of the chucks, but I am sure this is a rare happening. It is likely that in the past the grizzly dined on rock chuck more often than the black. The grizzly is a prodigious worker and has four times the strength of a black bear.

The hoary marmot may be awake only three or four months out of the year. The rest of the time is spent in a deathlike sleep. When it sleeps, its breathing practically ceases, the pulse becomes faint and the body temperature drops to between forty-five and fifty-five degrees. This whistler comes out of hibernation in April and may retire early in August. (In the case of the woodchuck the date for leaving the den varies with the area where he lives. Your chance of observing a marmot is limited to spring and early summer.)

Building up enough fat to last eight or nine months means a lot of eating, and that is just what the whistle pigs do, they stuff themselves all day long. When they first emerge they may weigh only half as much as they did when they retired, and have a lot of weight to regain. These chucks miss a number of seasons other animals enjoy, the lush time of Indian summer when the harvest of seed and nuts is on, sometimes even a part of summer itself. It certainly isn't cold weather that makes them retire to their dens as it is with the bears. But while they are awake they enjoy themselves. Of course, they have family duties which must be tended to in the short time they are up and about. A mother whistler will give birth to from three to eight young. They are sent out to forage when they are about the size of ground squirrels. There is no time to waste in a leisurely childhood, with bedtime coming in a matter of weeks. Mother will be sound asleep before they have learned very much. Quite a few youngsters will not survive.

As summer progresses the whistlers begin to bulge. The little ones bulge as much as their elders. Now the short legs cannot keep the furry belly from rubbing on the ground. At this stage you could probably run one of them down, but if you did you'd have a fight on your hands. When cornered he can and will make good use of his sharp chisel teeth. When they reach this degree of fatness they stay closer to their dens. Having earlier cropped the far grass they feed on that close to their dens.

Each of the killers has his own way of trying to catch a whistler. We have seen how the bear works it. The coyote will certainly use his "prairie dog" trick of pretending not to see the whistlers. He trots along, never glancing into the meadow where the chucks are feeding. If he is able to pass close enough without arousing the sentinel or one of the other watchful chucks, by pretending not to be hungry or interested, he may be able to whirl and cut off a chuck who has wandered too far out into the meadow. His rush will touch off a wild chorus and a mad rush across the meadow.

The grey fox and the desert fox stalk by creeping through the tall grass and weeds on their bellies. Clumps of rose-briar and lupine or columbine will be used for cover. The approach will be slow, edging forward a foot, stopping to lie still, moving another foot. If the sentinel or one of the other old chucks detects even a flash of gray fur or the unusual jerking of weed tops, he will spot the invader and sound off. Then the fox will find he has wasted a whole morning and still has an empty belly.

The bobcat will stalk much as the fox does, but the cougar's only chance to dine on a fat chuck is to come down over the slide and try a flank attack. His problem is to move down over the barren slide rocks without being seen, so that he can get close enough to leap into the meadow where he can cut off the retreat of the chucks. The cougar is a master at moving unseen across a slide or along a ledge. His color blends with that of the rocks, he glides and stops and glides again. From an elevation his leap may be forty feet, but it must carry him clear of the rocks, because he will be hurtling through the air and his impact when he lands will be enough to smash him on broken granite. I have found cougar sign near rock slides where chucks lived, but I have never found evidence of a kill. A cougar rarely dines upon whistler meat.

Red-tailed hawks will come in low over a cliff at terrific speed and dive low over a meadow looking for very young chucks. I have a feeling that they kill many of the babies.

As we have seen, marmots are community-spirited. Both the hoary and the yellow-belly varieties appear to post sentinels, at least there is always one watchful chuck who is specially alert. How these sentinels are selected nobody knows. Someone has suggested that there is always one or two worry-warts in every colony who just don't aim to be surprised. My theory is that the sentinel is an old chuck, possibly a grandfather, who likes to sit on a rock in the sun, and who is a lot warier than the younger chucks.

With the August sun beating down upon their meadows and the tall grass and herbiage beginning to dry up, the bulging whistlers will one day decide that their labors are over for the summer, perhaps their bodies will tell them that they have stored enough fat to last them for nine months, and they will curl up in their beds and go to sleep.

Small Bundles

If you are in the Southwest and tramping a slope studded with creosote bushes, rocks and stunted mesquite you may see what appears to be a wildly waving white tail moving all by itself. Of course, the tail is attached to a body and that body is brown or dun-colored and blends perfectly with the desert ground. You have sighted an antelope squirrel. The white fur of the tail reflects the sunlight making a flash similar to the flash from the white rump patch of the pronghorn antelope. Hence the name this little fellow goes by.

Watch for him if you make a trip through Death Valley. He likes plenty of heat and does not mind the extremes of Death Valley where temperatures rise to one hundred thirty degrees or higher. This little fellow dashes about below sea level or on slopes three thousand feet above the furnace heat of the valley.

One would think that an animal who braved such heat would be conservative in its movements. Not this twelve-inch, five-ounce hustler; he dashes about during the heat of the day like a locoed ghost, his wildly waving tail never still, even when he pauses to snatch a few seeds from a bush, or to look back over his shoulder or up into the sky. He knows that the semaphore he constantly waves will attract hawks aloft and advertise his presence to killers on the ground. He is only bite-size but no hunter will pass him up. The antelope squirrel is easily the most restless

of the ground squirrels; compared to him the chipmunk is almost
a sluggard.

The time to see this fellow is from seven or eight in the morning until noon. He is not an early riser, he wants the desert well
warmed up before he ventures out of his den. At noon he takes
a two or three hour siesta before setting out to find his supper.
He is always back before dark. His habits are the reverse of those
of the kangaroo rat who avoids even bright moonlight. It takes
all kinds to make up the world of the wild.

A suspicious and super-cautious approach to everything helps
the antelope squirrel to avoid most of his enemies. He just runs
all of the time, his gait a series of six- to twelve-inch leaps.

The antelope squirrel is not an efficient digger, he goes to
considerable trouble trying to find somebody's abandoned nest
or den. He will make his home in a badger hole, which is safe
enough because badgers dig dozens of holes they never return to.
He may have to settle for a cranny in a rock wall. But sometimes
he has to dig. When he does, his burrow will be just a tunnel with
no rooms, but it will serve as a place to sleep and for the storage
of seeds.

An antelope squirrel may have as many as a dozen brothers
and sisters. His birthday will be in April or May. A mother who
is constantly on the go has little time to spend with her children
and abandons them as soon as they are weaned. Without help or
guidance many of them fall prey to snakes, hawks and other
predators.

According to Victor Chalane, who kept a number of these
squirrels in a cage, they cannot be tamed. For him they remained
as wild and untamed as when caught.

Chalane might be wrong, as he admits. If you caught a baby
antelope squirrel, it might grow up to be an affectionate pet;
certainly it would be a lively one.

There is another interesting fellow to look for on pine and
aspen mountain slopes. He is the golden mantled ground squir-

GOLDEN-MANTLED GROUND SQUIRREL   *Roy E. Disney*

rel. This is also red squirrel country and they, also known as chickarees, are apt to announce your coming noisily.

If you watch carefully you will spot a golden mantle, but not in the way you spot other ground squirrels or chipmunks. Stop often and look around. You may see three or four of these small squirrels, each seated on a rock or a log with small forepaws folded over a fat belly. This habit of sitting still may be a protection against hawks, but it gives the impression that the golden mantle is a very thoughtful fellow who spends most of his time considering serious matters. For additional identification he has bold stripes down his back and his color is chestnut which turns golden when the sun is shining on it.

When he does get around to feeding, the golden mantle eats fast and continuously, using his forepaws as hands. Those living along the trails in Yosemite Park and other parks are prime favorites with visitors who feed them so lavishly that they get so fat they can barely waddle.

There is a tale told about the golden mantled squirrel and the 49'ers who came seeking gold. It was said that where a prospector found golden mantled squirrels he was sure to find grassroots gold.

These squirrels live in burrows. Though they keep their coats sleek and clean, they are very bad housekeepers. Their dens are very untidy though they are careful not to scatter litter outside the entrance where it might attract the attention of a weasel or a badger.

In most mountain regions, the young are born between the end of June and the first of August. They will be a quarter grown when you see them. There may be as many as seven in a litter. Once out of the den they soon learn to forage for themselves.

The golden mantles are neighborly, they talk and argue with each other when out in a meadow, but they prefer to live alone in their burrows. When I say "talk," I am just giving my impression, it certainly appears to be talk to me.

They have glands back of their shoulders which exude musk. This is left on twigs and leaves and conveys a message to other golden mantles who pass that way; perhaps they are at times love messages and at other times the announcement of the arrival of a visitor. Beavers leave similar messages on mud banks, coyotes leave theirs on bleached skulls, or rocks or stumps along a trail.

The golden mantles are among the most handsome of the small fur-bearing animals. Luckily for them, they do not live near farms where they would be sure to call down the wrath of the farmers and suffer the fate of the prairie dog.

We cannot limit the chipmunk to any one locality, his tribe has set out to inherit the earth. Look for the chip in the mountains, on the plains, on the desert and in the eastern mountain slopes and forested uplands. The western chip differs from his eastern cousin in that his color is gray, not rusty. The western variety is smaller and it has a longer tail. Its back stripes are finer and there are more of them. Otherwise a chipmunk is a chipmunk wherever you find him.

You are apt to first see this little gray elf when he flashes across a trail you are following through the woods. He darts swiftly along and when he slows down his bushy tail comes up for balance and to serve as an air brake. Watch one seated on a rock stripping the husk from a lupine seed. The chip is an expert at getting a seed out of a pod or a nut out of its shell. The little hands work quickly, a few swift turns and the husk is off.

The delicate hands of the chipmunk are of little value in digging, so he seeks a range where there are rotting logs. If no logs are available, he finds a pocket under a stone, or a crack in a wall or an opening under the roots of a tree where he will make his nest and store the seeds he gathers.

If you camp in the woods you can easily make friends with all of the chips in the neighborhood. They will come to your camp and if you scatter a few crumbs they will become very friendly. I have often piled up cherry pits and sat back to watch the fun. The first chip to discover the pile always filled his cheek pouches as full as he could but would hesitate to leave the treasure, picking up a pit and trying to force it into his cheek pouch. Finally he would dash madly away to empty his pouches. Every chip that discovered the pile did the same thing. I have photographed a chip inside the rind of a half cantaloupe I had placed on the camp table. You can't scrape the rind too close to keep a chip from making a meal of it. I once found one perched on a loaf of bread in my cabin. He was trying to figure out how to handle such a big meal.

I once thought I would catch one and examine it. I had a gold pan in my outfit and a fly rod. I made a deadfall out of the pan by propping it up with a stick and attaching my trout line to the stick. I scattered cake crumbs under the pan and reeled out thirty feet of line, then sat down to wait. I did not have to wait long. We had been in camp a week and the chips had become very bold. I was a little greedy about the matter; I waited until there

GROUND SQUIRRELS   *N. Paul Kenworthy, Jr.*

were four eager chips harvesting crumbs under the pan. They
were having a contest stuffing crumbs into their cheeks. Had there
been only one he would have sat there and eaten the crumbs.

The deadfall was set on a bed of pine needles under a big pine
tree. I jerked the stick from under the rim of the pan and it
dropped over the four chips. I felt elated but only for a few
seconds. Before I could get to my feet and slip on a leather glove,
four gray sprites exploded from under the gold pan sending a
shower of pine needles flying. The only chip I was able to catch
on that trip was taken by accident. I had left a window of the car
open a few inches and a chip ventured inside to see what he could
find. I discovered him there and promptly closed the window
after slipping inside the car. I learned that it was no easy task to
catch a chipmunk even in the confined space of a Model A coupe.
I caught him and tried to calm him down and gain his confidence,
but he was so terrified that I let him go, but not before daubing
his head with ink. He was back in camp the next day.

Chips need all of their speed, good eyesight and sharp hearing to avoid their many enemies. They feed by day, are never still, and often dash about in the open as well as climbing grass and flower stems to get seeds. They perch on rocks and logs to shuck out their meals. Hawks take many of them and so do weasels. I once had a chip rush wildly through my camp screaming loudly with a weasel chasing it. I threw a stick at the weasel but that did not bother it, even though the stick almost hit it. The killer darted into a thicket where the chip had vanished. I stood helpless and listened to the death cry of the chip.

It is good to sit and listen to a chip chorus coming from a few hundred yards away. The song will be a series of chuck chucks, varying in pitch and tone with every chip nearby joining in. The eastern chip is a much better singer than his western cousin. Where there are many eastern chips feeding, one of them may hop on a log and sound a chuck or two. The other chips will line up and they will be off on a gleeful chorus.

The chips are helped in their fight for survival by the fact that a female will give birth to two litters a season, numbering from two to seven in each litter. But the speed and alertness of this little seed-gatherer is also a big factor.

Chips eat a variety of food; nuts, seeds, and fruit of all kinds, whatever their range offers. In New Mexico they store binsful of pinon nuts. Any nut, berry, or seed is stored and eaten.

They make the woods merry with their chatter and colorful with their antics and they readily accept you as a friend if you do your hunting with a camera. Unfortunately some campers have to take along a .22 rifle. For a while I filled in as secretary to the Chamber of Commerce of Gunnison, Colorado, a town in the mountains on the Western Slope. I received a letter from a man in the east saying that he would like to vacation in Western Colorado, if there were any chipmunks his son could shoot.

The chickaree is the noisiest animal in the woods. This red squirrel is found in most of the pine woods of the west. Any wild hunter, even a man, will be greeted by angry chattering.

SQUIRREL   *Roy E. Disney*

"Tcher-r-r," repeated over and over again in a voice that carries
a long way. It is like the rattle of an old alarm clock with a de-
fective bell.

Even a bear receives an angry greeting. If the bear stumbles
upon the chickaree's cache of pine nuts, the chattering will include sputters, hisses and growls, uttered while the squirrel is
stamping his feet furiously on a limb. This is all bluff; no red
squirrel would let himself get close enough to a bear to nip him.
And no bear will leave a chickaree's storeroom until the last nut
is licked up. After the bear ambles away the chickaree will come
down out of the tree and search for nuts bruin might have missed.

Human thieves often search for the chickaree's storeroom,
which in the fall will contain a goodly supply of pine or pinon
nuts. The red squirrel is such an industrious nut gatherer that
each cache will yield a large supply of nuts. The Indians of the
southwest spend much time searching for the squirrels' nut bins.

If there is no creature around to scold, the chickaree will carry on a conversation with himself, cheerfully chattering away while he works. There will be spells when he is silent but they do not occur very often.

It is a tribute to this squirrel's sharp eyes and ears that it can detect a cougar slipping through the woods on noiseless pads, never snapping a twig or overturning a stone and always keeping to dense cover. But he knows somehow, and many a doe has been given enough warning to make off with her fawn to a secluded spot where she can hide the little one.

The chickaree is an unsociable fellow, keeping to himself except during the mating season. He is easily spotted because he is always on the move and very noisy most of the time. Red squirrels were hunted long before the white man came to America. The Indians have always eaten this squirrel, and the squirrel has learned a few tricks to protect himself. The most successful is his way of flattening himself on a limb so that it is difficult to see him. Pioneers killed the chickaree for food and for its skin and tail, which they used to decorate their hunting caps. It is killed today mostly for sport.

There is an interesting bit of history connected with the red squirrel's tail. In the early days men from the colonies used to organize game drives. On these drives the pioneers killed hundreds of deer and other big game. This wanton slaughter infuriated the Indians who killed only what they needed for food. They passed a sentence of death on all hunters. One sure way to recognize a hunter was by his cap trimmed with red squirrel tails. Going into the woods wearing a coon skin cap trimed with squirrel tails was a good way for a hunter to lose his scalp.

The red squirrel has many enemies besides man. They can avoid ground prowlers by darting up a tree, and the leafy branches protect them from hawks and owls. Of course, they do spend some time on the ground in hollow logs or stumps where they are exposed to coyotes, bobcats and foxes. However the log or stump is almost always in the open so that stalking is difficult, and it is usually near a tree the squirrel can reach in a few bounds. But when a pine marten spots a squirrel, that squirrel is doomed. The marten can climb faster and leap farther than any squirrel. And the pine marten is found in the territory of the red squirrel.

For the chickaree the mating moon rises in late winter and early spring. In some localities they will be chasing each other as early as February. The honeymoon is a frolicsome affair but does not last long. About five weeks later the young are born. There may be as many as seven in a family and they are entirely dependent upon their mother until they are one third grown.

The best nursery a red squirrel can find is a woodpecker's hole in a tree trunk. Such a nest is easily defended and is high off the ground out of reach of snakes and most other predators. You may see furry heads peeking out of a woodpecker's nest. Have a good look to make sure because the pine marten uses abandoned woodpeckers' nests the same as the squirrels do. If danger threatens her babies, the mother will move them one at a time to another hiding place. This is quite a feat if the youngsters are a third as big as she is, because she has to leap from tree to tree with a baby in her mouth, gripped firmly by the loose skin on its belly.

All that restricts the red squirrel's range is a lack of suitable food and shelter. Chickarees cannot manage where there are no trees. They are never found on the open deserts. It is known that the red squirrels may make mass migrations as do the gray squirrels. Why a whole population in an area should suddenly feel an urge to go someplace else is a mystery. They will leave localities where the food supply is adequate. The chickarees in the western mountains have pushed their range to the border between the forest and the desert. Here the nests are built high in the crotch of a tree, and will be made of sticks and leaves. This borderline timber does not attract woodpeckers.

A red squirrel often has three or four nests; perhaps a den in a hollow tree and a couple of woven nests. If one nest becomes infested with fleas, the squirrel moves to another that has been abandoned by the pests.

Thieves pose almost as big a problem for the chickaree as do his enemies, the hawks and the predators. Neighbors too lazy or witless to store food keep an eye open for a squirrel cache. Woodpeckers, nuthatches and other birds are fond of nuts. A bin of nuts is a real find, especially if the nuts are out of season. Gray squirrels and fox squirrels will steal from the red squirrel. Perhaps the chickarees do some thieving on their own.

If the cache is cleaned out late in the fall the chickaree will face lean days, even disaster during the winter months.

The chickaree's midden is just a pile of cones and husks which may be of considerable size if it has been used for several seasons. The squirrel places the nuts, berries, mushrooms and other items of food on top of the pile and the food often gets mixed with the debris so that the squirrel has to dig through the whole pile to locate the items he wants. This does not apply to the regular storerooms.

If you come upon a big brown mushroom lodged in the fork of a tree you may be sure that a chickaree put it there to serve as a snack later on.

In addition to nuts and seeds the red squirrel hunts for bugs, grubs and larvae found under loose bark. Abandoned wasp nests, torn apart by other animals, may yield wasp eggs and larvae. The half-eaten carcass of a deer killed by a cougar will be feasted upon no matter how carefully the cougar has covered the meat with sticks and leaves to mark it as his cache.

Winter is usually a time of leisure for the red squirrel, unless a thief has looted his storage bin. He hedges his chance of loss by having a number of separate caches. During the snow months there will be excursions so that the chickarees will know what is going on in the neighborhood, or to visit places where nuts and seeds have been stored. In snow country the record of the travels can be read by the tracks in the snow.

This little red squirrel can be said to be the voice of the pine forest as well as its eyes and ears, and as we have seen he does not take his duties lightly.

The gray squirrel is found from the Atlantic to the Pacific. The western gray has never been as numerous as the eastern. The forests along the Atlantic coast teemed with gray squirrels when the first colonists arrived. There were so many of them that they destroyed all planted crops where the forest surrounded the fields. A bounty had to be placed on them. During 1749, Pennsylvania paid for the destruction of six hundred and forty thousand gray squirrels.

In those days, the gray squirrel, like the lemming of the north, often made mass migrations. They crossed rivers and lakes. No obstacle stopped them. Thousands were killed by predators, were drowned or bagged by hunters, but still they marched on with bushy tails raised like crusaders' banners. In 1842 such a migration took place in Wisconsin which lasted a month. Seton has estimated that this mass exodus may have contained a half billion squirrels.

The western gray squirrel stays pretty much in one locality during its life. You will seldom find a gray in the territory occupied by red squirrels. The smaller red squirrel will attack the gray viciously and may even kill it.

The gray squirrel is notable for its big, fluffy tail. It forages on the ground a great deal, but is at home in a tree, which is its refuge when hunted by hawks or other prowling killers, the latter including man.

Park grays become very tame and are sure to visit your camp, again a reason for not staying at a motel. They are expert beggars and will do tricks to get your attention. You pay off with scraps and bits of bread crust. Grays can be seen on the lawns and in the parks of cities from coast to coast.

The gray has always been classed as a game animal, and has been hunted by men from the time they arrived in America. After hundreds of years of being pursued by men armed with guns, the grays have learned a lot of evasive tactics. Hunting for gray squirrels calls for skill and some knowledge of woodcraft. The wild gray is not lazy like the park squirrels, he is very alert and

GRAY SQUIRREL   *Ralph A. Anderson*

active. It may take a hunter eight hours or more to bag one gray squirrel. An alert old gray will circle a tree trunk, keeping the trunk between himself and the hunter, who will also be circling, or he may flatten himself on a limb of the same color as his body. Today a great many people prefer to watch the grays rather than shoot them.

Raising the family is strictly up to the mother; the father is a fickle fellow who will have as many as four mates. After the mating season he abandons them all and retires to a solitary life. The mother selects a tree to build her den in. The litter may number up to six young. They develop slowly, their eyes remaining closed for five weeks. It takes two months for them to develop enough strength to climb around in their home tree.

In the Sierra Nevada area of the west, the grays often rob the acorn caches of the California woodpecker. These are odd storehouses. The woodpecker selects a big tree and pecks round holes in the trunk into each of which it forces one acorn. The trunk will become speckled with holes each showing the tip of an acorn. Of course such a supply of nuts will not be ignored by a gray squirrel if one is in the vicinity. There are a number of these nut storage trees in a small park in Santa Barbara, California. I have never seen any grays in that park, but the last time I visited it the nuts were gone from the holes. I can only speculate as to whether squirrels made off with them or whether the rightful owner ate them.

Compared to the red, the gray squirrel is big, weighing up to a pound and a half as compared to the red limit of ten ounces. Little detailed description is needed. If you see a squirrel with a big bushy tail, gray in color, with short ears and bright shoe-button eyes, you know it is a gray squirrel.

Like flying fish, flying squirrels do not fly. They are gliders. A flying squirrel will leap into space from the top of a sixty-foot pine tree. At once the squirrel spreads all four legs at right angles to its body which extends its "wings." The wings are folds of loose skin covered by soft short hair.

The squirrel may glide as much as two hundred feet before landing, not a bad record for an animal weighing from three to five ounces. By changing the slack in a wing the squirrel can change the angle, speed and course of its glide. The tail does most of the guiding. If a fast ninety-degree turn is needed to avoid hitting a limb, the squirrel can make it. The only thing this squirrel can't do is to flap his wings and rise into the air as the birds do, but he has been trying for thousands of years and may eventually do just that. Bats are animals which learned to fly.

The flying squirrel is more agile than the red squirrel. It can take off from a limb while the red is trying to decide where to jump.

You can identify this big-eyed little fellow by his markings. The upper fur is brownish, the belly, vest and cheeks are white. Of course, if you see a squirrel leap out of a tree and sail away, you won't need to see any markings to know it is a flying squirrel.

If a flyer's nest is disturbed, she will grasp her baby by the loose skin on its belly, and launch forth to take it to another nest. Generally the young stay with the mother until another brood is expected.

A flying squirrel in the wild does not live much longer than three years. They have too many enemies; all of the hawks, the marten, raccoon, the weasel and other larger predators. However, in the flyer, the marten meets a squirrel who can out-jump him.

You may spend a lot of time in the woods and never see a flying squirrel unless you startle it out of its nest. They come out of their nests to frolic and feed at dusk and retire before dawn. And frolic they do, scampering up tall trees and gliding down. You might see them at dusk or on a brightly lighted night when there is a full moon.

Flying squirrels make wonderful house pets, but their night-time frolicking can make them a bit of a nuisance. Having a little flyer land on your forehead with a plop while you are asleep can startle even a squirrel lover. Catch a young one if you want to make a pet out of a flying squirrel.

Dog Town

Over five hundred million inhabitants once lived in a town a thousand miles long and two hundred fifty miles wide. They built wonderful underground houses complete with living rooms, bedrooms, toilets, pantries and dining rooms. Little hallways connected the rooms. A steep shaft led down in a straight drop to the living quarters six feet below the surface. The builders always fixed a little shelf just below the entrance so that the owner could sit and listen, occasionally popping his head out to check on the neighbors or any intruder. A mound-shaped dyke kept rain water from running into the house. Outside the doorway one tall weed, often a thistle, was allowed to remain standing as a door sign. Otherwise front yards were kept clear of weeds and grass.

This was a prairie dog town, a vast community of fat little animals looking like oversized flicker-tail gophers. Today, dog towns can be found only in isolated places. The prairie dog has gone the way of the buffalo on the western plains. I recently revisited an area in Western Colorado where I lived twenty-five years ago. In those days, by taking any country road, you could see thousands of fat dogs sitting on their mounds and barking lustily. The area is cattle and sheep country and the ranchers waged constant war against the white-tailed prairie dogs to protect their grazing lands. They bought hundreds of pounds of strychnine to poison grain, which they scattered in the towns. They killed more game birds and song birds than they did dogs. Then a rodent exterminator discovered a liquid which, when poured down the shaft, evaporated into a gas heavier than air that would creep into all of the rooms and suffocate the inmates. In this extermination program no town was spared, even though it was located on land worthless for grazing.

The prairie dog is now so rare that I saw a sign in Arizona advertising a "town" which could be visited if you paid admission. There are a few left. I found one on a side road on Cochetopa Pass in Colorado. I hope no exterminator reads this and starts out with his can of lethal gas. I passed that way three years ago; perhaps he has already located that town.

Besides the plains strip I have mentioned, Texas was once said to have a dog population of 800,000,000, who could eat as much grass as 3,000,000 cattle. So the little barker had to go. No slaughter was ever greater, even that of the passenger pigeon, and, once the weapon was found, no slaughter was easier to accomplish. The cost was nothing as compared to preparing missiles with nuclear warheads with somewhat similar capabilities for mass destruction.

In examining the marvelous prairie dog home, with its plunge-hole into which a dog could dive when an enemy approached, one is faced with a riddle. What do the dogs do with the earth they excavate? The mound at the entrance can account for only a small fraction of the dirt dug out to construct so many rooms. And how does the dog get the dirt up the perpendicular shaft, which in some cases may be as much as ten feet deep?

One thing is sure, the builders make a house that is safe from flood waters. Many farmers have tried to flood the dogs out of a field by turning irrigation water into their shafts. The little fat architects had foreseen this flood possibility and had excavated a number of rooms by tunneling upward before enlarging the chamber. It worked like an inverted bottle thrust into water, air

PRAIRIE DOGS   *Warren E. Garst*

was trapped inside the room and no water could enter. The dogs just sat and waited for the water to seep into the ground.

The way of life of a prairie dog is a lazy, happy one. There are troubles and crises, of course, but on the whole they enjoy a happy, noisy existence. None of them that I knew ever hibernated, even at higher altitudes. They stayed underground when the weather was bad, but were out when the sun shone, even when there was snow on the ground. They are sociable creatures and will actually kiss each other when two friends meet. They like to sit up on their mounds and sing a sort of song. When in a hot argument with neighbors they make a sort of "ske-skirr" sound.

Unwelcome visitors often seek to take up residence in a dog town. For a long time a fable persisted that prairie dogs welcomed rattlesnakes and little prairie owls, even furnishing them food. They probably do furnish burrowing owls and snakes some food, their own babies, but I am sure this is not a voluntary contribution on the part of the dogs. The fact is that prairie dogs hate and fear rattlers. If a rattler slides down a shaft into a house seeking baby dogs the whole town may be roused and rush to the den entrance. With much excited chattering they may kick stones and dirt into the tunnel, securely plugging it up. The snake, not being a digger is trapped and doomed to a slow death of starvation.

As for that comical little bird, the burrowing owl, who always bows politely to any creature that approaches it, it also will stir up a fuss if it selects an inhabited burrow. The dogs are apt to attack it and tweak out its tail feathers. The owl has to find an unoccupied house. There it can set up housekeeping without arousing the wrath of the town. But its eggs and chicks will suffer the same fate as baby prairie dogs if a snake or a weasel enters the burrow.

All of the big cats try to catch prairie dogs. They just can't resist, with so many fat morsels tempting them. Few of the cats ever succeed. The area around a dog mound is always cleared of grass and shrubs, so that an unnoticed approach is impossible. There will always be a number of dogs sitting on their elevated mounds. The instant they spot an approaching bobcat or cougar they sound off. Dogs feeding some distance away from their home will take a quick look to locate the thistle which marks their entrance and then be off. Down the plunge-hole go all of the dwellers except the ones who perch on the shelves close to the entrance. Weasels and in some places, mink may enter a burrow. If they do, they will kill the entire family and there will be another vacant house which a burrowing owl may use.

Prairie dogs can be sassy and they do not always use good judgment. I know of one, a fat lazy fellow, who had been secured to play a part in a picture. The crew made so much of him that he got the idea he was an important character, able to toss his weight around. This foolish dog walked up to a falcon and barked in its face. In a second the dog was dead, struck in a vital spot by a lightning thrust of the falcon's talons.

Enos Mills tells of watching dogs mob an old member of the town. He was forced into a hole and rocks and dirt heaped upon him. He also says that he has seen mobs put one of their number to death. He speculated on what town ordinance those dogs had violated. I have watched dog towns for hours but have never seen any mob action against one of the dwellers.

Prairie dogs were once considered excellent weather prophets. If they started to repair the dyke around the entrance to their den, that was an indication that a storm was imminent. A number of naturalists vouch for this, insisting that when a prairie dog gets busy on repairs, a rain storm will soon blow up.

The prairie dog is a grass and grain eater. He likes alfalfa and clover but can make out on any kind of grass. When they forage, they have to go beyond the limits of the cleared area around the den. When they do this they keep eyes and ears open for enemies, and often sit up to get a better look. This is called periscoping and is practiced by weasels and many other animals. They also make sure that their house marker is in sight. The dog also has to scan the sky. Sharp-shinned and red-tailed hawks and golden eagles can see a dog on the ground at a height beyond the vision of the dog. When they pick a target they come down at terrific speed. The sharp-shinned hawk is likely to come in low over a hill and burst upon the town without warning. They catch more dogs than the other high-flying hunters.

Fleas and ticks are pests which force the dogs to take many dust baths. They kick and twist in a bin of dust until the fleas are suffocated. This does not work with the ticks, they have to be scratched or bitten off.

Accepting the observations made of prairie dogs in captivity may not be a safe guide when applied to the domestic life of a wild dog. Wild prairie dog males begin trying to get a romance started a couple of weeks before the females give any thought to honeymooning. Some females mate when they are a year old, others wait until the second year. Romances start occurring about the first of April and, once begun, both sexes chase about the town and there is much loud talk.

A mother may give birth to as many as ten pups. When the young are a couple of months old, they begin to spend much time above-ground and start to eat green food. The brothers and sisters will stick together in a group. They are appealing little creatures, all eyes and ears open for anything interesting. If an alarm is sounded by the old dogs, the pups will huddle together and look wildly about. They soon learn about their enemies and where safety lies.

At about this stage the mother leaves the den and does not return. The pups have the house to themselves. She will move into a vacant burrow and live by herself. In every town there are always vacant apartments.

Prairie dogs are hearty eaters. It is this big appetite that has brought the wrath of farmers and ranchers down upon them. Two or three dozen of them will eat as much grass as a sheep. Prairie dogs can go for long periods without water. In some mountain areas there will be frequent showers and water will be no problem, but in arid places weeks may pass without a dog getting a drink. They probably get some water from succulent plants.

Trappers, Indians and explorers ate prairie dogs. If the hunter wanted to be sure of his dog stew, he had to be careful not to shoot the dog inside the crater of his mound. If shot there, the dog was almost certain to slide down his plunge-shaft out of reach.

The prairie dog is plump-bodied, has a flattened head, rounded ears, short legs and a short tail. Its total length will be from ten to fifteen inches, its weight from one-and-a-half to three pounds. The color is pale gray, the coat short-haired.

It is to be hoped that a remnant of the dog towns will be spared. Man does not use every isolated acre of land in the west. We spend billions of dollars in storing grains we cannot use, and grazing stock and dairy animals that pile up surpluses. Why not leave a little grass, a high mountain meadow or a rocky slope to the little barkers and let them add their voices to those of the other creatures which make the high country and the plains live and speak.

Quills and Hare

Few people who have hiked along wooded mountain trails especially in the western United States have missed seeing a porcupine. Hikers in the Rocky Mountains and the High Sierra certainly have met this gnawer of resin bark and so have hikers in the northern Atlantic mountain areas. His range extends north into Canada and Alaska.

When you meet porky and observe him, you may come to the conclusion that he is a dull-witted fellow. He has no sense of curiosity that can be noticed. I have never seen one of them frolicking or playing. He just ambles along paying no attention to anything, or sits swaying in the top branches of a conifer sapling gnawing bark. I once stretched out on a grassy bank after climbing a ridge and dozed off. I was awakened by grunting sounds. Looking around I discovered a porcupine in the top of the second growth pine I was lying under. He must have come close to stepping on me when he approached the tree.

Another time I was awakened by a porcupine who was chewing on the stirrup flap of the saddle I was using as a pillow. Salt from the body of my horse probably made the leather attractive. I have had porcupines sit on a snowbank outside my cabin window and peer in at me. They certainly do not avoid man and this sometimes brings disaster to them. A hungry man, far from supermarkets, and without a gun to shoot game can easily whack a porcupine over the head and roast it at his campfire. The meat will be a bit greasy but it is sweet and many people like it. It is one wild animal that a man without weapons can catch, and it is protected in certain areas for this reason.

If you go after a porcupine with a club he will shove his head under a log or rock and bristle the quills on his back while switching his quilly tail threateningly. This defense is enough to discourage any wild killer except the fisher. This big member of the weasel tribe has solved the defense of the porcupine. The fisher simply rolls porky over and attacks the belly where there are no quills, and he never eats the skin or quilly parts.

A porcupine is often called "quill pig" or just "porky." Its quills are white in color or ivory, with black tips. They vary in length from one to five inches. Close to the end the quills taper to a sharp point which is covered with barbs, each barb overlaying the other. A layer of muscle at the base of each barb allows porky to make them stand erect to meet an attack or to lie flat when no danger threatens.

An unexcited porcupine gives the appearance of being covered mostly by fur. The quills may be hidden in the fur except for those on the tail. Porky has an arched back which is covered with coarse guard-hair. In the western variety these hairs will be tipped with yellow. The under-fur is fine and brown in color. The head is blunt with small ears, and porky has no neck to speak of. The front feet toe in like those of a bear.

Dogs, lacking the instincts of a coyote or wolf, often attack a porcupine. The dog rushes in intending to grab the quill pig by his back and shake him to death. In a flash the porcupine reverses ends and his quill laden tail jerks up striking the dog on the chest and face. When the dog leaps back and starts pawing at his face he simply drives the barbs deeper into his flesh. I have seen dozens of quills in the faces and mouths of dogs. When a dog comes in loaded with quills, he will have to submit to the painful ordeal of having them pulled out with a pair of pliers.

PORCUPINE   *Yellowstone National Park Photo*

If the quills are not extracted they will work into the skin, some coming out, others working their way like arrows into the dog's vital organs and causing death. The savage wolverine has been known to die a lingering death after having devoured a porcupine, quills and all. But even a savage killer like Carcajou will avoid porky unless starving.

Once in a while an old cougar whose teeth have worn down to where he can no longer use them as weapons in hunting may be found with lips and face filled with quills. Theodore Roosevelt shot one on the White River in Colorado that was starving because its mouth and throat were studded with quills.

It may be instinct which makes the big killer avoid porky normally, or it may be because of a painful early experience or from a mother's training.

The loss of a hundred or more quills in an encounter does

not bother porky, he will grow others to take their places. Anyway he carries an arsenal of several thousand barbed arrows.

At one time there was much speculation as to how porcupines mated. There is a simple explanation. The female makes her quills lie flat when being caressed by a suitor. One thing is certain, he won't caress her if she does not want him to.

A pair of porcupines walking through the woods may appear to be carrying on a conversation, repeating over and over one word or sound, in half grunts.

Porky has an odd taste in food. He eats the resin-filled bark of any conifer, pine, fir, spruce, balsam or hemlock. He will girdle small and large trees and climb into the saplings to get at the more tender limbs. During the snow time he sits on the snow beside the tree and works around it. Woodsmen can calculate the depth of the past winter's snow by the height of the girdle marks. Porky will eat other kinds of bark but he prefers the resin-filled kinds. He will grind up bleached bones and eat them, probably to secure needed minerals in his diet. He likes salt and will eat anything that has come in contact with salt: floors, pick handles having a salty flavor left by the sweaty hands of a miner, or your shirt if you leave it outside unwashed.

Porcupines are not as stupid as many people think. Observers get this impression because porky has very poor vision. He just does not see many things other animals see. If a porcupine meets you on a trail and you stand still he will show no interest until he is a yard or so away; then if you move he will look bewildered for a moment before retreating at a clumsy gallop.

The gestation period of the porcupine is over two hundred days. The mother gives birth to one baby. It may weigh a pound which is more than a cub bear weighs at birth. Its eyes will be open and some of its teeth will be pushing through the gums. There will be many quills in its fur, some an inch long.

Within a day after its birth a young porcupine can climb, but until it is six months old it will spend most of its time on the ground sleeping. At the age of six months mother and her youngster part company. Young porky just wanders off or his mother leaves him up a tree and does not return to him. At the age of six months he will weigh about three pounds and be able to find food and shelter. To me the mountain trails would not be the same without this gnawer whose teeth are always gummed with resin. I am sure he never offends anyone with bad breath.

The snowshoe rabbits found in the western mountains are actually varying hares. They get the name, snowshoe, because of their big, well-furred feet which make it possible for them to move over deep loose snow. The term hare has never been much in favor in this country. They all look like rabbits so they are called rabbits.

The snowshoe is the fleetest runner in the woods. If pursued by a coyote he will stay well ahead moving along with effortless bounds. Occasionally he will leap into the air and look back. These hares do not flee in a straightaway course; they circle. A wise coyote may cut across the circle and intercept the snowshoe, or he may have a mate waiting in a ravine they know the rabbit will use.

The enemies of the snowshoe are all of the predators, including the golden eagle who can kill a snowshoe and fly away with it, its top weight being about four pounds.

An average litter will have four young in it. Their eyes will be open at birth and they can crawl to the mother to nurse. They develop steadily for a year when they will be mature. Their brown coats will turn to pure white when winter arrives.

The snowshoe rabbit population varies greatly from time to time. Periods of abundance occur every ten years. In times when they are scarce the number of bobcats and lynx will decline noticeably.

Winter brings a time of famine to the meat-eaters living in deep snow country. The ptarmigan and the snowshoe may be the only game the hunters can find and kill, and even this is no easy task until the snow forms a hard crust. The crust will also help

SNOWSHOE HARE   *Yellowstone National Park Photo*

the foxes, coyotes and bobcats. The snowshoe population does not vary as much in our western mountains as it does in the north, even though snow conditions will be much the same.

You may miss this fellow unless you pass close enough to his bed to startle him into bounding away. This is true in winter and summer. Once he has spotted you he will sit very still unless you move directly toward him. A white snowshoe on a snow bank is almost invisible and is as hard to detect in a thicket during the summer. His camouflage is almost perfect.

There is a big fellow who is called a rabbit but is also a hare, and that is the jack rabbit. Long ears like those of a jackass may be responsible for the popular name. The jack is found scattered over the western plains and east as far as the Dakotas.

The big jacks are swift runners. They can travel up to thirty-five miles per hour. Of the dogs, only the greyhound is fast enough to run them down. Like the snowshoe, the jack will circle when he flees, and this may be his undoing when chased by coyotes who know his tricks. A jack may run for a hundred yards and then stop to sit up and check his back trail.

Jack rabbits are great broad-jumpers. The black-tail can cover the ground in twenty-five-foot leaps and the white-tail can exceed this by five or six feet. Jacks can jump high as well as far. They have been known to bound five feet into the air.

A jack rabbit will measure about two feet in length and will stand a foot high at the shoulder, the weight will vary from four to twelve pounds. You cannot fail to identify this big fellow, his big ears will tell you who he is.

You can expect to find jack rabbits in the open, treeless areas of the west. One variety lives on the desert and is known as the antelope jack. This big hare can flash signals like a pronghorn antelope by spreading the white hairs on its rump. This is done by muscles which pull the skin over the rump upward which spreads the white hairs. This may be a heliograph warning to other rabbits or just a trick to make a wary coyote pause long enough for the jack to put a safe distance between himself and the hunter.

If startled while sleeping, the jack will bound high and far instantly. They seem to come fully awake at once. They like to bed down close to the head of a ravine or draw or on top of a ridge where a few long leaps will carry them out of sight of an enemy. Once out of sight they will circle back to their bed.

Although an efficient runner, the jack's range will be small, a circle no more than a mile in diameter is about his limit. If the grazing is good the jack does not yearn for far places. Water is not a problem for jack rabbits. They have adapted themselves to semi-arid regions and get their water from the juicy plants they eat.

A jack will have a number of beds scattered over his range. They will be shallow depressions scratched out near or under a

WHITETAIL JACK RABBIT   *Yellowstone National Park Photo*

bush. The jack uses the most convenient bed when he sleeps during the day.

Jack rabbits feed mostly during the night, but they will be about in the daytime if the sky is overcast. Moonlit nights call for a time of frolic, and on a winter night when the moon glistens on the snow they may gather in flocks. I once came to a place on the Blue Mesa in Colorado, where a truck loaded with loose apples had tipped over. It was night and a bright moon was shining on the snow. There must have been a hundred jacks gathered there to eat frozen apples.

In this same area I have seen haystacks toppled over. The jacks had literally eaten the foundation out from under the stacks. This probably meant that a large number of jack rabbits had congregated at the stacks.

If pursued, a young jack may take refuge in a burrow or hole.

The adult jacks seldom hole up, but I once saw one dive into a badger hole when attacked by a big hawk. The jack knew he could not outdistance the red-tailed bomber or get out of its sight.

In the southwest, jacks mate at any time during the year; in northern areas they mate in the spring. Under the mating moon four or five males will gather around a female and there will be a great deal of running and chasing and some pitched battles between rivals. Nights in the jack's range are never dark except in stormy weather. Even a half moon will light up the prairie and if there is no moon the heavens will blaze with stars. The ideal time for courting is under a moon, but the twilight under a starry sky serves as well. It gives light enough for these big-eyed Romeos to battle for the favor of a doe. When fighting, they stand erect and strike out with their big hind feet. One may leap over his rival and lash downward with both feet. Considerable fur is lost, because the feet are equipped with claws. There may be wounds inflicted, but I never have found a dead jack that I thought was killed in a battle with another rabbit, and I have never talked to anyone who believed the fights end in fatalities.

The battles are silent except for the thumps of big feet. I have never heard a rabbit give voice to a cry except a death wail. That I have heard and it is a cry no one is likely to forget. It is likely the rabbit's first and last cry.

A mother may give birth to from one to six young. The average is probably three. The young are well formed at birth except that their ears are short. Within five minutes they can take a few steps. The mother covers them with fine grass or some of her fur. She beds down nearby but not close enough to attract a killer to the nest. If a coyote comes along she will show herself and lure the coyote away from the nest. She feeds her babies at night. In a few days the youngsters will be wandering about nibbling grass and tender plants. In a few weeks they will be foraging for themselves and are not likely to recognize their mother should they meet her. But during this short span of family life the mother is affectionate and protective.

Where feed is plentiful a female may have two litters a season. Over much of the desert and mountain range the jacks are not plentiful enough to make rabbit drives necessary, except in the desert areas of Eastern Oregon. I have watched rabbit drives in Idaho and Eastern Colorado. Both areas have much grazing land and in both, a bounty on the scalps of coyotes upset the balance of nature, eliminating the coyotes and allowing the rabbits to multiply rapidly. Consequently, the rabbits themselves became pests, and in Colorado, the *Denver Post's* annual rabbit drive used to net four thousand jacks in one day. I have witnessed the slaughter of that many in a one-day drive in Idaho, too.

I have since seen signs on fences in that same Eastern Colorado country warning hunters that if they trespass and kill coyotes they will be prosecuted. These are heartening indications indeed. Tens of thousands of jacks can be as destructive to a range as huge bands of sheep. Like the sheep they can crop the grass so close as to kill it, and will when their numbers become so great that they are always hungry. On a drive they will bunch up ahead of the long line of hunters like bands of sheep.

Running jacks is considered a sport in many places, but has never been developed to the extent that red fox hunting has. A friend of mine, Bill Caulkins, and I used to run them in his fenderless, cut-down Ford in the sage-studded San Luis Valley of Colorado. Their darting, dodging flight made this a giddy sport, and once we turned the Ford over while trying to corner as fast as the jack did. Sometimes we didn't get a single jack in an afternoon of chasing, and as I recall it, we never bagged more than two. But it was exciting sport with the odds favoring the jack.

There is some market for jack rabbit fur. It is used by hatters and some of the better skins go to trim cloth coats. But the price is low, usually ten cents a skin.

The jack's most persistent and dangerous enemy is the coyote, although the bobcat is a close second where bobcats are found on the jack's range, much of which is country not to a bobcat's liking. The northern lynx cat will live almost wholly on rabbits.

Insect pests attack jack rabbits. The worst of these are the larvae of the warble fly which develop a swelling in the flesh of the rabbit and may blind the jack if they attack the eyes.

When I was a boy I sat many a moonlit winter night on the top of a haystack with an ancient double-barreled shotgun waiting for jacks to converge on the stack. The ejector was broken so I carried a ramrod to poke out the spent shells. For convenience I carried the cleaning iron in one barrel of the gun. Once I fired that barrel at a fleeing jack, forgetting in the excitement to remove the rod. The rod missed the jack and I was knocked flat. For a week I had a very sore shoulder. After that I carried a heavy iron bolt in my pocket which I could drop down the barrel. I have not shot a jack in thirty years, but I do not object to farmers defending their haystacks.

There are several species of cottontail rabbits, the little brush rabbits of the west and the more generally known cottontails, whose range extends into Canada and covers most of the United States. This latter species has been divided into a number of groups, mainly on the basis of color.

Everyone who has tramped in the woods knows the cottontail with his white powderpuff tail. In the summer you see it bounding away down a trail and ducking into a willow patch; in winter you see it sitting like a small ball of fur in a snow bank where willows rise above the drift.

The females of the tribe do their level best to provide a rabbit for every bush and rock pile along a creek. She is so intent upon fulfilling this destiny that she will lure four or five males into attendance upon her. When she picks a mate she soon tires of him and turns on him, biting him and pulling patches of fur out of him. In her single-minded devotion to her goal she will be able

COTTONTAIL.   *Yellowstone National Park Photo*

to produce four or five litters a year. Her young are born a month after she mates and she is likely to be out collecting suitors within an hour or so after delivering the babies. She will keep this pace up for six or seven months.

But there are many checks which keep her from achieving her purpose. From the day she is born her life is beset by adversity. Every blood-lapping, meat-eating killer hunts the cottontails. A weasel will wipe out a whole family, as will a mink or marten; hawks and great horned owls constantly hunt them. Diseases kill many, warble fly larvae burrow into the flesh during the warm months, tapeworms and round worms attack vital organs; coccidiosis infects the intestines, a disease chicken farmers are familiar with. Tularemia, a microbe disease, is highly lethal to all rabbits, ground squirrels and other rodents. It is also infectious to man, and may be contracted by handling an infected rabbit. Cottontail meat is delicious but it should be thoroughly cooked before eating.

Man's inroads on the cottontail population are reduced by the fact that during the summer the rabbits are apt to be the hosts to the warble fly larvae, making the meat unpalatable. Open season on cottontails starts when the cold weather arrives. In many states this tasty morsel has been declared a game animal and cannot be hunted except during regular open seasons.

Way back when I hunted, we ate a great deal of cottontail meat. It is white as compared to the dark flesh of the jack and is tender, the flavor equal to that of any wild game. The jacks I brought home usually wound up in mincemeat, if eaten at all, but the cottontail was fried, stewed and even went into the chop suey pot. Fixed with plenty of bean sprouts and water chestnuts cottontail chop suey is tastier than chicken.

The Pacific slope brush rabbits are small, very dark brown in color, with short legs and no white patch on their rumps. Otherwise they are quite similar to the cottontails found all over America.

You are apt to see a brush rabbit in the evening, possibly a pair frolicking close to a thicket. There is a pair living close to a place I rented in Santa Barbara, California. Everybody in this thickly populated area on the slope of a mountain has at least one dog and many have cats but this does not seem to worry the rabbits. One thing about the brush rabbits is that they have excellent cover. Probably the dogs had learned that chasing a little rabbit through tangled bushes all armed with barbs and thorns is a painful experience.

Brush rabbits are not hunted like cottontails. Going after them through tangled thickets of manzanita and chaparral is not easy. Anyone who has ever tried to penetrate a solid mass of manzanita knows it can't be done without using a brush knife or a hatchet. I once stood on a ridge looking down at our camp on the shore of a lake in Plumas County, California. The camp was less than a quarter of a mile below me, but there was a slope choked with manzanita between me and the lake. I walked two miles before I found a trail through that tangle. About the only animals which can penetrate such a thicket are the brush rabbits and the gray foxes.

The courting rituals of the brush rabbit consist of a series of dances. They face each other, then start hopping. One hops over the other, which in turn hops over the first rabbit. It is much like boys playing leap frog. If four or five other suitors join in they will put on quite a show.

In mating they are quite similar to the cottontail. The bride soon tires of her mate and drives him off her range, which will be a limited plot of ground she considers her private property.

As with the cottontail female, the female brush rabbit may mate hours after the birth of her young. The family develops fast and, as with the cottontail, the female may raise as many as five litters a season.

With admittedly fewer enemies than the cottontail, it would seem that the bush-choked hills on the Pacific slopes would swarm with these small brown rabbits. This is not true; in my tramping in the coastal range I have seen fewer brush rabbits by far than I have seen cottontails in their haunts. I have seen dozens of cottontails in one small, rock-rimmed gully but have never seen more than two brown rabbits together or in the same locality at one time. It is possible that they have more active enemies than I thought. In spite of such fine cover, spotted skunks, weasels, snakes and even hawks undoubtedly kill many of them. Breeding habits may have something to do with it; brush rabbits scatter out and tend to guard their grazing areas, thus making mating a bit more difficult. This is just conjecture, however, because the youngsters and males do feed together without quarreling.

Fires and floods are real disasters for brush rabbits. In the southern portion of their range the summers are rainless and the brush on the slopes dries to a tinder condition. Every year there are many brush fires which are a scourge not only to wildlife but

PIKA   *National Park Service*

to humans. Large areas where residences have been built in canyons and on slopes are devastated almost every summer, cities are even laid waste. A brush fire is likely to kill most of the brush rabbits living there and those that survive the flames will have nothing to eat. A flood may sweep away all of the rabbits in a narrow valley. But in spite of all of the dangers facing them, the brush rabbits manage to survive.

There is one hardy mountaineer who never leaves the high country of the west when winter blizzards drive most of the other mountain creatures to the lower valleys. He isn't a very rugged looking fellow, seldom over seven inches in length, and this does not include his tail because he has none. He seldom weighs over four ounces.

The coney, perhaps more properly known as the pika, is

usually lumped in with the rabbit tribe, perhaps because there seems to be no other place to put him and he does look somewhat like a rabbit though there is also a resemblance to a guinea pig.

His home is usually high up in the towering spires just below timberline. Coneys have been found at elevations as high as 13,000 feet. I have sat and watched them gathering grass within a hundred feet of naked granite. They usually pick slide runs or spots where loose rocks have piled up. This gives them cover from eagles and hawks.

If you come to a slide which appears to be deserted, too high and barren for birds or ground squirrels, with forage limited to clumps of scattered grass and occasional stunted shrub, sit down and remain still. You may sit in the open on a rock, but you must remain unmoving.

Very soon, if lucky, you may hear voices that sound like the creaking of rusty hinges. There is no use trying to locate the coney by looking toward the spot his voice seems to be coming from, he isn't likely to be there. The coney is a ventriloquist and quite expert at the art. But if he sees no movement he'll come out into the open and perch on a rock or scamper off to make hay. Even so, he is hard to spot, because his gray-black fur blends with the granite rocks. When he moves you see him, when he freezes he vanishes.

The high country summer is very short. The hay harvesting has to be pushed every sunny day. The hay stacks in the small caves have to be many and big. The coney does not hibernate during the winter; he is active and about no matter how deep the snow gets or how bitter the cold. The hay is cut and carried to the storerooms where it is cured. There may be as much as a bushel of hay in a single stack. The coney snips off weeds and grass and carries them to the next grass clump. When he has cut a bundle almost as big as himself he dashes to his hay stack.

The coney is not troubled by many enemies. His domain is too high for weasels, bobcats and coyotes. They find easier prey in the grassy slopes below his home. But eagles and hawks destroy many of the little ventriloquists. This happens because the coney likes to bask in the sun on top of a rock where he can be easily spotted by the killers of the air.

One exception to the coney range should be noted. Coneys may be found in lava beds at lower altitudes, but this is unusual.

The coney's world is very small. He will not wander far. His range will be limited to six hundred square yards, more or less. Of course, he has a magnificent view. From his perch on a rock, peaks and valleys are visible for a hundred miles. But I doubt if he ever notices the distant view. I have never seen a coney sitting staring off into space as the golden mantle ground squirrel and the black bear do.

If you are climbing the rugged slopes of our western mountains, linger a while beside a rock slide. Watch a mountain come alive, and listen to its voice.

Where it is Wet

Deep in a clear pool which is fed by a wide stream, a chunky animal swims along slowly. He has a black back, a pale brown face with eyes like black beads. He looks up at the surface and sees water skippers skating about, leaves floating, edged shoreward by a gentle breeze. As he nears the shore he sees a long-legged blue heron standing on the bank, long neck curved, head bent toward the water. A sucker swims past, moving sluggishly, a fish in no hurry. Suddenly the heron's long beak darts downward. Instantly the glassy surface is broken and the heron appears to be a writhing and distorted creature. This is the world as a muskrat sees it from his favorite vantage point, the underwater home where he spends much of his time. He surfaces, exposing just his face and watches the heron flap away with the fish in her beak, headed for her nest to feed her young.

The muskrat is a stocky animal. When fully grown it may weigh as much as four pounds, but two would be close to the average. Its pelt is valued in the fur market. It has fine underfur and outer-fur with long guard hairs, which is what the furrier is looking for. It is a member of the chisel-tooth tribe and like the beaver has a scaly tail, flattened but not very broad.

The muskrat's home may be in a bank or in a rush house but no matter where it is built, it will have an under-water entry tunnel. This gives it protection against most of its enemies except the mink which is an excellent swimmer and slim enough to enter a muskrat tunnel. A mink cannot see under water and must blindly follow the muskrat through the tunnel to his den where the killer can use his eyes. The furry water rat is no match for a mink and many of them perish in their own dens.

Bank muskrats like to live alone but will share a pond or stream with other muskrats. If they live in a house, as many as four or five may occupy the same room. These houses are piles of rushes stacked in shallow water. Inside the pile there will be one large room. Entry to the house is by a shallow canal which may be as much as six feet long. It opens under the house.

When I was a boy I used to visit these rat houses after the first frosts came. In order to find out how many rats occupied the house, all I had to do was to stamp on the frozen mud close to the runway entrance. The rats inside would flash past along the canal and I could see them through the thin ice.

I once caught a coyote by a toe in one of several steel traps I had set in the top of a house, and learned that coyotes dig into rat houses in attempts to catch the rats. My strategy was better than that of the coyote, I simply damaged the roof of the house and set my traps to catch the owners when they came up to repair the damage. The coyote in his digging would surely send the rats dashing out into the pond where the coyote could not follow. Perhaps, though, after opening a hole in the roof the coyote would lie in wait for the return of the muskrats.

Canada lynx and bobcats also tear the roof off rat houses before sleet and late rains soak them and frost hardens the roofs into unassailable masses of ice. Again I am sure the hunters do not catch many rats that way.

Mother muskrats may give birth to as many as nine young. This is a happy situation for the trapper, as it means the supply of muskrats will not run out. As he traps only when fur is prime, which is late fall and winter, he will not catch mothers having very young babies. By the time he starts trapping the youngsters will be on their own. The young rats develop fast after their eyes open, which will happen in sixteen days. These four-ounce little fellows take readily to the water and paddle about nibbling at water plants. They dive and play and soon learn to duck under a lily pad if a marsh hawk appears.

When another litter is expected, the mother drives the young-sters out of the house. She gets very rough with them, biting and sometimes crippling them. She knows they must not stay and must be made to understand that they cannot return. If they stayed they would devour the new babies.

Man is still the muskrat's worst enemy, but all predators prey upon them. When they go ashore to forage they are very vulner-able to land prowlers. It seems unlikely that hawks, even the swift-flying sharp-shinned hawk, ever take many except very young ones. A swimming muskrat does not expose much of him-self and he can dive in a flash. Sanctuaries and closed seasons have helped to keep this expert swimmer from going the way of the beaver.

I am sorry to say that during my grade school days I trapped muskrats. Their skins were worth ten cents each, if prime, and it was a big day for me when I shipped my bundle of furs off to a St. Louis fur house. But I learned a lot about muskrats. I cherish some of the memories, like the fall visits to a big marsh near our home. Hard frosts would have laid a thin coat of ice over the big pond. The trees would be in fall glory of color and just starting to drop their leaves. All around the pond there would be big rush houses and the activity would make me sit for an hour and watch. I could see half a hundred or more muskrats. Some of them sat on the ice, others worked on their houses, dragging in rushes to add to the pile, some paddled in the bit of open water in the center of the pond. They all seemed to know that within perhaps a few days they would be locked in a world limited to their houses and the areas under the ice. It was one time when I could check up on the number of rats to be found in one pond. I suppose I was multplying the number of rats by ten cents, dreaming of the fortune I could make if I caught them all. But visiting that marsh in late fall is a memory worth having. As I sat there, mallards on their way south would glide in and land on the open water, flocks of blackbirds would burst into eager songs of farewell to the swamp where they had raised their families during the summer, the cattails would be alive with them, red wings, yellow wings, and just plain black ones. When I stood up to leave, the mallards and the blackbirds would swirl up toward the gray, storm-brewing sky, but the muskrats would not seem to mind me, they would go on with what they were doing.

Running trap-line let me observe many animals. I got interested in studying them, at first in order to catch them and then because they fascinated me. I soon found that I had a whole community of interesting creatures around me when I wandered in the woods. I guess my days as a boy trapper laid the foundation for a lifetime of wildlife study and half a hundred books written about animals.

I had my first contact with a lynx cat at a muskrat house where I had set some traps. Like the coyote, the lynx was trying to dig into the house. I had placed a fallen tree trunk between the shore and the rat house because the ice was too thin to sustain my weight. I was half way across the slender log when I discovered the lynx and he became aware of my presence. He reared up out of the hole he was digging and we stared at each other. The only weapon I had was a thin-bladed skinning knife. The lynx wanted off the house and I wanted off the log. Neither of us wanted to jump on the thin ice and go under for a cold ducking.

I could tell that the lynx had been eating a rat caught in one of my traps. He had blood and rat fur on his cheeks. The log was hardly more than a pole so my footing was tricky. I backed along the log slowly. Seeing that I was retreating, the lynx moved out on the pole and followed me. When I reached the bank and jumped aside the big cat shot past me and vanished into a thicket. That was my first close look at a lynx cat.

I discovered later that the old lynx used a stream which ran through our farm as his hunting domain. My brother offered to lend me his rifle so that I could shoot the big, tufted-eared cat. I decided not to shoot him right away. There was a lot I wanted to know about him. I finally did get him and always felt afterward that I had murdered a friend.

Mountain beaver and their workings can be seen in Marin and Mono Counties in California. They are also found in western Oregon and Washington and a small portion of western British Columbia.

Few of the trappers and explorers who opened up the west were naturalists. But when they saw an animal new to them they gave it a name which usually became the name the animal is known by. A jack rabbit was so-named because his ears resembled those of a jackass, the big mountan deer became mule deer because their big ears resembled those of a mule, the bison's popular name has always been buffalo. The mountain beaver's official name is Apolodonita Rufa. We'll go along with the trappers and miners and call him mountain beaver.

He isn't a beaver, hasn't even a tail that is noticeable. The Oregon name is "boomer" but he does not boom. Some people call him "whistler" but he can't whistle.

Perhaps he is called a beaver because he does occasionally cut down a tree, but no mountain beaver ever cut down a tree bigger than a sapling.

Mountain beavers are great burrowers. The work of one pair gives the impression that at least a dozen have been busy. Trails and tunnels often lead from one beaver's workings to those of a neighbor. But trespass signs will be up and woe to any uninvited fellow who shows up. However, two mountain beavers have been known to live together so they are slightly more sociable than pocket gophers, but they do not go in for social activities as do otters and real beavers.

Much of this digger's range was once covered with dense

forests of pine and spruce and redwood. It prefers such an environment and sticks to lower canyons where there is water. It always takes up residence close to a stream.

A mountain beaver is about the size of a muskrat. It has short legs, almost no tail and its body is chunky. Its ears and eyes are small and its fur stiff and coarse. The color is cinnamon brown. It will weigh from two to three pounds.

The runways of the mountain beaver are erratic. Like the pocket gopher it just goes ahead digging, not caring much where the tunnel leads, knowing it will encounter plenty of roots which will guide it to the plant above. It also uses the tunnels for cover. On his range, deep penetrating frost is not a problem, so the digger seldom burrows more than a foot beneath the surface of the ground. Above-ground it is clumsy and slow, an easy victim for any killer. As it is big enough to make a meal for most of the predators, it is hunted and waylaid by them when they get a chance. Quite a few of them are caught by coyotes, bobcats and lynx.

The beaver opens holes along the tunnel which are used in tossing out excavated dirt. If the earth is loose the tunnels may be as much as ten inches wide and the same in height.

The mountain beaver has very poor eyesight and seldom ventures more than a few feet from cover. Cut-over forest areas are soon covered with a tangle of brush and second-growth trees which conceal fallen logs and discarded trunks of trees left by the lumber crews. These areas offer excellent cover for the beaver. It gives him cover from hawks and eagles as well as from ground prowlers. All members of the weasel family, except the land otter, prey on these little beavers.

Beaver tunnels may be as long as three hundred feet. They may follow along under a fallen tree, and the nest chambers are likely to be built under stumps or rocks for better protection. When this beaver wants to explore above ground he simply digs a hole in the tunnel roof and climbs out.

All that is known of the romantic life of a mountain beaver

is that it lasts about six weeks. Like bull fur seals, the male becomes very thin and lank during this period, probably because he neglects eating while gripped by the excitement and spell of the mating moon. It takes him about a month of stuffing to regain his usual fat condition.

Each mother produces two or three young. It is thought that the young leave their mother's care when two or three months old. The information about their domestic life has been pieced together from bits and scraps.

The area where the mountain beaver lives offers a variety of green material it likes to eat. When eating, it sits on its haunches like a squirrel and handles its food with its forepaws. There is much food wasted. The beaver hauls into its tunnels twice as much as it can eat.

The mountain beaver has a voice he uses when in combat with a rival. It is a series of angry squeals. When in pain it whines. There seems to be no voice communication between mountain beavers aside from the abuse they hurl at each other when fighting.

About the only major disaster that can happen to this beaver, aside from being snapped up by a coyote, fox or bobcat, is a brush or forest fire, or a controlled burn designed to remove bushes to make room for range grass. In case of fire the little animal is luckier than most wild dwellers in the forests, in that he can take refuge in his damp tunnel. But when he emerges he finds his food supply gone and he has to migrate over burned-off slopes exposing himself to hawks, eagles and big owls.

The body of the mountain beaver has not developed over the ages as other animals have developed. Like the possum he is still a primitive. But he has survived while others which lived a million years ago are long extinct.

Beaver Water

True beavers were once found along most of the streams in northern areas of the American continent, their range extending well into the southwest territories. Today there are only scattered colonies left in the mountains of the west and a few other protected spots.

Studying a beaver colony is a rewarding way of spending a few hours close to nature. There isn't a more interesting animal alive than a beaver, or a more amazing one. Hundreds of thousands of years ago there lived a giant beaver that was bigger than a bear. We do not know much about how this giant beaver lived, but if he worked as our modern beavers do he must have built some amazing dams on waterways. If he had survived we might have been spared the expense of building some of our big dams.

A beaver never stops growing but its growth is slow, and it does not live very long in the wild, not over ten years. A beaver may attain a length of three feet and weigh from fifty to seventy pounds. If it is old and cage-fat, it may weigh more. Beavers built dams, canals, and snug lodges, and stored food for winter use when our ancestors were living naked in caves, storing nothing, building nothing. Beavers were doing things like surrounding their lodges with deep water moats thousands of years before kings thought of surrounding their castles with moats to keep enemies out.

Beavers work in icy mountain streams fed by melting snow but they are never cold. A beaver is protected by a heavy, warm suit of underwear in the form of under-fur. His body secretes oil which makes the underwear waterproof. Over the under-fur there is a coat of long fur with a sprinkling of guard hairs. Even so, after leaving an icy stream, if the temperature is near zero, the beaver will at once comb the water out of his fur and, in doing so, restore the oil to it.

A beaver has webbed hind feet and a flat, broad, scaly tail; both are useful for more than just swimming. The tail, six inches wide and a foot long, serves as a rudder and a brake and as a means of warning other beavers of danger. This is done by smashing the broad tail down upon the water. The result is a boom like the blast of a shotgun. If you hear that boom when dusk is settling you will know there are beavers in the vicinity. The boom is followed by a loud splash as the beaver dives. Trappers on the beaver trail considered a beaver tail, roasted in coals, the most delicious meal they could get.

On land the tail serves as a prop to keep the beaver upright while he is cutting down a tree. It is also useful as a trowel while he is building or repairing a dam.

The beaver does a lot of swimming under water. To make this comfortable the beaver has valves in the nose and ears which close tightly behind the protruding front teeth. This allows the beaver to cut up limbs and logs from his stockpile at the bottom of his pond without getting a mouthful of water. Large lungs and liver allow the beaver to retain oxygen in his bloodstream in sufficient supply to allow him to stay under water for as long as fifteen minutes. His favorite food is the bark of the quaking aspen tree.

His big chisel teeth are his work tools. Nature knew that if a beaver broke a tooth he would be out of business, so she pro-

BEAVER

vided him with teeth that will grow whole if broken and he can even replace a lost tooth. I know of no other animal that can do this; perhaps there may be some I have never heard of.

Beavers cut down scrub willow, alder and aspen trees for two reasons, one is for winter food, the other is to get materials for building dams and repairing them. The tough trunks and gnarled branches of the scrub willow serve the same purpose as reinforcing steel rods do in concrete walls. Again the beaver was thousands of years ahead of the modern engineer.

After spring repairs have been made on the dam and the lodges, the beavers toil at cutting down trees, the tempo increasing as fall approaches. Old timers say they can tell by the size of the beaver's harvest how hard the winter will be. If the beavers work frantically the last couple of weeks before their pond freezes over, the coming winter will be a really bad one.

Felled trees are cut into lengths the beavers can handle, and the limbs are removed. If a tree is big, most of the main trunk will be left where it fell. Getting the limbs and logs to the pond is often a problem but the beavers solve it. As the standing timber becomes farther and farther away from the pond due to cutting season after season, the hauling problem gets tougher. Trees from eight to twelve inches in thickness are usually selected, but beavers have been known to cut down a tree five feet in diameter at the butt. If the colony has been living in a pond for a number of generations and the standing timber is quite a distance from the pond, the beavers solve the problem by building canals down which they float logs and limbs.

In felling a tree the beaver usually works alone, but sometimes two beavers work on the same tree at the same time. After selecting his tree, the beaver sits upright facing the tree, propped up by his tail. He makes a gash in the soft green bark with his teeth, then makes another just below the first. The next step is to rip away the bark and wood between the gashes. In biting, the upper teeth are used to anchor the head while the big lower incisors chip away at the trunk. Soon the ground around the beaver will be littered with chips. It may take all night to fell a big tree, smaller ones are felled in a few hours. When the tree begins to shudder and give forth its death snap, the beaver leaps away and slaps its tail on the ground which is his way of shouting, "Timber!"

The crash of the falling tree will ring through the surrounding forest. This is a signal for the whole colony to rush to the pond and plunge in. Up their heads pop and they listen and peer into the night warily, for a bobcat, bear, coyote or cougar may have heard the crash and come to investigate. If they hear nothing and see nothing they soon return to their work.

The fallen tree will be stripped of limbs and cut into pieces from two to six feet long. These will be dragged or floated to the pond where they will be buried in the mud at the deepest spot in the pond and well-anchored with water-logged limbs and mud.

A careful check of a beaver-cut slope will convince you that a beaver does not control the direction the tree falls. Sometimes it will land in a nearby tree and never reach the ground at all.

In the fall, when the beavers are busiest, skid trails will be worn to a width of three feet, and they will be hard and smooth.

The beaver's canals are the work of engineers. They are usually built on a number of levels with locks at intervals to maintain a proper water level. The first level will be filled with water from the pond, the other levels may be fed from mere trickles of water coming from a spring, thus assuring that no water is wasted. The locks perform this service as well as maintaining water deep enough to float a log. The dam usually gets most of the attention of a visitor, but the canals are more difficult to lay out and build properly. I would rate them the most remarkable thing the beaver does. They may extend for seven or eight hundred feet. I have paced off the length of two canals that would measure more than eight hundred feet. The grade has to be just right and the beavers get it that way without the help of a transit or a level. They are usually a couple of feet deep and the same width, but I have fallen into canals concealed by tall grass that were at least five feet deep. While fishing for trout on Tomichi Creek in western Colorado, I fell into a deep canal which had enough water in it to fill my hip boots. The hay ranchers along the Tomichi were never able to get rid of the beavers. They were conscientious ranchers and called on the state Fish and Game Department to come and catch the beavers, which were transported high into the mountains and turned loose. But more beavers always came in from the Gunnison River so the ranchers had to put up with canals in their timothy fields and they had to tear out dams the beavers built across their own canals and ditches.

Some students of wildlife rate the beaver as only half as intelligent as a dog. I am sure there are some stupid beavers, as I am sure there are some stupid dogs. I admit there have been some poorly located dams and some badly built, but I have seen hundreds that were well located and beautifully built. I counted twenty-four in one Colorado canyon and I rode no more than seven miles up that canyon. It was one spot the trappers had missed and where ranchers had not cut and destroyed the dams to get a summer flow of water. Every one of those ponds was occupied by a colony of beavers. That was thirty years ago and I have never been back, but I hope that isolated and nameless little canyon is still a haven for beavers. Every dam I saw was a masterpiece. I admit that beavers are doing things today the same as they did a thousand years ago, but so are dogs and they have had human masters to teach them and to improve their instinctive skills.

A beaver builds a dam because he needs to have a deep body of water the year round that will maintain a constant level. Deep water is one place where a beaver is safe from his many enemies. It surrounds his lodge and protects it and it furnishes a big storehouse for his winter food. Three feet of depth at the center will do; more at the face of the dam will be fine.

No two beavers are ever exactly alike in their approach to dam building. No two locations will be exactly the same nor will the construction of the dam be the same. Materials for building

BEAVER   *Yellowstone National Park Photo*

a dam are never exactly the same and the beaver has to adapt himself to what he has available. There is one fixed requirement;
there must be a spring or a stream with a good output of water.
A beaver may start building his dam when the stream is low.
Disaster may come when the spring runoff hits the dam.

The beaver, sometimes with the help of his family, will build
the dam. They heap up rocks, mud and water-logged poles, aspen
logs stripped of bark, anything handy. Four or five foot poles may
be laid side by side along the down-stream side of the dam, and
parallel to the stream. Water may trickle through the structure
as it rises, but all beavers hate leaks and will soon find and plug
them. In the west much scrub willow, which has many gnarled
and twisted branches, will be used to bind the mud. The dam
may eventually be fifteen feet wide at the base and twelve feet
high. Generation after generation of beavers will add to it. Of

course the water will have to run over the dam at some point. The beaver's dislike for leaks makes him keep patting mud and willows on the overflow spillways so the dam keeps growing higher and higher every year. In a well-kept dam there will be no leaks on the face of the dam. One group of construction engineers hit on a way to stop a leak in an earth-fill dam which they had not been able to locate. They put a few beavers into the reservoir. In a very short time the beavers had located and plugged the leak. Some day a beaver may learn to build a spillway. If he does, beaver dams will stop growing as they do now.

I was once given a good lesson in dam building by two beavers. I was driving my car up a dim trail leading to a cabin which I planned to use on a day's outing. I found a ford across a small stream flooded with three feet of water backed up by a beaver dam which had been built just below the ford. The water was too deep for the car so I had to spend several hours opening up the center of the dam in order to drain off the pond. The dam was less than fifteen feet long and about four feet high. No one except a person who has tried to take a beaver dam apart with a hatchet and shovel can have any idea how well built a beaver dam is. Branches were interlaced and packed with mud so solidly that even with a hatchet and shovel I had a tough time getting the center open. As I watched the muddy water flow through the opening I felt a bit ashamed of myself. I could have gone fishing somewhere else; there are eleven hundred miles of trout streams in Gunnison County. For one day's fishing I was causing the beavers two or three weeks of hard work. A dedicated fisherman probably would understand. I had located a virgin trout stream nobody else knew about.

I had a fine morning fishing the next day and packed my gear. When I reached the ford I was amazed to see that the dam was completely restored, looking just as it did when I first saw it and there was a pond four feet deep across the road. I hated to discourage such industry but I had to get back to my courtroom where I had a hearing scheduled for that morning. At that time,

I was a County Judge, and judges are supposed to be punctual. I set to work and again removed the center of the dam. The repair job had been no makeshift piece of work, that dam was as solid as the original. Out of curiosity I returned to the spot the next week-end and found the dam again restored.

Some beavers are called bank beavers because they do not build dams. They burrow into the bank of a stream or pond. Usually this den is only a temporary lodging built by a young beaver who has just started out in life and has not had time to build a dam, perhaps because of the lateness in the season.

The lodge of a beaver may not be close to the dam, but it is sure to be located in fairly deep water. When construction starts, sticks are laid in a circle. The walls are built of logs, stones and mud. They rise to a height of three feet and will slope inward, finally meeting overhead. Masses of brush and scrub willow branches will be piled on the walls and plastered down with mud. As long as the lodge is used, the beavers will keep adding mud and sticks to the outside. At the base of the house there will be a slide hole connected to openings on several sides.

The beaver scoops up mud with its forepaws and flexes its tail to hold the armload. Building a lodge is a job which requires hundreds of trips to willow patches and mud banks, but like the repair of the dam I cut, it will be accomplished quickly.

There will be only one room in the lodge, but it will be big enough to shelter a man. It may be as wide as five feet with a four-foot ceiling. There will be an air-vent at the top. Only the babies have a soft bed; it is made of shredded grass. Later, after the babies get bigger they will eat the bed. It is seldom that a lone beaver builds a lodge and lives in it; there will be a group who work together and later live in the lodge.

It is usually the father who repairs the dam and the lodge, but in case of damage to the dam by a flash flood, the whole family will pitch in and help.

Mating among beavers takes place in January or February and the union will last for life. The courtship will be a very serious matter. A young male starting out in life will travel about seeking a mate, leaving pats of musk-scented mud along streams and on the banks of ponds where a female is sure to find his love messages. After a period of wandering he will meet a female who has read his messages and they will seek a colony to join.

Four months after the mating the young will be born. They will stay with their mother for two years. She will be an affectionate parent, but as we have seen, when the arrival of a new brood is imminent she will drive the youngsters out. The father, too, will have to leave.

Soon after departing from the lodge the youngsters will start seeking mates of their own. Father will take up quarters with other exiled husbands until the new babies are able to get around, at which point he is permitted to return.

Old males who have lost their mates may become surly and have to be driven out of the colony. It is suggested by some observers that a council is held to decide what is to be done with the trouble-maker. I doubt this. I think that the surly old one has for some time been nipping and snapping at other beavers and finally goes after a beaver's wife, or challenges another beaver. When this happens the whole colony pitches in because they have reason to dislike the old one. I have more than once discovered an old beaver living alone in a bank den, not caring enough to even plug the land opening to his den.

During the summer, beavers have many enemies that prey upon them. When a beaver is on a slope far from his pond cutting down a tree, he is very vulnerable to an attack from a coyote, bobcat, or cougar. Its powerful teeth may help it to escape death, it will put up as courageous a defense as it can, but it has no chance of running away from an enemy as it can move no faster than a dog-trot.

But in winter the mud-plastered lodges freeze solid and protect the beavers with an armor plate no predator, even a cougar, could break through. A bear might do it, but at that time of the year the bears are sleeping peacefully in a cave. A killer, driven desperate by hunger, may stop and sniff the warm beaver-scented air coming up out of the air vent and be driven by the appetizing smells into attacking the lodge, but no matter how strong he is or how sharp his claws and fangs, he won't be able to break through the foot-thick layer of frozen mud.

For years beavers were trapped for their fur. The pelts were much sought after by European hatters for the hair. Actually the beaver hat opened up the American trails West. In seeking new beaver water, trappers and scouts explored every river and all of its tributaries as far west as the Pacific coast. The first overland road and most of the mountain passes were found and used by men on the beaver trail. Aside from admiration for his ability to build, we owe the beaver a great deal. But the beavers were almost exterminated in the process. No conservation was practiced, the rule was to clean out every beaver in a stream or pond before moving on.

The passing of the beaver hat helped some but it came too late. What has saved them is the complete protection they have been given. There is no open season on beavers, and it is a crime to sell a beaver skin. Westerners have learned that there is no better water conservationist than a beaver. Many arid western states have copied their methods by building small dams which hold back rain water and let it sink into the ground where it raises the underground water table. This is exactly what the beaver has been doing for years. Stray beavers who wander down into farm-lands are now carefully gathered up and transported to high country where they can build dams.

If you can locate a fairly isolated beaver pond you may see the beavers working by day. Now that they are no longer trapped they are slowly beginning to return to the habits of the past when it was safe to work by day. But even if they are night-workers they will be out very early in the evening, long before the light fades.

Bear Facts

If you set out to watch bears there are many things you will see. You are not likely to see all of the tricks a bear does, but you may come up with some new antics which can be added to the stories about bears which have been recorded. At any rate I am sure you will change your ideas about these shaggy brutes.

You may come upon a black or a brown bear when he is in the mood to just sit with his back to a tree and look out over the mountains and forests. Black and brown bears are naturally lazy. The grizzly is the only really energetic bear, and he is rarely found in the United States except in Alaska. His haunts are now Alaska, British Columbia and the Yukon. The only place you can find him without traveling far north is in Yellowstone National Park, where there are only a few, and on the California state flag. He became a state symbol and was rewarded by being destroyed. The 49ers must have admired the strength and courage of the grizzly, but he was a bear and the easiest of the bears to find and kill because he liked open country and seldom stayed close to cover.

The history of the discovery and development of our west is filled with stories and legends about this hump-backed grizzly-coated bear. Many of them are fanciful accounts of hand-to-hand combat with a grizzly bear, exploits of courage in facing the monster. In the light of what we now know, most of the yarns must be discounted. The usual pinch of salt is not enough if you try to swallow most of them.

Grizzly Adams as far back as the middle of the nineteenth century demonstrated that the big bears could be amiable companions. He had a pair, Benjamin Franklin and Lady Washington, who were his constant companions. He slept with them, used them for pack animals and paraded them down the streets of many cities. Thousands of people saw them. True, he did find a few grizzlies he was unable to win over by kindness, and his death is attributed to a mauling he received in trying to tame a wild grizzly. But with Ben Franklin and Lady Washington, he demonstrated that grizzlies could be less dangerous in captivity than a black bear.

William Randolph Hearst once sent a *San Francisco Examiner* reporter into central California to catch a live grizzly. This reporter was not an outdoorsman and had never in his life seen a tame or a wild grizzly. It took the reporter about a year to round up a wild grizzly, chain it to a sled and drag it down to a Southern Pacific Railroad station. I am not going to vouch for the stories which appeared on the front page of the *Examiner,* sent in by the reporter while he was pursuing grizzlies, but the fact is that he did deliver a wild grizzly which lived for years in the San Francisco Zoo. "Monarch" was real enough and someone caught him.

When California was Spanish territory, vaqueros often ran down and lassoed grizzlies which they turned loose in pens with the wildest bull they could find. One bear and one bull in deadly combat. Generally their trouble was wasted because the grizzly would break the neck of the bull with one smashing blow and the fight was over almost before it started. This proves several things, first that a few cowboys with lariats could overcome a grizzly and second that a grizzly is a dangerous and courageous fighter when aroused.

GRIZZLY   *Yellowstone National Park Photo*

The preceding goes to show that a grizzly is not the frightful monster portrayed by the early historians and yarn-spinners of the west.

Despite their size the big bears are very agile. Kodiak browns demonstrate this when fishing for salmon, and so does the grizzly. They are able and willing to do a prodigious amount of work to secure food they like. One grizzly will practically overturn a slope seeking rodents and roots.

The grizzly is not a tree-climber and he is not a clown like the black bear; he is serious at all times, working hard all day long to get food enough to fill his big stomach.

When grizzlies roamed our mountains the black bears had to be alert because the grizzly hated a black bear and would kill one if he could catch it before it reached a tree.

Over eighty-four species and subspecies of bears have been described, their range covering North America. The Kodiak and the polar bear are easily distinguished but the others are less easily separated.

We will concern ourselves mainly with the black and brown bears because they are still found almost all over the United States where there are forests and can be seen in the wild without taking a trip north.

There is no difference between the black and brown bear except color. A mother black bear may give birth to a black and a brown cub in the same litter. If you see a black and a brown cub together they will certainly be from the same litter.

There are certain signs to look for if you are in bear country and want to know if there is a bear in the area. If you come to an ant-hill that has been torn apart and scattered you should start looking closely for bear tracks; there will be a resemblance between the bear track and the track of a barefooted man. While teaching a country school on Owl Creek thirty miles east of Neiber, Wyoming, I had a disgruntled bear hunter drop in one afternoon after school. He had followed what he was sure were bear tracks for two days only to discover he was following the wife of a man who owned a small band of sheep. She was barefooted because the shoes she had ordered from a mail-order catalogue had not arrived. She was moving the sheep along a stream to new grazing grounds.

If you find a rotting log that has been ripped apart it is almost sure to be the work of a bear searching for grubs. If flat stones along the trail have been overturned you may suspect that a bear has passed that way. Bears flip stones over looking for beetles, crickets and bugs. If the stones are large you can be sure. If they are small it may be the work of a raccoon. Raccoons seldom pass a flat stone without flipping it over if they can move it.

Margins of ponds and streams are fine places to look for bear tracks. You may even find a wallow where a bear has taken a mud bath. But if you later catch up with the bear you will find that he is not muddy. Bears take mud baths to clear vermin from their shaggy coats and afterward wash away the mud. Finding fish heads along a stream is a good indication that a bear has been fishing there. If you are able to watch a bear fishing you will learn that the stories about how bruin fishes are not always true. Many people believe, including some authors, that a bear tosses the fish out on the bank with a paw. This is not true. Bruin smashes a paw down on the fish and then thrusts his muzzle into the stream and sinks his teeth into the fish. In Washington and Oregon, bears catch many salmon but over the rest of his territory the brown bear is able to find only an occasional fish though he may come upon a mountain pool well stocked with suckers.

If you are in the aspen belt examine the light green bark on the trunks of the trees. The soft bark may show claw marks made by bears climbing the tree. If the scars are blackened they will be marks made during the past season. If the scars are bright green and oozing sap your bear will not be far away. The condition of the scars can tell you much. If they are very fresh you should move silently, keeping to cover and listening often. The bear will not bother to walk very silently.

Old bears often mark a tree as high as they can with their teeth. Some woodsmen think this is a challenge to other bears. The king puts his mark higher on a tree than any other bear. And kings there are, savage old males who have ceased to be interested in female bears, and who attack any bear they meet in their domain.

In the fall, dung filled with chokecherry seeds tells you to look for your bear in a wild cherry grove. Abandoned mountain apple orchards are good places to look. You may be sure that if there is a bear within miles he will know about that orchard and visit it as soon as the apples begin to ripen. A bear is an expert at shaking apples out of a tree. Those he can't shake out he climbs up and picks.

If you look for bears in the winter your approach will depend on where you look. In high, snow-clad mountains you won't have much luck. The bear will find a cave and hole up there, letting snow drifts close and hide the entrance unless the cave is a big one. In southern areas the bear is apt to hibernate in a hollow tree. If he is far south he may not go to sleep at all.

A bear does not actually hibernate in a death-like trance as many wild animals do; his breathing and body temperature will be about the same as in normal sleep and he may be partly awake at times. If it is a she-bear who expects cubs, she will be almost awake for three or four weeks toward the end of the winter after her cubs are born.

It is not wise to enter a big cave where one or more bears are sleeping, even though you feel sure they are asleep. At times a bear will be semi-conscious and aware, but will not be disturbed by movement or sounds around it. But the bear may be wide awake and resentful of intrusion, ready to swat or bite. Even in the coldest places a bear may leave its den if the day is warm, and wander about until the temperature drops.

If you are looking in early spring, say in March or April, when the high country bears are coming out of their twilight sleep you will notice a change. The bear's coat will be shedding patches of hair. He will keep moving, eating snow if there is any left or drinking some water. He will ignore food for a time but when he does start to eat he will have a big appetite. If the bear you spot is a mother with a couple of cubs, she will spank them and make them dash away or she may send them up a sapling, but she will not desert them. This is one time when a shy and timid black bear can be an ugly customer. Driving the cubs to safe cover is what she is most likely to do. Cubs are fast on their feet even though out of the den only a few days. They have had three weeks inside the den wrestling with each other and tumbling over their sleepy mother. No attempt to catch a cub should be made. A mother bear will meet any animal with a savage attack, even the father of her cubs, should he show up.

The mother is very affectionate, yet she is firm and will not hesitate to spank the cubs if they disobey her. They soon learn

BEAR CUBS   *National Park Service*

that when she sends them up a tree, they are to stay there until she returns from foraging. And they learn to take off fast when she sounds a warning. Up a tree is the safest place for the cubs when she is away; preferably a small tree which an old male bear cannot climb. Any old male would make short work of them if he was able to catch them, as would any other predator. Later, when mother thinks it is time for them to be off on their own she may send them up a tree and go away. She will be miles away from that tree before hunger makes them come down and start looking for food.

As I have mentioned, there was a time when black bears had to be alert at all times against an attack from a grizzly. Trappers and hunters often found the mangled remains of a black bear with grizzly tracks around it.

Suppose you are out on a day in early June. The location we will select is in the aspen belt on a mountain slope. The leaves are bursting on the aspens and willows. You have spotted a bear and have taken up a position from which you can watch the slope below where the bear is getting his breakfast. If there is a pond nearby he may sit for an hour and watch a pair of mallard ducks. Black bears are very curious fellows. Their bump of curiosity is bigger than most wild animals possess, exceeded only by that of their small cousin, the raccoon.

It is evident that the bear is just too lazy to try to catch one of the mallards. After a time he may pull a few wild onions and eat them or he may sniff about in the grass and find a mouse's nest taken over by a wasp or a bumblebee. He will tear the nest apart and lick up the larvae. If the angry mother wasp or the bumblebee fastens upon his snout, he will lick her off with a flick of his tongue and she will join the larvae he is chomping upon.

If you can stay with your bear you will experience a delightfully lazy morning, and you will be amazed at what a bear will eat. Mother nature's cupboard is stocked with an amazing variety of food, each adapted to some animal's need. But bruin isn't choosy. He prefers wild honey to a big brown mushroom or a puffball, but he won't pass up either. He has a feast if he finds the carcass of a deer which has lain in the sun until it is really ripe.

He passes up a few tasty morsels such as ground squirrels and gophers. He would very much enjoy them but the labor needed to dig them out of their dens does not appeal to him. A grizzly would uproot a whole hillside to get a half-dozen ground squirrels, but not the black bear.

A black bear may occasionally kill a fawn if he accidentally stumbles on one hidden in a thicket, but this does not happen very often. If the doe hid her baby under a bee tree, which the bear would smell a long way off, the bear might find it while studying the bee tree.

Lazy as black bears are, they are still pranksters. If a black bear sees another black sitting with his back against a tree snoozing and sunning himself, the visitor may creep up behind the tree and reach around and clout the napping bear, at the same time voicing a coughing roar. The sleeper will take off, tumbling end over end down the hill. The prankster will amble off without a glance at his victim. He will act as though he didn't know there was another bear on the slope.

You may come upon your bear up a tree. If you do he is apt to stay up that tree. I have talked to woodsmen who have tried to take half-grown cubs out of trees. They just don't come unstuck no matter how strong the man is.

I once knew a family who lived high on a mountain above Somerset, Colorado. There was a man and his wife and two sons. The country around them was wild and they had no neighbors closer than about fifteen miles. The two teen-age boys were great hunters and they lived right in the middle of bear country, so they hunted bears and had killed a number of them.

They were hunting in a canyon where there was an abandoned saw-mill site. The younger brother decided to stay at the mill site and look for fishworms while the older brother went on up the canyon with the rifle. He was looking around for a likely spot to dig when he looked up into an aspen tree and saw a half-grown bear clinging to the trunk looking down at him. The boy picked up a mill slab and rushed to the tree, shouting at the top of his lungs for his brother to come with the rifle. The shouting excited the bear and it started to slide down the trunk. The boy whacked it on the rump with the mill slab and it went back up the tree, but would not stay there. It came down again and the boy whacked it hard. This time the bear just turned loose all holds and dropped, landing on the boy and bowling him over. Instantly the bear leaped off the flattened boy and charged away. The only damage to the boy was that he had the breath knocked out of him. When his brother arrived they started trailing the bear but they never sighted him again although they spent the whole day looking for him. Those boys had a number of bear skins to prove they were expert hunters, but they were no match for an alerted black bear.

Black bears can do quite a few things people do. They can stand erect and take a few steps. They can remove honey as expertly from a wild bee tree as a man can. They spear fish, using their long claws as a spear. And the carcass of a bear with its shaggy coat removed looks startlingly like the naked body of a heavy-set, short-legged man. Indians were aware of this, and always were careful to apologize to any bear they killed and to offer prayers for its soul's speedy and safe flight to the Happy Hunting Grounds.

A bear knows that he has only one place to store food for the winter which is a time of famine for most predators. He has never thought of storing it in his cave; anyway, he'd be too sleepy to eat. So he devours an enormous amount of food during the summer and builds up layers of fat under his shaggy coat. That means he has quite a bit of work to do, much as he would prefer to sit in the sun and drowse. Where there are many oak trees he eats quantities of acorns and adds pine nuts for variety. Once in a while he is able to raid a squirrel's storeroom.

GRIZZLY   *Yellowstone National Park Photo*

The black bear has only two real enemies. He has little to fear from other wild animals. The two enemies are man and forest fires. Over the years bears have come to know that a man with a rifle is a deadly enemy. The resinous conifer timber on the slopes of our western mountains may turn the bear's range into a place of death in case of fire. The avenues of escape are fewer in the southern mountains where there are few streams and where the forests are not drenched by frequent summer showers. A bear caught in a canyon on the eastern slopes of the Sierra Range has only one avenue of escape, he has to outrun the flaming holocaust. In the north he may join a multitude of forest dwellers in a river or a lake. At such a time fear of each other vanishes, the hunter and the hunted huddle together, the rabbit next to the bobcat, the doe beside the cougar.

It is true that the bear avoids certain wild neighbors. He will quickly yield a trail to a porcupine or a skunk. I have never seen a bear with a face full of porcupine quills. It is well known that a bear is quick to step aside when he meets a skunk. He may stand on his head and do a lot of tricks when at a safe distance just to try to bother the skunk but he won't get close and he will make off fast if the skunk stamps his feet and elevates his plume.

Being a very smart and cunning fellow the black bear manages to live, often with human neighbors nearby. Unless he takes to killing sheep or pigs or to breaking into cabins to get at the good things stored there, he may live out his full span of life. But if a bear takes the easy way he is doomed. Pigs are probably his greatest temptation; all black bears love pork. I am sure his shyness and fear of man help him to escape from man's rifle. I had this shyness illustrated for me once.

I was fishing in Rosebud Lake high in the mountains of Montana. I was working my way around a steep cliff which rose out of the lake. The ledge I was on was not more than a foot wide and there was a thirty foot drop to the water. I rounded a corner and found myself face to face with a good-sized black bear. We almost collided. I could take a thirty foot dive into the lake or try to back off. I was sure I couldn't turn around on that narrow ledge. I didn't have to do it, either; that bear executed a lightning turn which seemed impossible on such a narrow strip of granite, then charged away. Shaken but able to move, I got off the ledge in time to see him charging away up a steep slope. He turned aside only for big trees, smashing down brush, charging over saplings and sizeable second growth pines.

His action was typical of all wild black bears I have ever met. I think this is what any bear will do when he meets a man. If he has a choice he will run up-hill. I once watched a half-grown bear who had no choice but a down-hill run to escape a hunter. He tumbled head over heels twice before he reached level ground, but each time he landed on his feet still running.

As I have said the black bear hates to exert himself one bit more than he has to to secure a meal. He will debate quite a while before starting to dig, even for skunk-cabbage roots. And he will search diligently for a rotting carcass rather than try to catch some fresh meat for his dinner. Once in a while he will make an attempt to slap down a rabbit, and when he does he exhibits re-markable agility. I once saw one leap over a four-foot tree in an attempt to land on a snowshoe rabbit he had spotted sitting in the shade of the tree trunk. He missed the rabbit only by inches.

We should all be glad that there are still black bears in our woods and be thankful that most states have laws protecting them. May their numbers increase.

Ring~tailed Bandits

The raccoon is sometimes credited with being a distant relative of the bear. If there is any relationship, it is distant indeed. This little animal with a black mask, and ringed, furry tail is far more intelligent than a bear. Having a raccoon for a pet will prove that to anyone. Weecha quickly solves the problem of latched doors and closed drawers. He will unscrew bottle caps and Mason jar tops. His small forepaws are as adept as hands. I had one that I kept in a screen cage which had a complicated cupboard catch on the *outside* of the door. He was a mature raccoon and I had little hope of being able to make a gentle pet out of an old male, but I wanted to watch him and study him. My son had caught him and handed him over to me. He was grumpy, but not above accepting a couple of eggs and a saucer of fresh warm milk when I milked the cow. Within two nights he had solved the problem of the latch and left the cage. He helped himself to eggs in the henhouse but did not bother the hens. He returned to the woods where he belonged and I often saw him starting on his rounds in the evening. Oddly, he did not return to the henhouse for more eggs.

Recently I wrote a script for Walt Disney about a raccoon and a redbone hound puppy who grew up together, raised by a mother raccoon. I felt that the trick was to get a newly born raccoon and a newly born puppy and put them together the day they were born, hoping the mother would tolerate the pup in lieu of the rest of her brood, save one. The only hitch came when the property man started phoning all over the United States and Canada looking for pregnant raccoons and redbone hounds. Nature's timing being what it is, we needed quite a few of both to make sure we had babies that were born at the same time.

A tiny red pup is a sure-fire scene-stealer and when combined with a baby raccoon we had a real pair of actors. And the pup didn't steal any scenes from that little raccoon. They took to each other like brothers. Teaching the raccoon to do tricks was an easy matter. He got a cherry out of a Mason jar on the third try, he learned to ride a hobby horse in a couple of hours. It wasn't necessary to teach him how to unlatch doors, or pull switches in a machine shop and start all the machinery in the shop. The only concession in making the shop scene was that the handles of the knife switches were painted in bright colors. He didn't miss a single switch. The usual tiresome retakes when making an animal picture were not necessary.

Bonuses came by the hatful because that raccoon did things I wouldn't dare put in the script. He unlatched the doors on a row of rabbit hutches and let the rabbits out. He was curious about everything and had to find out how it worked. Our cameraman was about convinced that he could teach the raccoon how to run a camera.

I am sure that those who saw the movie will agree that the raccoon is a real actor.

In the wild, this fellow is just as curious and capable as when he is kept as a pet. No raccoon ever passes a hole in a tree trunk or in the ground without poking his snout or his paw into it. Any shining thing will be picked up and examined carefully. Trappers often fasten a bright bit of metal or shell to their trap pans if they are making set for raccoons, knowing that if a raccoon passes that way he will reach down into the water for the bright object and get caught. Every flat stone he comes upon is turned over, the raccoon has to see what is under the stone. He is often rewarded by finding a beetle or a bug which he can lap up.

While living in the Santa Cruz Mountains of California in a house that had a rock fish-pond in the front yard, I learned a bit more about raccoons. I had stocked the pool with a dozen fat goldfish. One morning I went out to feed the fish and found not a single one there. I suspected a kingfisher I had seen the day before until I discovered small, wet tracks leading away from the pool. They were raccoon tracks. I had furnished a banquet for a pair of raccoons.

One of the hazards of being a raccoon is danger from sportsmen who hunt them with packs of hounds. Unlike the red fox, the raccoon cannot outrun a pack of hounds; all he can do is climb a tree (unless he can reach a pond or river), and wait until the hunters arrive with their flashlights and guns. His eyes reflect the light and he makes an easy target. I said "sportsmen"; perhaps that is not the right word to use. Webster says that a sportsman is "one who in sports is fair and generous."

If a raccoon falls out of a tree wounded, he will fight savagely for his life and will inflict many deep slashes on the legs and bodies of as many dogs as he can get his teeth into before he is torn apart.

If there is a stream or pond handy a wise old raccoon will take to the water where he is more than a match for a dog. Raccoons have been known to climb on the back of a swimming dog and hold its head under water until it drowns.

Some hunt clubs take the raccoon alive so that it can be chased another night. Having a live raccoon in a cage makes certain the chase will end with a raccoon up a tree. In the wild the hounds often do not find a hot trail.

A few hunters will trick the raccoon into coming to them. They learn to utter a cry like that of a wounded rabbit or bird. This is certain to bring any raccoon within hearing to the spot

RACCOON   *Warren E. Garst*

on the run. Before the raccoon discovers his mistake he is shot.

A male raccoon may mate with several females but he will always be affectionate to the lady he is romancing at the moment. Females are true to the male they choose, but they are not willing to romance with just any male that comes along. I discovered this while looking at "out-takes," i.e., scenes taken on location but not used. I wanted to get a scene where two raccoons, a male and a female, were fighting. I needed it for a sequence where the mother who had adopted the puppy protects him against an old male who hates all dogs, as all old raccoons do. If I could pick up the scene from the library I would save time and money.

I got my scene, and a very lively one, from footage shot for another Disney feature. The script called for love scenes between many wild animals during the season of the mating moon. A young female who was ready and eager to mate was introduced to a big male who at once started acting like an eager suitor. But the lady didn't like his looks; she tore into him, and a handler had a thumb bitten parting them. I had my fight scene, even though it wasn't planned that way. But it taught me something about the nature of raccoons.

In the southwest, the mating season is December, in the north, February. Nine weeks later from three to six babies will be born. The average would be three or four.

The home is usually in a hollow tree but caves are not spurned. The nest will be used for a couple of months; by that time the youngsters will be foraging for themselves.

Shellfish, frogs and insects are eaten as well as any small fish the coon can catch. They are very fond of green corn and can make deep inroads into a patch if it is near a wooded area. They eat other grains, as well as fruits and berries. If near a stream, spring or pond, they will wash each morsel of food carefully before eating it. They sit up and handle the food with their forepaws as a person would eat a roasting ear or an apple.

The raccoon is widely distributed and adapts itself to the surrounding conditions. It may even be found on the plains of Texas where there is little water and no trees. There, abandoned badger holes and coyote dens serve as homes.

The wanderings of a raccoon family will start at dusk. It will be a slow-moving journey with many stops. If a clutch of turtle eggs is found, time will be taken for a feast. As everything they come upon has to be examined, their progress is slow. A cricket chirping in a bush has to be found and snapped up. Each stone they find in shallow water has to be turned over and the snails attached to it licked off. Every shallow pool has its muddy bed searched by their small hands for crayfish and mussels. Banks of soft loam have to be dug over because such ground yields many earthworms. Grassy parks and meadows yield tasty mice. There is no hurry; actually they are not really going anywhere. They have no appointment so there is no need to worry about being late.

The youngsters are safe from most dangers as long as they are with their mother. A bobcat or a cougar may snap one up and sometimes a dog will try it, but usually a dog will hesitate to face the fury of a mother raccoon. The youngsters will stay close to their mother through the first winter and by spring will be able to take care of themselves, as they have been well trained in woods lore.

The raccoon is one of the most rewarding animals to watch, and it is easy to see the wild ones and to make friends with them. I hoard stale bread and crusts before going camping. You need quite a big sackful if you plan to stay a couple of weeks. You can make friends with many chipmunks and coons if you have a supply of dry bread. They will visit your camp or cabin in increasing numbers as the word gets around that you are a generous host.

The coati should be considered along with the raccoon. Their range is southwestern New Mexico and southern Arizona. Their long tails remind you of a raccoon. In fact, they are caricatures of raccoons. They are long, rather slender animals with grizzled brown fur. They may reach a total length of four feet, their tail accounting for half their length.

The first thing you will see when you spot a coati is the elevated long tail waving above tall grass or shrubs. If you sight one you may expect to flush a whole band from cover. When startled they will dash up palo verde trees, as agile as a band of monkeys, where they will leap from limb to limb, growling and hissing, baring their sharp teeth and glaring at you.

The male coati is about twice as large as the female, and is a loner except during the mating season. The females, on the other hand, like company and the bands you see will be made up of mothers with four or five youngsters each.

The real home of the coati is tropical America. Only the hardiest members of the tribe brave the chill winters of New Mexico and Arizona.

Coatis are always hungry. They hunt day and night and eat

anything and everything that is edible. They sleep part of the night and through the mid-day heat. Lizards are a favorite food but they will eat any small animal they can catch as well as birds and bird eggs.

The ringtail cat is usually lumped with the raccoon and the coati. The ringtail is a most appealing little animal weighing a couple of pounds. It has a delicate, pointed face which appears to be all ears and big eyes. Its ringed tail may be twice as long as its body.

Although its range is a large area of the southwestern United States, few people have ever seen it. It is very shy and keeps to cover, seldom coming out except after dark. I have seen them in Yosemite National Park and a friend of mine in Colorado showed me one he had shot in the rugged country above Gunnison. He said he shot it because he didn't know what it was, something more than one man armed with a gun has done. I identified it for him and suggested he just watch the next ringtail he saw.

Those that have been kept in captivity are said to be filled with curiosity and interested in everything around them. But as pets they do not fit in well with man's habits because they like to sleep during the day and if awakened remain drowsy.

The ringtail eats lizards, and in some parts of its range most of its diet will be wood rats. Of course, mice make up a part of their food any place they live.

The ringtail has been called the "miner's cat" because no wild creature is as thorough at ridding premises of rats and mice as the ringtail. Miners like to have them take up residence under their cabin or near it.

A ringtail has few enemies, although a big rattler or an eagle may take some of the babies. The high flying golden eagle sees every moving thing on the ground and may catch even an adult ringtail if it ventures out before dark, but their way of life offers good protection. Their fur is not valuable so they are not sought by trappers. So elusive an animal will probably always be with us.

RING-TAILED CAT   *N. Paul Kenworthy, Jr.*

The Cats

When writing about North American cats of the wild, it is usual to start off with *Felis concolor*, the cougar, the most expert stalker that roams the western mountains. I prefer to save the cougar as a climax and will start off with a reddish-gray kitty who seldom weighs more than twenty pounds. This fellow gets his name, bobcat, from his stumpy tail; he is also called a wildcat.

I first became acquainted with bobcats while teaching in a one-room, log schoolhouse on Owl Creek in Wyoming. I was familiar with the lynx cat as there were a number of them which lived along the Dakota stream where I ran trap-line as a boy. I boarded with a widow who ran a sheep ranch. Her home was a half-mile from the schoolhouse and in going to supper I always followed a path that skirted an alfalfa field. Steep slopes crowned by sandstone rimrocks overlooked the hay field. I have never seen so many bobcats in one place as there were living in those rim-rocks.

Rabbits were attracted to the succulent alfalfa, and where there are plenty of rabbits, bobcats are almost sure to be found. I usually walked from the school to the ranch late in the evening as the family always ate a late supper. This is the time of day when the bobcats start prowling. Almost every night I would see one or more bobcats burst out of the alfalfa field and bounce up the slope to the rimrocks. Once in a while I would almost step on one who was intent upon stalking a rabbit. They would cover the slope and vanish among the rocks in a remarkably short time.

One of my pupils owned a pair of greyhounds he used for catching coyotes. Old Charlie, the larger of the two, was a scarred veteran with a face laced with claw marks. Old Charlie liked to come to school and lie at the open door looking in, and he often lingered after my six pupils had gone home, so that he could walk to the ranch house with me. I had taken a great liking to the lank old hound and he appreciated the attention I gave him. If he was with me when we flushed a bobcat from the alfalfa field, Old Charlie would streak after the cat. He was always able to overtake a bobcat before it got very far. Then began a comedy which was played every time the old hound sighted a bobcat.

When Old Charlie reached out to fasten his fangs into the neck of the bobcat, it would flip over on its back and rake his face with four sets of sharp claws. Old Charlie would leap back, howling mournfully, and the bobcat would roll over and be off again. Old Charlie would overtake it and get repulsed again. This would happen perhaps three times before the bobcat reached the rimrocks and vanished into a jumble of rocks. I have seen Old Charlie kill a number of coyotes but I never saw him bag a bobcat.

Bobcats are supposed to be wild and ferocious, spitfires who refuse to be tamed, even when taken as kittens. This may be true of some of them. I once extended a hand into a box where a kitten was lying, thinking it was a house cat the zoo keeper was keeping as a pet. I was greeted by a harsh mew and a series of spitting sounds and two small paws lashed at my hand. This little bobcat was living up to his tribe's reputation.

But a friend of mine living in Cupertino, California owns what must surely be a bobcat. It has the build, the markings, the bobtail, the ears and legs of a bobcat. This cat has the run of the farm and enters the house where it acts like any house cat. It mixes with this woman's other cats and one female has had a

BOBCATS

litter of kittens with bobtails and other bobcat markings. I know this is a controversial statement to make, but it is difficult not to believe one's eyes. I once wrote what I thought was a very fine short story about a bobcat who lured a pedigreed Persian puss into the woods where they romanced under the stars. Scientists and editors on the Pennsylvania Game news magazine rejected the story with the statement that it is impossible for a bobcat to mate with a house cat. Since then I have seen a cub tigrello, the result of mating between a tiger and a lioness. The last time I heard of this tigrello, he was in the Salt Lake City zoo.

I met a number of bobcats on location where Disney was making a film. One of them was the biggest and tamest bobcat I have ever seen. It acted just like a big house cat, purring when stroked, rubbing against my leg like any tabby. It was so mild and loving that it did not fit the part of a fierce bobcat which it was supposed to play. In order to arouse its wild nature a rabbit was dropped into the cage. Apparently this bobcat had never seen a rabbit before. While the rabbit crouched fearfully, the bobcat walked over and sniffed it. Then he lay down with his head against the furry belly, yawned lazily and closed his eyes.

Trying to get a bobcat to act is more difficult than handling a cougar. The producer had one that was fierce enough to play the part but every time the boys turned him loose, he ignored the bait he was supposed to chase and climbed the nearest tree. It is not difficult to get a two-hundred-pound cougar out of a tree, you just climb up the tree and prod him down, guiding him by his long tail. But you don't do that with a spitting twenty-pound bobcat. The boys had to chop down four trees to recover their bobcat the first day they tried to work him. It was the only way they could recover their bobcat, which was rented. Had the studio owned him the producer would have gladly allowed him to return to the wild.

Bobcat footage was finally secured but dozens of bits and pieces had to be spliced together to make a good chase scene. The film editor labored long in fitting the scenes together. All of which proves that a bobcat is an independent fellow with a mind of his own.

The bobcat is a night hunter, especially in settled areas. This caution and wariness makes it possible for him to live in agricultural areas if there is brush and timber for cover.

The color of a bobcat will vary with the region where it lives. In the north and northwest the color will be dark, on the desert it will be pale. This is an adaption to be expected.

A bobcat is not much of a tree-climber but will go up a tree if chased by dogs, or if it spots a bird's nest it suspects may contain eggs or fledgling birds. It gets most of its food on the ground and much of it is rabbits and mice, with an occasional meal on the eggs of a ground-nesting bird, such as sage hens, grouse, quail and larks. On the desert the bobcat catches lizards and ground squirrels, but even there mice will outnumber other prey by a thousand to one.

In Arizona and New Mexico the bobcat will catch a few peccaries but grabbing one of the little javelinas is a risky venture. A herd of peccaries are savage and aggressive. The setting has to be just right, with a high ledge or a tree handy, or the bobcat may wind up in the stomachs of the wild pigs. The usual way of stalking these wild pigs is for the bobcat to lie on a limb or a ledge and wait for a piglet to wander close enough so that the bobcat can leap down, snatch the prize, and leap back to safety before the herd closes in on him. A tree with spreading branches is ideal; the shade will attract the little pigs.

Barnyard fowl will often be carried away by bobcats if there is brush cover close to the area where chickens and turkeys go hunting for grasshoppers. But there is one barnyard fowl the bobcat does not get; that is a guinea hen. Night or day a guinea hen will instantly set up an infernal racket if approached even in the most stealthy manner. This explosion of sound shatters the bobcat's sensitive nerves and sends him off fast. At night a bobcat will not hesitate to enter a henhouse or barn if he can get inside.

A bobcat will kill sheep and may slaughter more than one

when he attacks a sleeping flock. On the whole, though, a bobcat is a small menace to farmers or ranchers. The toll he takes of mice and rabbits more than tips the balance in his favor.

The temperament of these cats varies with the different individuals; there are probably no two alike. Whereas one will kill only animals smaller than himself, his brother may unhesitatingly attack bigger animals. There are cases on record in which a bobcat has killed a mature deer, although a fawn kill would be more likely to occur.

It is the opinion of most hunters that, given good cover, none but the biggest and most savage dogs can get the best of a bobcat. An ordinary dog would not have a chance of killing one.

Friends of mine who live in Three Rivers, California, tell me that the canyon where they live, which is some distance from the village, was once infested with domestic cats, many of them running wild, others roaming far from home to hunt birds and mice. A bobcat moved into the area and soon there wasn't a cat left except those kept indoors. Bish is a keen observer and I believe him.

There is some evidence that bobcats are sociable. Groups of from two to six have been seen on what appeared to be hunting forays, though they may have been simply social outings.

The bobcat has about the same voice and vocabulary as that of a domestic cat, but it is harsher and louder. When angry, it spits and hisses; when giving vent to the urge to seek a mate or just to let off steam, it yowls long and loud. Its yowl lacks the wild ferocity of the lynx; I have never heard any big cat that could out-yell a lynx.

The bobcat has as much curiosity as the cougar or the lynx. Like the cougar it may follow a man through the woods just to see what he is doing, or to figure out what manner of creature this upright walking animal is.

Bobcats mate in February or March. In about seventy days, two to four young are born. The father leaves or is driven away from the den at this time. No one has come forward with evidence that he returns to help raise the family. The den is usually on a ledge or in a rock slide but a hollow log will do, even a standing tree. The babies open their eyes in nine days and are weaned in June.

This tailless hunter is often seen by day. He moves from one range to another, across open slopes and valleys during the day. I once came face to face with one while walking through knee-high grass in a mountain meadow. He was probably there hunting mice. A blur of brown fur burst out of a clump of grass not more than a yard away from me. I was as startled as the bobcat. He must have been very intent on what he was doing to let me approach and almost step on him.

The chance of survival for the bobcat seems good. As long as there is cover he will be with us.

The lynx confines himself to the northern areas of the United States and Canada and Alaska. He is well adapted to snow country and has to have a range where there are rabbits. He eats so many rabbits that he seems to have taken on some of the traits of a rabbit. When rabbits on his range diminish so do the lynx cats.

You could be awakened on a moonlit night by terrible cater-wauling, lusty, blood-chilling shrieks and screams. It is as though a couple of demons were staging a battle to the death. If you are able to summon the courage to investigate, you will find two big lynx cats crouched with their noses a few inches apart, mouths open, vocal cords vibrating as they hurl insults at each other. This will go on until one of the big toms has been out-cursed. He will then slink away, humiliated, no doubt.

But there will be no slashing with claws or fangs. No trapper ever took a lynx that has a single scar that could have been caused by a fight with another lynx. That is the word that comes from the Hudson's Bay Fur Company. Skins never come in marred and scarred as they do with other big cats.

But the lynx is aggressive as a hunter. It carries on a year-round feud and will kill any fox it can catch. The fox is smarter and swifter than the lynx and can easily avoid him when there is no loose snow on the ground. Deprived of his speed and ability of maneuver, the fox has to fight to the death if he meets a lynx on a snow-covered meadow or park. The lynx respects the snapping jaws of the fox and will use every trick he knows. It will not be a fast-closing, slashing attack such as the weasels use. It will be a circling, stabbing attack, with the fox trying to retreat to the nearest timber while the lynx keeps cutting him off, waiting for the fox to tire before he moves in for the kill. No one has ever been able to account for the hatred the lynx has for a fox.

A lynx can be easily identified by its big furry feet, its tufted ears and its long side-burns. It has thick, sturdy legs and a tail like that of a bobcat. The winter coat is a pastel gray. It may weigh up to forty pounds but the average will be closer to twenty.

The lynx does not see well in bright light but it has excellent vision in dim light or in the green dusk of the forest. I was once called into a projection booth to look at some lynx footage shot in Canada. "Something's wrong with that cat," the producer said. "Can you tell what it is?"

After studying the footage it came to me that the director, who was shooting in color and needed as much bright sunlight as he could get on the subject, had moved the big cat into sharp sunlight. Its eyes were mere slits and it was plainly cringing. Now that fast-index color film is available, I am sure very natural footage will be made of a lynx, but it will have to be taken in shaded areas.

This big cat is a silent hunter, keeping to forest floors littered with fallen trees and limbs. It prefers the dim light of the stars or slice of moon where its superior night vision gives it an advantage over its quarry, but it will also hunt in the green twilight of a dense forest. It slips along, pauses to listen, and to test the breezes funneling through the forest. It checks every shape and shadow around it. During the summer the big rabbits it hunts are gray and not easily seen in dim light. In winter they are as white as the

LYNX   *Hugh A. Wilmar*

snow they sit on. But the lynx has a keen nose and ears as well
as eyesight. The scent of a rabbit will give its general location,
and the eyes will seek it out. Once located, the snowshoe will be
stalked slowly and silently, movements on the part of the hunter
being kept to the minimum.

It is very difficult to slip up on a snowshoe rabbit. If it is
napping it may be doomed but if it is awake it usually spots the
lynx and bounds swiftly away. A lynx may have to stalk a dozen
rabbits in a night to catch one.

The lynx is always out after rabbits but he will kill any
bird he can surprise. At all times, when moving along the trunk
of a fallen tree or over a carpet of pine needles, the lynx stays
crouched down so as to be as inconspicuous as possible, and he
takes advantage of wind-fallen trees, depressions in the earth,
rocks and stumps.

A lynx gets most of his venison by killing fawns who have strayed too far from their mothers or when he is able to locate a very young one the mother has hidden in a thicket. In this case his keen sense of smell will not help him any. During this period the fawn will have no scent at all. But the lynx knows where to look and checks every dense thicket. This period in the life of a fawn is its most critical time. The lynx makes its chances of survival less.

One might think that killing a fawn after it has started following its mother would be easy as she has no antlers for defense, but she has other weapons, better in many ways than lances of bone. She has slender and powerful legs, capable of letting her make terrific bounds, and those legs end in sharp hoofs which she will use like knives if her fawn is attacked. Her lightning blows can slice through the body of a lynx to his heart or other vital organs. So the lynx has to wait, and goes without venison most of the time.

During the romance period, male lynx indulge in serious vocalization. I have already described a duel between two males. When gripped by the ardor of wooing a lady, their cries of passion have chilled the blood of many a wayfarer passing through the woods at night. The females answer just as loudly.

Imagine the weird noise when a half dozen lynx cats get together on romance bent. The number may be even greater. When a couple finally stop serenading each other, they go off on a honeymoon. About sixty-five days after mating the young are born. There will be from one to four and their eyes will be open at birth.

After the young have been suckled for two or three months they will set out on their travels with their mother. There is some evidence that the father, even though he is not with them, will stay nearby. During the summer the kits will learn to hunt by joining their mother when she makes kills. They are also likely to learn a lot from the mistakes they make. After a young hunter has missed a rabbit a few times because he popped his head above the grass too soon, he will learn to keep it down. The same is true of snapped twigs and scuffed stones. The family continues together through the autumn and may even stay together until March, when the mating urge will cause the mother to leave. The young ones will feel it, too, and a new cycle of lynx life will start.

The ocelot is considered by many observers to be the handsomest of cats. No two are marked exactly the same but there will be some markings and stripes which will be found on all of them. The background color is gray becoming darker in the winter, with splotches and dark stripes. For this reason it is sometimes called a leopard cat. Its weight is from ten to twenty pounds. Ocelots found in our southwest are all of one species, and are a little smaller than the tropical species.

The favorite haunts of the ocelot are the impenetrable thorn thickets which give dogs a lot of trouble and which man cannot penetrate. In one square mile of chaparral, two dozen ocelots might live out their lives without being known to people frequenting the area.

The ocelot prefers darkness, the darker the better; it may stay holed up on moonlit nights. They like black, stormy nights when the wind is blowing with hurricane force. On such nights ocelots have been known to boldly raid a chicken house. This hunter even manages to catch sleeping birds on such nights, although how he does it is a mystery, with the tree limbs lashing and swaying. It may be that a bird struggling to keep from being blown out of a tree would make such a fuss that the ocelot could easily find it. Ocelots climb as well as domestic cats but are not in a class with monkeys and squirrels. They can move fast in a tree, and hunt or take naps in the upper branches.

On the ground an ocelot is swift. If a hound picks up his trail, he is full of tricks and does not dash off to his den but leads the dog a merry chase, back-tracking and double-crossing his trail which he will make sure leads through thickets of cactus, mesquite, and nopal, armed with edged barbs and poison points. After a few hours of this the hound slinks back to the hunters in a condition which might have been caused by the ocelot's claws and fangs, as well as the terrain through which he has traveled.

Tragedy comes to this courageous fellow only when there is a very large pack of hounds and cover is light. He is fast but he is a sprinter and the trail hounds are bred for the long pull. Within a mile, if he finds no dense cover the dogs will overtake him. Like all cats harried by dogs he will then take to a tree. The combination of a pack of hounds and a man with a rifle spells his doom. The intrepid hunter, safe on the ground and armed with a high-powered rifle will shoot this small tiger-cat out of the tree and call it sport.

When you look at an ocelot you immediately think of the savage jungle tiger and the leopard, and are ready to credit it with fierceness and savagery. You will be mistaken. The ocelot is mild and gentle. He makes the finest pet you can get. He will love you and try to please you. He has come into such high esteem as a pet that today in the United States there is a National Ocelot Club which publishes a magazine for those who have this spotted charmer as a pet. I do not say own, because more than likely if you get an ocelot, he will own you. He's just a big simple cat.

As many as a dozen ocelots may be kept in the same cage. They will spend most of the day curled up in furry balls sleeping. At night when it is natural for them to be active, they frisk and play but they are never quarrelsome and never fight, even in crowded quarters.

At one time it seemed that this little tiger-cat would be exterminated except in inaccessible jungle areas. But many people have come to know him and hunters have learned that an ocelot is worth more alive than dead and skinned. The pelt is worth about six dollars, but a live ocelot will bring ten times that much. This has helped to diminish the slaughter.

In all of their habits they are like house cats. They wash their faces, relax on your hearth, express their wants in the same way your tabby cat does. Like all of the cats I have come in contact with, they have mastered the art of relaxing completely. I have a feeling that the bigger the cat the more thoroughly it will relax. When we worked cougars in making a film, on a warm day they would find a spot of shade and stretch out, legs sprawled and extended, the entire body in repose within seconds.

The game caught by a wild ocelot will include birds of all kinds, and poultry taken from their roosts, rabbits, wood rats, mice, and reptiles, such as lizards and snakes. An ocelot has been known to kill a seven-foot boa. They have a habit of plucking the feathers off a chicken or bird before eating it. This may not be true of the northern ocelots but has been observed in the southern species.

Most of the dens of ocelots which have been examined by hunters and naturalists were in rocky caves. Very few have been found in hollow trees. They are always well lined with grass and soft materials.

Not much is known of the courtship and mating of the ocelots but it is safe to believe that it is much like that of the other cats, big and small. September arrival of the young indicates a June honeymoon. Family life follows the way of all cats.

Our information on ocelots is somewhat scanty because most people simply shoot the animal as soon as they sight it. And the habits of tame ocelots cannot be accepted as those of wild ones who have had to struggle to find food and to stay alive. I have noticed this where zoo or pet cats have been worked when filming a story. The keen scent and sight of wild cougars is absent from the tame cats used on location.

You may see an ocelot seated in a car beside the driver, or strolling along a street with its owner. When taking an ocelot for a stroll a leash is needed. This summer I saw one strolling along a Santa Barbara beach tugging at a leash held by a little girl.

The jaguarondi is a small animal with a formidable name.

Actually it looks more like a big weasel than a cat. It has a small head with a pointed snout, a long, slender body, a long tail and short legs. It will weigh from ten to twenty pounds.

A few of these hunters will be found in southern Texas. Their range is mostly south of the border. Here, where the hot sun beats down upon thorn thickets, it lives in dense, barbed cover much as the ocelot does. This brushy cover is steadily being bulldozed away and when the cover goes, the jaguarondi will vanish from our borders.

Partly due to its living in jungles neither man nor dog can penetrate, and partly because of its shy and elusive habits and also because it hunts at night, the jaguarondi has been studied very little. There are few reports from people who have watched them. Most of those seen were young, and had not yet learned to keep to cover. I do not know of anyone who has ever tamed one. They can climb trees but probably do most of their hunting on the ground. Evidence of their tree climbing comes from hunters who have shot them out of trees after spotting reflected light from their eyes. Other reports state that these odd cats will take to water readily and cross streams and lakes.

Their food is undoubtedly like that of the ocelot as their ranges are the same.

I have lived all of my life in areas where there were cougars but have been able to watch only a few of them in the wild. They are found in all of the mountain areas of the west and northwest. My friend, Milt Holt, of Gunlock, Utah who has been taking cougar-hunting parties out for years, tells me that there are still plenty of them in that area. He proved it to me by taking me out on a hunt, after I made him promise that the cougar would be taken alive and unharmed. This he readily agreed to. His hounds treed one the first morning out, a big, snarling old tomcat who took refuge in a tall cottonwood tree. It took Milt and his friends longer to get that big cat off the high cottonwood limb than it had to run the cougar down. Milt is full of tales about cougars he has trailed and taken, but I have seen more free and untreed cougars than he has.

We took Sheba, a young female cougar that Milt's teen-aged daughter had raised, with us. Milt had given Sheba to his daughter when the cougar was a kitten. A hound pup was raised with her, the usual way of handling the taming of a cougar. Sheba was about two-thirds grown at the time. She was friendly but full of pranks. I learned not to move too swiftly past her if she was stretched out napping. Out would flick a paw and there would be a rent in my trouser-leg, and once she got a bit of skin. But she loved us all. She loved us so much that she always tried to get into a sleeping bag with one of us at night. This would have been highly uncomfortable. Sheba was all cat and when she got warm and happy she did what your own cat will do, she unsheathed her claws, flexing them in and out on any solid thing beside her, which might be your arm or leg. With her that meant an inch-and-a-half of sharp-tipped claws to caress you with. We had to pen her up at night.

Sheba and the hound she had grown up with were very much attached to each other. The other hounds considered her just another cougar but they left her alone because Pete would defend her if they bothered her. Backed by Pete, Sheba made a danger-ous opponent for the hounds. She liked to climb a tree in the yard of the hunting lodge where she would stretch out on a limb. From her perch she would watch the hounds stretched out in the shade under the tree. Like all hounds they flopped and snoozed when not running or eating. When she decided that they were all asleep, she would spring down upon one of them. She never used her fangs or claws, but having a cougar land on one of the dogs was enough to start an uproar of baying and yelping. Before the hounds could get into action Sheba was back up the tree with a ring of angry hounds bounding about below. She would lie on the limb with the black tip of her long tail twitching and wait, an hour, two hours, until the hounds went to sleep again, then she would stage a repeat performance.

In taking the cougar alive on our hunt, Milt climbed the tree and lassoed the big cat. It took some tugging to get the angry tom out of the tree and a lot of maneuvering before Milt could give him a shot of tranquilizer. Milt refused to use a tranquilizer gun, he said it made the big cats sick. He used an ordinary four-inch hypodermic syringe. The cat's jaws were not wired shut and he was not trussed with ropes. He was just tossed across Milt's saddle and Milt rode with a hundred and fifty pounds of cougar in his lap. The trouble was that he waked up when half-way out of the canyon. Even a cougar-trained horse will not stand still with a clawing cat on his back. That sorrel bucked lustily and sent Milt and the cougar flying.

Milt's dogs were too smart to tackle a cougar on the ground. They backed off, waiting for the cougar to run. He was too groggy to head for a tree and one of the men lassoed him. A second shot put him to sleep for long enough to get him into camp. The boys stretched him out in the shade of a tree and he slumbered peacefully. It was the first time I had ever seen the black flag at the end of a cougar's tail stop waving. It was the black tufts on the tips of his ears that kept twitching.

Sheba was very much interested in the big tom. She rubbed her cheek against his and licked his face. She may have thought we had rounded up a husband for her.

That cougar did not wake up until we got back to Gunlock and put him in a cage. When I went to look at him the next morning he was eating a jack rabbit Milt had tossed into his cage. He was as savage a lion as I have ever seen, aside from a few females with cubs.

On that hunt I cranked out roll after roll of 8 mm movie film with my Bell and Howell, which, added to the shots I took on location while the big cats were being filmed, gave me a nice home movie which I could study. I have one hunt film where you can actually see the cougar running through the trees, something Milt tells me he has never seen in a real hunt. You see the dogs but never the cougar. I simply spliced in running shots of a cougar and hounds taken on location.

The range of the cougar covers the western states and as far north as British Columbia. In primitive times, when the continent was beginning to greet white settlers, this big cat was found in large numbers everywhere and was known as puma, panther, catamount, mountain lion and cougar. The name cougar is the one most commonly used. In the early pioneer days animal drives were organized which resulted in the wanton slaughter of all animals caught in them. A typical drive was one organized in Pennsylvania in 1760 in which forty-one panthers were killed along with one hundred and nine wolves, one hundred and twelve foxes, one hundred and fourteen wildcats, seventeen black bears, two elk, ninety-eight deer, three fishers, one otter, twelve wolverines, three beavers, one hundred and eleven buffalo and upwards of five hundred smaller animals. This bit of recorded history throws much light on the numbers and distribution of wild life in the days before they were wiped out in many places. This hunt covered a circle thirty miles in diameter. The report says that the choicest hides were taken, and the tongues of the buffalos. The carcasses were heaped up along with pine limbs to the height of a tall pine and burned. I have mentioned the Indian's attitude toward these hunts and how they retaliated against hunters.

These drives did not cease until most of the wild life in an area was exterminated. Records show that many hunters killed a hundred or more panthers during their active careers. Z. M. Pike says, "Standing on a hill, I beheld in one view below me, buffalo, elk, deer and panthers."

The cougar is the peer of all wild hunters. He is endowed with maximum power, speed and endurance, all that can be contained in a one-hundred-and-fifty-pound body that is lithe and graceful.

Toward evening, when the deer and the elk have come out of the forest to browse in the parks and meadows, and long shadows from tall pines begin creeping out across the tall grass and low shrubbery, the cougar slides out of a cave or a thicket where he has spent the day sleeping. He moves silently on big padded feet; eyes, ears and nostrils alert. He will not stake out close to a water-hole or salt lick or a stream where deer come to drink, and wait to ambush his prey. He is a hunter who matches his wits with his quarry, stalking it and striking swiftly.

He will move in great circles through the woods of his domain swiftly and so silently that in many places in the east he was known as "sneak-cat." He will pick up trail scent and follow it but what he is seeking is body-scent carried to him on a breeze, and he does not need to see the game to know what it is. Once he picks up the body-scent he starts a slow, stealthy approach, directly up wind.

He will glide like a shadow over fallen trees, around heaps of brittle twigs which would snap under his weight, avoiding leafy bushes and shrubs where the rustle of his big feet might be heard. He will pause often to look and listen and test the wind as it brings stronger body-smell. He is now making a slow, stealthy approach. Finally he will hear the champing of the deer's teeth as it snips off and chews twigs and leaves. If the sound stops, the cougar will wait patiently as much as half an hour for the sound to start again, telling him that the doe or buck has satisfied itself that the sound it heard was made by the wind or a falling branch dislodged by the breeze. A cougar may make half a dozen approaches before he gets into the position he desires.

When he sights the feeding deer he will study it. He prefers a doe but if the quarry is a buck with a rack of antlers, he will not break off the attack; he will wait until the buck has his back toward him and thus will be unable to meet the leap with daggers of bone. Of course, he may have a choice between a doe and a buck; if so he picks the doe. His next move is to check the ground between himself and his quarry carefully, spotting small land-

marks, a rock beside which his first leap will land him. The final distance for the last spring must land him upon the back of his unsuspecting victim.

He will not hurry, patience is one of the virtues he possesses. Cougars have been known to lie in wait for a day and a night on a ledge or limb to get a chance to make a kill. This time limit was established by a cougar that had taken up a position on a rock. Twenty-four hours before the attack there was a snowfall and no tracks led through the snow to that rock. There was only the evidence of the kill and the tracks leading away from the rock and the kill.

Deer are alert creatures. Mule deer, which are a large item in a cougar's diet, have big ears and keen eyes. When feeding they raise their heads at intervals and prop their big ears forward. If the cougar makes any sound at all, they will hear it. When the head starts up a cougar crawling on his belly through tall grass will freeze. Only the black flag on the tip of his tail twitches back and forth. Some outdoor men say this is a warning to other cougars to move on and not interfere.

The deer may hear a sound and spot movement of the tawny body before the cougar can freeze. The deer will be off, bounding high, moving so swiftly that chase would be fruitless. A whole night may pass without a kill, but eventually patience and careful planning will bring success. Without the cougar's menace the deer would lose their bounding grace, their alertness, and would become slothful and lazy like park deer.

After the cougar is set he bunches his powerful leg muscles which are like steel springs. The first long, high leap is made and then the second. With terrific impact the tawny body hits its target, a paw reaches out to the deer's muzzle and jerks it back, snapping the neck bones. The deer collapses and the big cat rips at the jugular vein and is soon lying beside the carcass lapping hot blood and purring as it takes the finest fruit of the kill. Only cats purr and someone has suggested that they learned to do this by breathing deeply as they enjoyed the warm blood of a victim.

This makes a bubbling, purring sound which they have learned to make when contented or happy.

The female is the better hunter as is the case with cats big and small. She is also more aggressive in many ways.

Winter hunting when the snow is deep is another kind of hunting. During early winter when the snow is loose and deep, the cougar often goes hungry for days. The deer's slender hoofs drive down through the snow to solid ground and it can bound away as fast as it can in the summer time, while the cougar flounders. With the slopes covered by a deep white blanket of snow the cougar cannot fall back on mice, although he may catch an occasional snowshoe rabbit. But here again the snowshoe has the advantage of moving fast over the loose snow on his big furry feet. But when the snow crusts enough to hold the weight of the big cat the story is reversed, now the hunter can move fast while the deer are handicapped. This is the time when most deer kills are made. But the cougar kills only when hungry so there is no wanton slaughter as in the case of the weasel tribe.

The best description I ever got of the courtship between cougars came from an old trapper who had watched a pair in New Mexico. He said that gentleman-longtail was always the reluctant one. This confirmed my observation from watching a pair in the Denver Zoo. The female called coaxingly from the wood while the male sat at the edge of a meadow and ignored her.

She was down-wind from him and knew exactly where he was. His indifference soon irritated her and her coaxing call changed to a harsher, throaty rumble as she loped out of the woods. The big tom continued to ignore her, his interest centered on a park below. When the she-cat closed in she tore into the big tom, who was almost twice her size, and clawed him, then slapped him soundly. After quite a bit of this the tom slapped back and they rolled and tumbled on the grass. Breaking off their wrestling they loped away side by side into the timber.

But like the little female raccoon mentioned earlier in the chapter on raccoons, the lady cougar does not always fall for a big and handsome male. Tom and Sally were leading stars in the cast of *Killers of the High Country*. Tom is the biggest cougar I have ever seen, Sally is a trim little female. In the story they were supposed to be brothers. We were all sure Sally would be smitten by Tom. Their first scene together was a run down a slope. The distance was about a hundred yards and they were lured into making it by one of the crew who had a live chicken in a sack at the bottom of the slope. He shook the sack and the chicken squawked and flapped its wings. Even at that distance Tom and Sally heard the chicken and came down the slope in graceful, long bounds which seemed to make them float along.

When they were halted by the screens of the crew, they were close together. Tom showed a definite interest in Sally and tried to be nice to her, thrusting out his muzzle eagerly. She would have nothing to do with him. She reared up and snarled, then swung a paw at him. Tom backed off hastily. If Sally had been in the mood she might have accepted his advances, but I doubt it.

One thing about these cougars which had been kept in captivity since they were cubs was that they learned fast, possibly in part through instinct. None of them had had a chance to learn to hunt in the wild. Sally had grown up as a house cat owned by a woman. She was released from her crate close to a band of thirty head of sheep. I doubt if she had ever seen a sheep before. On her first run she dashed among the sheep, scattering them and batting at a few but never selecting one for a kill. But on her second run she selected one sheep and pulled it down. She would have made short work of it if an Airedale the handlers kept handy had not arrived at once and nipped her rump. She turned to strike at the dog and the sheep was rescued unscathed.

These cats on location had plenty of freedom. Only on rare occasions was a fenced area used; they were just turned loose and lures were used to get them to move in the right direction. If one ran away, Milt Holt's hounds soon treed it, but even without hounds a cougar unused to rustling its food would soon come back to camp for a meal. They had learned that chicken-wire

fencing meant a cage so they could be stopped and guided by
flimsy frames to which chicken wire had been tacked. If a cat
charged, you would set the screen down at arm's length in front
of you and the cat stopped when it reached the barrier. When
new hands were hired who had never been around the big cats it
took some convincing to get them to rely on a flimsy screen.

Every cougar in the cast was interested in horses and eager to
get at one. The saddle stock had to be kept away from them. Tom
knew what to do when he saw a deer, even though he had never
hunted one. He also stalked a beaver and rushed it. On that occasion there was a bonus. When the beaver dived into its pond
through a hole in the ice, Tom dived right in and would have
gotten the beaver if the boys hadn't grabbed him by the tail and
dragged him out of the pond. The director thought it was a fluke
but on a retake he did the same thing. I am convinced that a wild
cougar would do the same thing and probably does if he is
hungry enough.

I got the idea that these cougars instinctively did the same
things a wild cougar would do. The only weakness in them
seemed to be that, through lack of use, their senses were not
sharp. I know Tom's sense of smell was not keen, but he could
hear a chicken flapping a hundred yards away. And he did not
seem to be attracted by movement as a wild cougar would be. He
was lured down to the top of a cliff overlooking a slope where
sheep were moving about. He was supposed to react like a hunter
when he saw the sheep. The reaction shot was gotten when the
sheepherder rode by below the cliff on a gray horse. Tom saw the
horse and came to life at once.

In the wild, three months after the honeymoon the cubs are
born. There may be as many as four but two is the usual number.
In securing cubs the studio was able to get only two cubs in a
litter although they combed the United States and Canada.
Taken away from the mother they proved to be friendly and
playful little fellows, but not very sure on their feet for a long
time. They did a good deal of pouncing at objects tossed to them

but seldom hit the target. They fell over their feet and were unsteady when they tried to charge a ball or a feather.

The cougar's den is usually in a cave which is located in an inaccessible place such as a cliff wall or high on a ledge. Often the mother has to reach it by making long leaps. It will be littered with bones of deer and other animals she has brought in to teach the cubs what to do with meat.

The cubs are born in early spring. They arrive with soft yellow hair liberally covered with black spots. These spots disappear when they are about six months old but this is not a fast rule, the spots may go at two months or may last for a year. The mother takes them on hunting trips and they learn the things a cougar must know to secure a living for itself. There is some evidence that the father will kill the young ones, especially the males, if he can get to them when the mother is away hunting. This is true of many old tomcats of the alley variety. Cases reported are rare, however, and mostly come from observation of caged animals.

The mother cougar is a loving parent, devoted to her young and savagely protective of them. It is rare, indeed, for a mother to desert her cubs when hounds close in. A fight between a grizzly bear and a mother cougar was witnessed by two miners near Murray, Idaho. One day one of the miners noticed a bear moving along a ledge where he knew there was a cougar's den with kittens in it. The bear was not interested in molesting the cubs, he was just interested in getting around the cliff face by a short route. The mother could have let him go his way but she didn't; she leaped down from the cave entrance, and landed on the bear's back. He tried to toss her off but both fell from the ledge with the cougar trying to get at the bear's throat. The miners found them in a creek bed, both dead, and each badly torn and mauled.

The big cats are a model of muscle and bone structure. Running down-hill a cougar will outdistance the fastest dogs for a half mile, but he is not a long-distance runner and he does not have much staying power on a hot day. On a hot day the big cats worked by the studio had to rest after each short run. After fifteen minutes of work in the hot sun, they just quit and sought shade. A medium-sized cougar will flee down-hill taking thirty to forty foot leaps. On the level, twenty foot leaps are common. I have seen a cougar leap straight up from a flat-footed stance to a height of at least eight feet.

Cougars seldom climb trees except when chased by dogs. They are perfectly able to climb a tree but seem to prefer to stay on the ground most of the time. Once in a while a cougar will be found who refuses to be treed by a pack of hounds. Such a cougar may live a long time. On the ground a pack of even a dozen dogs would find it difficult to kill a cougar. There is a case on record where a hunter trailed such a cat for two years before he was able to kill it.

These tawny hunters are great travelers. Many of those hunted by my friend in Utah have come up from Mexico, following mountain ridges. They cross the border in the vicinity of Douglas, Arizona where they are hunted extensively. Many of the ranchers in that area keep packs of trail hounds. I talked with a number of them and none claimed that cougars destroyed cattle, those ranchers simply hunted them for sport. The home of one rancher I visited was decorated with pictures of treed cougars and mounted heads. There were cougar-skin rugs on the floors. At the time of my visit he had a young female in a cage. She weighed about forty pounds. His dogs had treed her and he had taken her alive. She was used to train the young dogs. Turned loose, she would head for the nearest rims and timber. After a number of runs the little she-cat learned that a tree was not a safe refuge and would face the pack with her back to a rock wall. She was promptly shot because her usefulness was over and she might even ruin some of the young trail hounds. Some packs will have at least two Airedales, dogs that are fighters, not trailers. An Airedale will tangle with a bear or a cougar.

Full-grown cougars caught alive remain defiant and savage.

They cannot be handled and are usually sold to a zoo where they are stared at as they send shivers down the spines of youngsters. Guides who take parties out cougar-hunting may guarantee that the hunter will bag a cougar, for a handsome fee, of course. In this case the cat has been caught alive, then put to sleep so that it can be safely handled. The guide turns the cougar loose at a spot he has picked. The hounds easily pick up the trail and after a proper length of time on the trail, enough to convince the hunter that he is really roughing it, the dogs tree the cat and the hunter shoots the cougar as it crouches on a limb. The guide may not turn his cat loose until the second day, depending on the hunter's ability and desire for roughing it in rugged country. Of course, the hunter does not know he is bagging a planted cat. Again I must point out that there is little sportsmanship involved in shooting a cougar off a limb. The rule of English sportsmen, never to shoot a sitting duck does not apply here. During the chase the hunter never sees the cat and is seldom able to keep up with the dogs.

The work of the modern state hunter, whose job used to be the extermination of cougars, wolves and coyotes has changed in most western states. He now hunts mostly predators which are known killers of stock. If an old bear goes bad and starts killing calves and hogs or sheep, the state hunter goes out and ends his career. Coyotes are encouraged in areas where rabbits threaten grazing lands. The modern way is tending toward conservation and control. Admittedly there is a lot yet to be done, but some progress is being made.

As this chapter is being written, today's newspaper reports a story about a wild cougar who wandered out of a canyon and into a suburb of Salt Lake City, Utah. Swarms of police are out after him. One officer said he wounded the cougar and it leaped eight feet into the air when the bullet hit it, but managed to escape. This could have been a fine story if the Utah Fish and Game boys had been called in to catch the cougar and return him to his mountain home. They would have handled the matter, I know. I met quite a few of them and found them excellent wild life managers.

Much fiction has been written and quite a few movie scenes have faked attacks on people by cougars. Seton found only two authentic cases in the forty years he studied cougars. In one of these two cougars attacked a man who had caught three cubs, presumably the mother and her mate attacked to rescue the cubs. More recently a man-killing cougar was hunted down and shot on an island off the coast of British Columbia. This instance seems to be well-founded, although magazine stories were written about it which contained much that came out of the imagination of the authors. Most of the reports have turned out to be instances of a mounted man being attacked at dusk or at night. At these times the cougar undoubtedly was after the horse, and probably did not know or notice that there was a man on the horse. In one case in which a girl and her two brothers were attacked by a cougar, the lioness was suffering from rabies, which the girl contracted, causing her death later. Only in the case of the island man-killer has a cougar ever acted as some leopards and tigers do, becoming a man-eater with a long record of killings. Cougars often follow a man walking through the woods but they do it out of curiosity. Once I was certain I was being followed and tried my best to catch a glimpse of the beast trailing me. Finally I back-tracked and found the pad marks of a cougar at the edge of a pocket gopher mound.

The life of the cougar will continue to become more hazardous but the big cats appear to be in no immediate danger of going the way of the gray wolf. Their haunts are rugged mountain areas and they will continue to go hunting under the stars, gliding over crusted snow or over green meadows for a long time to come.

Wild Dogs

Down through the ages the wolf has been cast in the role of villainous killer, a savage enemy of man. For centuries man has waged war against the wolf. In the United States, except for Alaska the species has been practically exterminated. Its last stand was in the Colorado Plateau area: Colorado, Arizona, New Mexico, Utah and Montana. It seems to be prospering in parts of Canada and Alaska and in Mexico. But man also made use of the wolf. The dogs owned by the American Indians must have descended from wolf stock. The descendants of the wolf in the United States alone probably number better than fifteen million. In some western states there is one dog for every eight people.

Yet the wolf is a kind and devoted creature; both parents give much attention to the pups. A wolf likes to hunt in company with other wolves, and captive gray wolves are affectionate toward a man who has tamed them. Wandering wolves leave messages for other wolves on rocks, stumps or the bleached skulls of elk and deer. This killer can be playful when not on the trail of game.

When a blizzard comes hurtling down out of the north, whirling masses of icy snow before blasts of chilling wind, a band of wolves is apt to seek an unprotected knoll where the wind and driven snow lashes at them. Grouped together, they will howl gleefully and defiantly, their muzzles pointed toward the sky as they defy the elements. Such a chorus, swept by the wind to a trapper's shelter of boughs, has wakened many a hardy man from deep sleep.

A gray wolf or lobo is somewhat similar in appearance to a big German Shepherd dog. Its head is broader, forelegs heavier; the difference is in the face and ears. The wolf's coat is thick and grayish or even reddish-brown in color. Its length will be from four to seven feet, and it may attain a weight of as much as one hundred and seventy pounds. It has powerful jaws lined with teeth and fangs.

While wolves band together they do not always extend a friendly greeting to a stranger who seeks to join them. They may accept the stranger at once or they may test his mettle by roughing him up. If the dislike is strong, they may gang up on him and kill him. If accepted, the visitor will become a part of the band and may select a mate from among the she-wolves, being careful to pick an unattached lady. It is likely that only an unattached she-wolf would accept his advances.

Many naturalists contend that wolves mate for life. One thing is certain, they do mate and stay together for more than one season, the male helping to feed and protect the pups. Looking back to my boyhood days I remember how my father used to locate a wolf or coyote den. If he spotted a lone male sitting on a high point doing sentinel duty, he would circle until he found a well defined trail. This would lead him to the den. Usually the sentinel would trot away, trying to decoy us into following him away from the den. This is definite evidence that a pair work together after the pups are born.

Wolves form bands in the winter, during the summer they are busy feeding and training their pups. A band of four or five seen together in the fall is likely to be a family. Winter bands will be hunting parties.

The chase is deadly but it is also sport for the gray killers. Even if you cannot see them chasing a deer, you can follow the course of the chase and tell how it is progressing by the tone of their howls. First one wolf will sound off with a call which tells the others he has picked up a fresh trail and they will all be off, the tempo of their cries increasing as they lope along. They are not silent hunters like the cougar; they do not care if the prey hears them. Their savage howls add to the fear and panic of their intended victim, reducing its chances of escape. You can tell by the change in tone when the grays sight the deer, elk or caribou they are chasing. Then they will sound the cry of the kill, and presently this savage chorus will change to a series of short barks, snarls and growls. Then you will know they have pulled down their quarry and are dividing it up.

Big animals like the moose or elk may make a stand and have to be surrounded. Wolves leap in from every side but leap back when the besieged moose or bull elk whirls with sweeping antlers and slashing hoofs. This feinting attack will go on for hours, accompanied by howls and snarls, being broken off at times to invite another retreat. Finally, even a bull moose is likely to become exhausted unless he can reach a lake or river, and the attackers will be able to leap in and sever the tendons on a leg. Once the quarry is down the end will come quickly. A big kill may mean that the band will camp near the carcass until the bones are stripped of meat; the smaller bones being cracked so that the wolf's tongue can lick out the marrow. It may take as long as a week to consume the carcass of a moose. The wolves seek winter-weakened animals, those slowed by old age, or crippled, but if desperately hungry they will attack a big animal that is in the prime of life and strength.

The howl of the gray wolf is quite a musical sound. It is as much a part of the wolf as his bushy tail. He howls at the moon, the stars; he howls in defiance of a storm; he has a special howl which calls for help, telling other wolves that he is up against game too strong for him to handle alone; he sounds his cry of the kill as his fangs reach for the throat of a deer. The howl may be two notes, high-pitched and vibrating which is undoubtedly his hunting song. A pair of wolves running under the mating moon will pause on a hilltop to sound off in a happy duet.

But under certain circumstances, wolves become silent hunters. Many old lobos became legendary characters, eluding guns, traps and poison baits for years while they lived off the ranchers' cattle.

Just as there have been famous bandits in the west, there have been famous wolves. It took wolf hunters ten years to end the career of the White Wolf of Pine Ridge, South Dakota. This wolf was a big female and a double bounty was placed on her head. It is likely that old age rather than the ability of the hunters brought her to her doom. Slowed down by age, her senses dulled, she was finally run down.

Another famous wolf lived for ten years in the vicinity of Sentinel Butte, North Dakota where many herds of cattle roamed. Dogs refused to hunt him, he scorned traps and balls of fat loaded with strychnine pills. No range rider ever got a good shot at him, though all carried rifles in the boot under their stirrup flaps. Elaborate schemes were tried. Chunks of unpoisoned horse meat were scattered over the range for a week, then poisoned squares were scattered. The old lobo ate his fill of the unpoisoned meat but refused to take the chunks containing the strychnine pills. But one day he leaped off a bank and one forepaw landed in a steel trap.

The account of his capture carried by the St. Paul *Daily Dispatch* says that "Mountain Billy" measured seven feet, ten inches from the tip of his muzzle to the tip of his tail, and that he weighed one hundred and sixty-eight pounds. Ranchers who had suffered losses from his depredations estimated that he had killed five thousand dollars worth of beef. And that at a time when a steer wasn't worth much.

The *Yearbook* of the U.S. Department of Agriculture, 1920, tells of a wolf called the Custer Wolf. He roamed over a large area in the vicinity of Custer, South Dakota. So desperate did the cattlemen get because of his destruction of young stock that the bounty on him increased until it reached five hundred dollars. Like other famous wolves, the Custer Wolf spurned poison baits, avoided being seen and kept his paws out of steel traps. The U.S. Biological Survey finally sent in one of its best trappers after the

WOLF   *Hugh A. Wilmar*

ranchers had resigned themselves to having to put up with the lobo's raids until he died of old age. Like Mountain Billy he finally stepped into a steel trap and his career ended. It was thought that he was well over ten years of age, and had lost much of his cunning and wariness.

There were many other famous wolves. When an old lobo got a reputation and a name, he was hunted not only by ranchers and state hunters but also by sportsmen. Any sportsman who could shoot a famous wolf made a big reputation for himself.

But the big grays vanished from the western range; there were not enough cunning and wise ones among them to keep the strain from dying out. I remember when the last Colorado gray wolf was killed. I believe it was about 1930. Her range was on Blue Mesa above Montrose. Like many of the others, she stepped into a steel trap. It was a trap which had been forgotten and had lain rusting on a trail for over a year. This may be why she didn't detect it.

This incident inspired me to do a book, *Gray Wolf,* which was a fictional account of the life and death of Colorado's last gray wolf. In creating the book I used many of the exploits of a number of famous lobos.

The mating of the gray wolf is true romance. When a pair decide to cast their lot together, they start running. They will flash across early spring hillsides, over patches of snow and matted dead grass. They will run on and on, ignoring tempting game, pausing to make love and to howl at the North Star. Finally they select a den spot. They have been to Niagara Falls and now is the time to set up housekeeping.

The she-wolf, possibly with the help of her mate, will select a den. A coyote or fox burrow may be selected. It will have to be enlarged and carefully lined with grass and other soft materials. The den is sure to be well concealed, but there will be high ground near or above it from which the father can watch the surrounding country.

The father does not share the den at this time or after the

pups arrive. He will be busy bringing in game, grouse, rabbits, even small tidbits like mice.

From four to fourteen pups will be born in April or May. They will be fuzzy gray little fellows. Their eyes open when they are from five to nine days old. They are fed only their mother's milk for the first three weeks. They quickly become alert and able to tumble about. The world around them has to be explored and they cannot long be confined inside a den; they spill out when their legs are still wobbly, and very soon they are ready to go with their parents. If they discover a steel trap or a deadfall, the parents show terror and avoid the trap and from this the pups learn that such an object is dangerous. When the parents pull down a deer, the pups join in the chase, outdistanced undoubtedly, but arriving in time for the feast. They soon learn, after a few hard knocks, that caution is better than valor. In many cases they will be seen with only the mother caring for them, but the father won't be very far away. They may remain pups for a year or even a year-and-a-half. They will not begin to feel the urge to seek mates until they are two years old. Thus you may see two sizes of pups in one family group, though this is not common and may come about as a result of a mother adopting the pups of a she-wolf who has met with an accident or been killed by a hunter.

There can be no doubt that in a cattle country, the gray wolf takes naturally to killing calves and yearlings and even young cows. There is also definite evidence that gray wolves sometimes kill for the sport of the chase. In this their record is better than that of domestic dogs who, when they run in packs, destroy as many calves and sheep as they can pull down in one night. This problem is serious enough that the Agriculture Department has issued a very complete booklet on how to cope with dogs who leave home at night and gather in packs to raid farms. This booklet is available through the Government Printing Office. When we lived on a small ranch in the Santa Cruz Mountains above Los Gatos, California a neighbor had two pedigreed Dobermans, a bitch and a dog. They had to be kept securely penned up, but a number of times they got loose and spread terror, pulling down pigs, calves and even attacking grown stock. The man who cared for our orchard had a dog that often left for days at a time to run through the woods. He would return limping, his feet sore from running.

The gray wolf is a shy creature; if it wasn't for his love of howling he might live close to the dwellings of man without the people knowing he was around. But today you'll have to visit our forty-ninth state or Canada or Mexico to see this courageous, graceful wild dog who has within him love, loyalty, fidelity and friendliness, even though his kind are maligned and treated as bloodthirsty killers. Remember that when they kill cattle they are doing only what the man who raises the cattle intends to do as soon as they grow up and he can fatten them.

The coyote is a slender-bodied little wolf with head narrowed and muzzle more pointed than that of the gray wolf. Seen at a distance, the coyote can be distinguished from the wolf by its pale yellow color as contrasted with the wolf's grayish-white coat; also it has a very bushy tail which it carries low, while the gray wolf's small tail is held high. And the coyote will never be much over a third as big as a gray wolf.

The coyote is one wild animal whose domain has extended in spite of the destruction of the forests and the clearing of brush-covered areas for farming purposes. It is an open ground animal and can find cover where there seems to be none. It goes abroad during the day but also hunts at night. It is also fond of hearing its own voice, though in parts of California it seems to be almost voiceless. There is a pair in the Hollywood hills who sing almost every night and I have heard another pair in the Santa Barbara hills.

Through the years I have spent in coyote country I have always loved the song of the coyote. One of my best remembered memories of boyhood is that of the evening and morning cho-ruses of the coyotes. The song-dog of the dawn sings when the mood strikes him. Two coyotes can create the illusion of a whole pack in full cry. The coyote is the only one among the wild dogs who really barks; sometimes the fox comes close, but the coyote really barks.

Some of the calls are no doubt messages or signals to companions, but much of the music, I am sure, is prompted by a desire to express an overflowing zest for life. The most striking choruses come at dusk or just before dawn. These will begin with a series of barks, increasing in power and pitch until it changes into a prolonged series of high, clear notes. One coyote on a hill will start off and immediately others will join in, filling the dusk or dawn with sound, making travelers, unacquainted with this little wolf, think there must be at least a hundred scattered over the countryside. Lone travelers crossing the plains in the early days have written about the hordes of savage wolves circling their camps at night. One traveler who rode from coast to coast on horseback tells of sitting up at night with his rifle across his knees, waiting for the savage beasts to attack.

My first contact with the little wolves came when I was a boy on our North Dakota farm. A pair of coyotes used to play a game with my shepherd dog, Bobus. They would appear on a knoll close to the house and bark. Bobus would rush up the hill after them. The coyotes would vanish over the crest with Bobus in hot pursuit. Within a few minutes Bobus would come charging back with the coyotes close upon his tailless back-end. When they had approached as far as they thought safe, they would turn and retreat with Bobus again chasing them. The three would keep this up until they were tuckered out. Neither dog nor coyotes ever got nipped.

Enos Mills was sure coyotes had a complicated communications system worked out; orders, warnings, calls for assistance. He was positive that they relayed their information over vast expanses of prairie. I am not sure there is an understandable code of signals they use, but I do know that they answer each other. Frank J. Dobie has written a whole book about the vocal accomplishments of the coyote. It is a fascinating book; its title is *The Voice of the Coyote*.

In Colorado I often returned from trout fishing at dusk. One canyon I liked to fish was Mill Creek, a Colorado Game Refuge. Towering granite spires rose high above timberline, topping high cliffs which bordered the creek. It is a very narrow canyon and a beautiful one, sheltering mountain sheep, deer, bear and many other wild animals.

As I trudged along with my creel of trout slung over my shoulder, I always waited eagerly for the first sharp bark of a coyote. It always came and soon a chorus was in full voice. Within the confining walls of the canyon, the effect was thrilling. The voices of the coyotes echoed back and forth from the faces of the cliffs, which increased the volume a hundred times. It was beautiful bedlam and I was serenaded all of the way down the canyon.

To my way of thinking, no other animal is so much a symbol of the great and still unfettered west. I wish I could do justice to this shadowy body from which comes the voice of the plains.

The coyote is a kindly creature. If caught young it soon becomes attached to the person or persons who care for it. It can be taught any trick a dog can do, and no dog will show more loyalty. It is also a sociable little beast, though I have never seen more than a half dozen coyotes together at one time. Usually you will see a pair or perhaps three or four. I never heard of over a dozen being seen together. I have learned for certain that they go in pairs, and that if one is shot, the other is often also killed, because it will not desert its mate.

You do not have to study coyotes long before you realize that here is a fellow who loves to play. a prankster who enjoys a joke on another coyote or wild creature with less imagination.

A coyote will pester a badger, trailing along after this serious-minded digger of gophers and ground squirrels. There is nothing the badger can do about it except to ignore the little wolf. Teasing a badger may be profitable as well as fun for the coyote. All gopher and squirrel burrows have exit tunnels apart from the main entrance. These are escape tunnels. Startled by the furious digging of the badger, the gopher may dart out of his escape exit, only to be snapped up by a waiting coyote. It is a rather easy and lazy way of securing a free meal.

A pair of coyotes have been watched teasing a gray wolf, one darting in front of him while the other nipped at his heels from behind. Certainly the pair had no intention of tangling with a big wolf; there was no point in what they were doing except mischief.

Anyone who says that man is the only creature with a sense of humor hasn't met and watched a coyote. If two coyotes get into a serious struggle, the victor will anoint the vanquished scornfully with urine.

A husky coyote has been known to challenge a bobcat and force the fight, many times routing the bobcat. But as a fighter this little wolf is always ready to break off the fight and race away if the going gets too rugged.

However, a coyote cornered by hounds, outnumbered and outweighed by every dog in the pack will fight savagely, even though the outcome is hopeless, which the coyote probably knows. His courage is of a high order when the chips are down. This is true even though many many authors writing on western sports, describe the coyote as cowardly. None of the so-called sportsmen will match his dog against a coyote in a fair fight, even though the dog might weigh twice as much as the coyote. Greyhounds are deadly killers of coyotes but the ordinary dog has no business tangling with this little wolf.

I used to ride with a pupil who attended a school I taught on Owl Creek in Wyoming. I have mentioned his hounds in connection with bobcats. If we flushed a coyote, these two greyhounds would overtake it and kill it unless it could duck into an arroyo. I am happy to say the latter happened very often. The hounds ran by sight and as soon as the coyote got into a wash or an arroyo, it managed to disappear from sight. I could not blame the boy, coyotes killed many sheep on his mother's ranch.

I also used to ride a lot alone; it allowed me to dismount and sit on a hilltop watching the rugged sage slopes below. I was often rewarded by watching the drama being enacted daily in that wild country. I came to the conclusion that a coyote is possessed of considerable wisdom. I once watched a pair take a jack rabbit. They knew exactly where to look for that rabbit and the strategy needed to catch it. They knew they could not outrun the long-legged, speedy jack; they had to outwit him.

They knew that jacks bed down at the head of a draw where a few long leaps will get them out of sight if they are flushed. The pair I watched split up as they approached the draw, one slipping down the ravine, the other circling and approaching from above the head of the draw. Sure enough, the circling coyote flushed a big jack rabbit and it bounded over the rim and into the ravine. I could not see what happened in the ravine but when I went there to look for signs of a kill, I found rabbit hair and blood some twenty yards down the draw. It was clear that the rabbit had been ambushed by the waiting coyote. This strategy is also employed by gray wolves when hunting deer in pairs.

Another proof of wisdom on the part of the coyote is his willingness to approach a house or cabin in the daytime, but never to come within rifle range. I have been told by plainsmen that a coyote seems to know if a man is armed with a gun.

I have seen hybrids among coyotes which indicates they cross with dogs. It appeared to me, in all those I examined, that the coyote was the dominant character. They were all larger than true coyotes, they had certain dog markings, but they were definitely prairie wolves.

Like dogs and gray wolves the coyote likes to roll in carrion and dope himself until he smells like a very ripe carcass. Carrion has a strong attraction for wild and domestic dogs. They are not carrion eaters, they just seem to like the smell. A close friend of mine once owned two Scotty dogs. They were pure-bred, high-class dogs. He laughed at me when I said all dogs doped. The next day as we walked up the street with his Scotties roaming

COYOTE   *Yellowstone National Park Photo*

ahead, he was horrified. His Scotties had found a pile of fresh horse manure and were happily wallowing in it.

The coyote is a hunter by choice but he will eat any dead animal, bird or fish that he finds. In his western haunts he lives mainly on small animals. If hard pressed by lack of mice, rabbits and prairie dogs, he will raid barnyards or pull down sheep in a pasture or on the range. As the coyote does not hibernate, the northern winters are perilous. In the southwest where snow is not a problem, he gets along very well.

At one time prairie dog towns were plentiful all over his range and coyotes spent much of their time trying to catch the fat little dogs. There are still a few isolated places where a coyote can hunt prairie dogs, but in farm areas the prairie dog has been exterminated. So now the coyote's dog-hunting is confined to areas the professional exterminators haven't found.

When a pair of coyotes approach a prairie dog town, they separate. One coyote keeps out of sight, crouching back of a bush or in a depression; the other walks toward the town, making no effort to conceal himself. He approaches a prairie dog seated on his mound barking loudly. The dog plunges into his tunnel but does not go all of the way down. He has fixed himself a shelf six inches below the opening where he can sit and listen or poke his head up and look. He has a look and sees the coyote trotting away and not even glancing back. He thinks the hunter is on his way and pops out of the hole. That is the moment when coyote number two, who has crept up close, rushes forward and snaps up the dog. Sometimes this method works, sometimes it fails.

If one lone coyote sets out to catch a prairie dog, he will saunter through the town apparently not interested in any of the yapping dogs. He will pass one without looking at it. If the dog feels there is no danger he may move away from his mound. If he does the coyote whirls and rushes to cut off the little dog and snap it up. If his timing is right, the hunter dines on a fat prairie dog.

The antelope jack rabbit offers sport as well as meat. This big, long-legged hare can easily outrun a lone coyote, but even a lone hunter can catch an antelope jack by using brains and a knowledge of the way a jack runs when chased. The jack always circles and as soon as the coyote knows which way the hare is circling, he can cut across and ambush it.

If two coyotes are running jacks, one will try to intercept the hare or they will run it in relays, one waiting until the hare swings around on his circle. A jack rabbit is no long-distance runner and will soon tire.

When big bands of woolly sheep came to the western ranges, coyotes could not resist such easy kills. During the lambing season they killed many lambs and still do. It was as though the sheepmen had placed food on a table and invited the coyotes to dine. The sheepherder may sleep with his flock, his dogs and his gun beside him, but that will not stop a cunning coyote from stealing a lamb and making off with it.

Again we must remember that dogs running wild are worse sheep killers than coyotes; they stage mass slaughters where the coyote will steal only one lamb.

Full-grown cattle and horses are safe from coyotes, but newborn colts and calves may be killed. Once, while going after a load of hay, we came upon a coyote feeding on a colt one of our mares had dropped the night before. My brother was driving and our hired man was sitting beside me on the edge of the hayrack. My brother whipped the team to a gallop and gave chase. The hired man caught up a pitchfork. The coyote had gorged himself on so much horse meat that he could not outrun a team of work horses. As we passed him the hired man killed him with the pitchfork. I was nine or ten years old at the time. I got so excited I fell off the hayrack.

Deer need not fear coyotes unless there is five or six feet of loose snow on the ground. As I have mentioned in speaking of cougars, the deer can manage fine in loose snow, but this means snow which is only three feet or less in depth. Once the snow becomes so deep that they sink into it up to the shoulders and backs they flounder and can move only at a slow pace. I have come upon them in deep snow while skiing and have in several instances been able to lay a hand on the deer's rump. Bucks at this time have dropped their horns and are usually weak after the strenuous rutting season. Bucks and does are easily killed by coyotes under such conditions. A coyote finding a snow-bogged deer may call his friends to help with the kill.

The pronghorn antelope is the swiftest runner found on the western uplands, but coyotes do catch and kill some of them. A lone coyote has no chance, but a pair or a small band may be successful. The band scatters and one coyote starts an antelope, the others take up the chase one at a time, each running the pronghorn as fast as he can, letting another hunter take up the chase when he is outdistanced. The antelope will finally collapse from exhaustion. This is possible because an antelope always circles back to his home range.

A pair of coyotes may run an antelope, each running a little distance on each side of the speedster. This causes the antelope to zig-zag between them and it will run twice as far as the coyotes. Like most sprinters the antelope can maintain top speed for only a relatively short distance and soon has to slow down. The coyotes then close in.

The coyote's marriage customs are much like those of the gray wolf. When they form a union it will be a lasting one. As with the wolf the father helps care for the pups.

Coyotes usually dig their own dens, burrowing into a bank, but occasionally they will enlarge a badger hole. When the burrow is lined with grass the mother will occupy it, the house is her property. As a boy I helped dig out quite a few litters of pups. As I have mentioned, we usually found the den by spotting the father on watch. He had a bachelor den nearby where he could sleep. The dens I helped dig into were all roomy and well ventilated and they were all located on banks.

I remember, in one den we found seven pups. The time was about the middle of April. Their eyes were open and they were very lively. Father judged them to be about two weeks old. We had quite a tussle with them before we got them into a burlap sack. Their teeth were sharp and they used them. We saw no evidence that they had left the den to play. They looked like gray, furry puppy dogs.

I am sorry to say that we made no attempt to tame any of them. Father considered them seven predators who would, if left alive, grow up to harass our band of turkeys and our little pigs, all of which ran loose on the prairie, before the wheat was up and after it was harvested. I do not know how Father disposed of them; he did not let me watch, but I suspect they went the way of surplus kittens, into a deep hole in the creek. Father was very much a nature man and I am sure he did not relish dropping a ballast-laden sack of coyote pups into the creek.

When two months old the pups will go hunting with the mother, and sometimes the father will accompany them. While they are denned up, both the father and mother will bring game to them.

The parents' domain for hunting will be staked out and they will have used it since mating. When the youngsters grow up and leave their mother they will seek new range, as the area used by the parents will be only enough to support one pair.

There is much satisfaction in knowing that this free-roving spirit of the West has been able to adapt himself and prosper, that his human brothers have become more tolerant toward him, that many have come to love him. Long may his joyous voice be heard under the stars on our western plains and mountains.

The kit or desert fox is the smallest of the foxes. It is also the most guileless and the least wary of any of the tribe. It will snap up a poison bait that any coyote would avoid, and can be caught in the simplest of traps. It may not have learned about man because it avoids his haunts. In every way but one, the desert fox is inferior to other foxes; that one thing is its speed on the ground. It can run faster than any other fox.

This speed is its defense against coyotes, cats, eagles and dogs. When the kit spots an enemy, away it flashes, ducking and twisting, making itself as poor a target as possible. It runs first in one direction then in another, slowing down its pursuer as he makes the turns. No other runner can change direction so swiftly. But the great burst of speed will be of short duration, just long enough for the little fox to find a hole or a cranny in a rock pile. This may not be necessary because the pursuer may become so baffled that he gives up the chase.

The desert fox will have a number of dens, one of which will be within reach at all times. Without them the kit would soon be caught and eaten.

This fox is slender and has big ears. It has a bushy tail which is black at the tip. It may reach a weight of five pounds and a length of two to three feet. Its color is buff gray.

The kit is not an efficient digger, its den must be dug in loose ground or desert sand. In order to enter it quickly it will have several entrances. These also offer handy exits if a killer is small enough to enter the burrow.

As its home, the kit chooses sandy plains and desert areas where there are many small animals. It hunts at night and catches mice, kangaroo rats and wood rats. It will not refuse a snake or a lizard. It also eats insects, grass, fruits and seeds.

On a hunt, the kit fox moves swiftly and detects its prey by smell and sound. It makes a stealthy stalk which ends in a swift rush.

Little is known of the mating or home life of the kit fox. The litter will number from two to seven and the young will stay with the mother for ten weeks or more.

This fascinating little fox is one of the rarest of our mammals.

"Grayback" is a fox with traits borrowed from the raccoon, the red fox, the bobcat and perhaps from the brush rabbit. He is shy, cunning, and a desperate fighter when cornered. But he will run away and hide in a burrow or up a tree if he can. He is the only one of the fox tribe who climbs trees. He may climb a tree for a better look over his domain or to escape an enemy.

The gray fox likes heavy cover of a thorny nature, like manzanita thickets and other tough barb-laden shrubs. He is not an open-field runner like the red fox. There would be no sport in running a gray fox with hounds. He is never found far from growth which horsemen could not penetrate and where even hounds would have trouble.

The voice of the grayback is like that of his red cousin, except coarser. A few notes resemble some made by the coyote. It may give a few short barks at night. While living in the Santa Cruz Mountains of California I often heard them barking after dark.

The gray fox is shy and pretty much a night prowler, but I have seen them early in the evening. They move swiftly, but I have had them pause and look shyly at me for as much as a minute. Some boys once brought one to me which they had

FOX   *Hugh A. Wilmar*

caught in a trap. He made no effort to squirm loose from the
sweater they had wrapped around him, nor did he utter a sound
or bare his teeth. He seemed to be a fatalist who had resigned
himself to his fate.

My son brought me a half-grown gray fox which, judging by
the smell of it, had tangled with a spotted skunk. The little
spotted skunk probably looked like easy prey to the young fox.
It did not have a wound on it but it was a very sick fox. We put
it into a box and offered it water and some meat, which it refused.
It died within a few hours.

As with the coyote, this fellow is often accused of being cowardly by writers who know little about him. He is shy, yes, and
prefers not to fight, but does not lack courage when he has to
defend himself. I consider it a wise and sensible fox who chooses
to run when flushed by a dozen hounds, each weighing four times

what the fox weighs and backed by men on horses. The gray just has better sense than the red fox who takes to the open fields when chased; he ducks into an impenetrable thorn thicket as fast as he can.

What little we know of the mating and home life of the gray fox indicates that they mate for life or for at least a considerable length of time. Hunters report often shooting them in pairs. Trappers say they have seen pairs together during all seasons of the year. One incident has been recorded in which a gray fox lured the barnyard dogs into a long chase while his mate raided the chicken yard.

Dens have been found in rock piles and in one instance in a burrow under the roots of a tree. The only one I ever found was in a hollow stump. It was unoccupied but there was ample evidence that it had been used by a gray fox.

Litters will number from three to six. When they are six weeks old, they will start eating meat and at that time the father joins the family circle and catches game for the young. It is believed that the youngsters will seek mates at the age of nine months.

The gray fox does not sleep out as does his red cousin. He will have a number of dens, especially in winter. In the Pacific Coast area the dens will be crude shelters.

The gray fox will eat anything any animal will eat, but his preference is for meat. His diet varies, of course, according to the area where he lives. He simply eats what he meets and can master. Rabbits, mice and even weasels are eaten by the gray fox. He likes snakes, lizards, clams, shrimp, frogs and fish. He catches grasshoppers and digs grubs from logs. He will lick up maggots if he can find them. Only on rare occasions does this wise hunter go near barnyards. I have related the only case of barnyard raiding that I have on record. I once found one of my hens in the woods close to our barn. It had been partly eaten and could have been killed by a fox. However, the head had been bitten off and that is something a coyote usually does.

The habits of the gray fox are those of most wild dogs. He is a night hunter but if game is not plentiful he will hunt by day. He can be easily caught in a trap as he is less trap-wise than the red fox or coyote. Where a coyote would detect a trap and avoid it or kick sticks into it and spring the jaws, the gray fox just steps into it.

I have never heard of a gray fox storing or caching food. That is probably because he lives where food is available all year round.

The way of life of the red fox is entirely different from that of the gray fox. There is no heavy thorn cover in the east and middle west where he lives, and the dangers he faces are a hundred times greater than those faced by grayback. Trappers set their steel traps along his trails, farmers will shoot him on sight as a poultry bandit, dogs like to chase him, he is run by packs of hounds urged on by galloping horsemen. His skin is prized and his tail is a trophy of the hunt.

The red fox could retreat to deep forests where there would be safety but he does not. He lives in woodlots and farm lands where he has to expose himself, or in fields and meadows with very little cover. It is true that he will live close to timber and make a den on a rocky hill, but farmed fields and pastures are more to his liking.

Any other animal, except the coyote, who tried to live under these conditions would soon vanish, wiped out by its enemies. The red fox manages to live under the noses of all who seek to destroy him. He just uses his wits, and he seems to enjoy getting the better of trappers and hounds. In fact he will make a game out of confusing the hounds on his trail and will flash past a safe den to prolong the sport.

The red fox is larger than the gray. He has a more elegant coat of fur. It is long and soft, golden-reddish in color with black feet, legs and chest. Its long bushy tail is tipped with white. There are also foxes of this species that are pure black. These used to be rare and very valuable but are now raised on farms.

Fox hunting by horsemen and hounds dates far back in history. In this country it is still considered a fine sport. If a hound-dog man dislikes jolting along on the back of a horse, leaping over hedges and rail fences as he tries to keep up with the hounds, he can sit on his porch or around a campfire and follow the chase by listening to the baying of the hounds. A good hound-dog man knows the voice of his own hound.

The home life of the red fox is much like that of the gray fox, except that he does cache food for later use. The red fox is credited with being faithful to his mate for at least a full season.

The red fox is a friendly fellow and will even try to make friends with farm dogs. It has been known to play with other wild animals. Such a fellow deserves more friends than he has.

The arctic fox is not large; it will weigh from six to twelve pounds. It has a small head, small ears and a bushy tail. Its coat is deep brown in the summer and near white in the winter. It has adapted its habits to the far north where it lives.

It moves through the arctic night unseen, its blue-white coat blending with the snow and ice. During a large part of the year it makes a den wherever it chooses by burrowing into the snow. Even during the brief arctic summer it does not bother much with a den. But it does store up piles of lemmings by putting them into the world's largest refrigerator, a snow bank.

Arctic foxes do not swim but they take long voyages, floating on floes and icebergs. If a polar bear takes up residence on the floe, the fox is indeed fortunate. He just follows the big, white bear around. A polar bear seldom eats all of a seal kill. This leaves a real banquet for the fox, meat enough to last perhaps a week. Of course, the fox is discreet, a polar bear would as soon dine on a fox as on a seal.

If he is alone on the floe, the fox has to catch gulls and little auks that alight on the ice. During the summer, cliffs swarm with nesting sea birds and there is a limitless supply of eggs and young birds that can be caught before they learn to fly. This is a time of lazy feasting for the arctic fox.

The mating habits of the arctic fox are about the same as with other foxes. The male helps his mate and stays with her at least as long as the young are following her.

Bears and wolves are the most dangerous enemies of the arctic fox. They may succeed in digging a fox out of his den, but there are ways of avoiding the big predators and, being a fox, this fellow is wary and smart. His defense lies in spotting the bear or wolf soon enough to put a lot of distance between himself and the killer.

Domestic cats and foxes on the Pribilof Islands used to grow round as butterballs from feasting on the discarded portions of the carcasses of fur seals slaughtered for their hides. Foxes sat amid billions of swarming black flies and gorged themselves in company with the island cats. Now carcasses are processed for fertilizer.

The white fox is easily trapped and for the Eskimo its silky pelt is a big source of income. But the fox population does not seem to diminish, even though the natives have long ago discarded primitive methods and now use steel traps.

There is a lot we still have to learn about this fox; perhaps somebody like Henry Elliott will come along and do for us what he did in describing the way of life of the fur seal.

Big and Little Stinkers

Most of us are familiar with skunks. They rate very low on a popularity poll, and they are generally considered dull-witted stinkers who taint a pleasant summer night with a distinctly unpleasant odor. Most creatures, including man, avoid them, knowing that most of them will fire their weapons upon very slight provocation. This comes from the fact that most of us know only the big striped skunk or the hog-nosed skunk. The most common skunk is the striped skunk, with two white stripes down his back which meet at his shoulders. This is the common swamp skunk which is found in all parts of the country. Its aim is deadly and it seldom misses its target; looking at the enemy, it sets its sights, twists its rear-end around and fires one or both of its guns. But it often gives a warning by stamping its forefeet before firing.

When trapping as a boy, I never tried to catch a skunk, but I often did have one step in a trap and get caught. I learned at once that the story about the way to handle a skunk by lifting it by its tail, was unreliable advice. Whoever started that story had never lifted a skunk by its tail. If you have to handle a wild skunk, get him by the head and point his tail away from you. If a long pole was available I always tried to depress the trap spring and let the stinker make off. The biggest problem always was to get a pole long enough so that I could remain at a safe distance when the angry skunk was freed.

One of the hazards of mowing alfalfa on my father's ranch was skunks. You started around the outside of the field and moved inward with every swath. As the strip of standing alfalfa narrowed, you might hit a skunk or a rabbit taking refuge in the remaining alfalfa. I could feel badly about the rabbits but when I hit a skunk with the slashing blade and he fired a broadside at me and the team, I felt little sorrow. If I could halt the team fast enough they got the blast, if not I shared it with them. Unharnessing a horse that has been sprayed takes a strong stomach. Cleaning a horse and a set of harness with soapy water and kerosene was always a job I hated.

Once I gathered a skunk up with a hay rake, the big wheeled kind of rake that was pulled by two horses. Luckily he was tangled up in so much rolling and piling hay that he couldn't get a good shot at me as he tumbled over with the hay. Needless to say I dumped that load without waiting to reach the windrow.

When I was a boy, a few of my friends trapped skunks. It was a sure way of getting sent home from school. One boy who attended school with me had only one pair of boots. He often missed as many as three days of school in a week.

I have had trappers tell me that you can talk a skunk out of firing at you by approaching gently and talking soothingly. This may be true of some skunks but none I ever caught could be soft-talked. As I have said I never wanted to catch a skunk and always freed it if I could, but sometimes, rather than lose a trap, I had to kill the skunk in it.

My mother never could understand why I caught skunks. I tried to tell her that a lot of skunks lived in our swamp and along our creek as well as muskrats—mushrats, we called them. I always came in smelling of skunk when I had to take one out of a trap.

Even though skunk skins brought fifty cents as against ten cents for a muskrat skin, I never skinned one. I would trade the skunk to the boy with the smelly boots for two rat skins.

Skunks hunt at night and sleep most of the day. They move at a leisurely pace and generally bed down wherever they are

SKUNK   *Warren E. Garst*

when daylight comes. During the winter they may den together for warmth.

The striped skunk likes brushy country, meadows, swamps and streams, but it will also live in the woods. The destruction of the forests has not bothered this skunk. It eats all kinds of insects found in meadows, catches frogs in swampy ground and may catch a few mice.

A skunk's den may be a badger hole or some other animal's abandoned burrow. The skunk will carry in a large bundle of grass for a bed, and as a plug to keep cold winds from blowing into the nest. Here the skunk, with perhaps a dozen others, will sleep during cold weather. This will not be true hibernation, it will be a deep drowsiness. In the deep south these drowsy spells will last only a few days; in the Northwest and Northeast, the skunk will not venture out until spring comes.

When spring comes, the females will be ready to mate, and the males will be roaming about looking for them. They will roam many miles during a night looking for a lady skunk. Males during the mating season often fight and spray each other. When they battle they squeal loudly. Eventually the skunk finds a mate.

The young are born about eight weeks later, probably in June in the North, possibly sooner in the South. Their eyes will open in three weeks and they soon have good coats of fur. Within five weeks they will be trailing along after their mother, usually in single file. Much time will be spent catching grasshoppers, beetles, crickets and their larvae. Skunks also eat fruits, berries, and many kinds of small animals.

The skunk is an excellent mouser. During the spring and summer, mice make up a large part of its diet. It is accused of robbing bird's nests and of stealing hen eggs. Any sort of fence will keep it out of the henyard as it cannot climb. Its value as a mouser far outweighs any damage it does. Add to this the potato beetles, army worms and tobacco worms it destroys and it well earns the protection it does not get.

Skunks are apt to wander into places where they are not wanted. A large number of them moved into the city of Sacramento recently and caused quite a stir; in some places quite a stink. More recently one wandered into a theatre just as the feature, *Come Blow Your Horn*, was about to be shown. The theatre emptied promptly.

Skunks make fine and gentle pets but it is best to have your pet de-scented, which can be done. They are playful, happy creatures and become attached to people who notice them.

The pelt of the skunk is not worth much more than it was when I was trapping as a boy. Dyed, it has long been used in making coats and as trimming fur. Only recently have fur dealers come right out and called the fur "Skunk."

In the wild, the striped skunk has the right of way on most trails. Few predators will kill it; most simply move aside and let it pass. Seton had a test he applied to tough killers of the wild. What will the bully or the tough do when he meets a skunk?

Pioneers used skunk oil as a medicine, much as they used snake oil or bear grease. It was supposed to cure rheumatism and other aches and pains.

The skunk's reputation is bad but the bad name is an unfair and unearned stigma. Actually this rotund creature is a charming animal. Calling a person a skunk might actually be taken as a compliment.

The little brother of the big skunks is the little spotted skunk. This skunk goes by many names, phoby-cat, polecat, civet cat, marten-skunk and many others. His habits and disposition are vastly different from those of the big swamp stinkers. He is well armed with musk guns but seldom uses them. When we lived in the Santa Cruz Mountains of California a pair set up housekeeping in a poison oak thicket close to my henhouse. When I visited the henhouse to close the door for the night I could hear them chirping to each other, but never did smell them.

One of them dug a hole under the wall of a pen where I kept three dozen baby chicks and killed ten of them. It ate several of them but did not carry any away. I set a steel trap at the entrance to the hole and caught the little bandit. It had not scented the trap. It looked at me appealingly and I didn't have the heart to kill it. I put a foot on the spring of the trap and released it. It dashed into the poison oak thicket without firing a shot.

The only one I ever knew to use its musk guns was one that got trapped in a garbage can. A friend of mine got sprayed while trying to rescue it from the can. He simply used bad judgment, he should have tipped the can over and let it walk out. That skunk was highly excited and panicked because it could not climb out of the can.

The striped skunk is a rather dull-witted fellow but his little brother is witty. Big skunks do not play but this fellow does. He likes to frolic and play tricks on other animals, and he is so full of

SKUNK   *Dick Smith*

curiosity that he will investigate everything in your house if he manages to get inside of it.

One of his favorite tricks when he meets you, or a wild neighbor, is to stamp his front feet and elevate his tail, then do a handstand with his hind feet pointing skyward. This is enough to send any other wild animal scurrying. When one of them does this to me, I give him the benefit of the doubt and back away.

In the Southwest this skunk has the reputation of being a hydrophobia carrier, and is often called a phoby-cat. Any skunk can be stricken with rabies, but the spotted skunk is no more prone to have this dread disease than any other wild animal. A dog or coyote suffering from rabies is far more dangerous than this little skunk.

The little spotted skunk hunts diligently during the night and also by day, catching insects and mice. One little skunk has been known to clean the rats out of a henhouse without molesting a single chicken. Any barn or woodpile infested with rats and mice will be free of them in a short time if a spotted skunk moves in. It is true however that baby chicks would not be safe with one around as proved by my own experience.

The spotted skunk is abundant in many parts of the country east and west. It is found in California and Florida as well as north along the Atlantic Coast. It likes wooded slopes where there is plenty of brush and low cover. The worst enemy of this little fellow is the great horned owl. This killer is swift and silent in flight, as keen-eyed as a lynx and as deadly as a tiger. He has no fear of a musk gun and he strikes without warning, plummeting down through the evening dusk with big talons extended. Tangled, thorny brush is the skunk's protection. If he leaves it, death may strike from the sky. He seldom does leave it until darkness settles.

Those who know only the slow moving, calm, swamp skunk must recast their thinking to fit the spotted one. He is one pound of restless activity, bounding here and there, ducking into crannies and holes, racing along logs, diving out of sight like a weasel, and reappearing again in a flash. On the desert the spotted one will duck about in a bed of cactus, stop and peer out at a person, certain of the thorny protection.

The little spotted skunk is merry and frolicsome at all times. It is difficult to think of him as a carrier of rabies, a creature to be barred from houses and yards, an animal to be destroyed. The better you get to know him the more you will love him.

I have used the little spotted skunk in a number of stories. I wrote an entire book about one who set out to see the whole world before he settled down to family life. It is fiction, but it fits the way of life of the spotted skunk. He frisked down the side of a mountain and came to the ocean. It was fantasy, yes, but what happened to the hero in my book, *In Happy Hollow*, I have a feeling, could have happened to any little spotted skunk.

The romancing and mating among spotted skunks seem to indicate that they do not pair permanently. The male will romance as many females as he can find favor with. The den is a natural cavity or a crevice under a rock pile, or a hollow stump, any convenient place, such as the deserted burrow of another animal. The young, from two to six in number, grow up about the same as the young of the big skunks, and are looked after by the mother until they can shift for themselves.

Here is a fellow worth knowing and watching. You won't be able to predict what he will do next.

The Badger

One animal I remember well from the boyhood prairie days and from later meetings is the badger. He is a specialized hunter with methods different from other wild hunters, except possibly the grizzly bear. He digs out his quarry—gophers, ground squirrels, and any small animal that burrows into the ground. He even tears apart the castles of the kangaroo rat to get at the dweller inside.

The badger is an amazing digger. With his long claws raking wildly and his teeth aiding, he can sink into the ground faster than any auger can dig a posthole. I have spotted many badgers starting to dig. If the badger was a hundred yards away, by the time I reached the spot he would have disappeared into the ground. The last glimpse you will have of a badger will be his stumpy tail sinking from sight.

The badger is low slung, chunky and pigeon-toed. It has powerful jaws and sharp fangs which are backed by a courage and aggressiveness which makes this digger a dangerous opponent. A man in Texas once owned a badger that licked all of the pit-bulls and other fighting dogs it was matched with. It was finally defeated by a dachshund, whose infighting was too much for the badger. One reason a dog has trouble with a badger is that its skin is loose. It can just about turn around inside its skin.

When a dog tries to get a hold on the neck or back of a badger, all he gets is a mouthful of loose skin.

When attacked, a badger hisses and acts much like a big skunk. Its tail goes up and it emits an odorous musk. It has very little tail and cannot squirt its musk as a skunk does.

It is next to impossible to drag a badger out of his hole. He will brace his feet and you can't budge him. Also it is a dangerous thing to try as the badger may reverse himself and sink his fangs into your hands, piercing even the toughest gloves. Even if you got him out you probably couldn't handle this fifteen-pound bundle of fury.

On the Dakota prairies the badger lived mostly on flickertail gophers. In the Southwest they hunt prairie dogs, pocket gophers, mice, ground squirrels, wood rats and kangaroo rats. They will rob ground birds' nests and eat carrion. In higher elevations of the west they dig out hoary marmots if they can find dens where slide rock does not balk them. The badger can dig fast enough to overtake those champions of diggers, the mouse and the pocket gopher.

As a barefoot boy, I once met a badger on a plank which served as a foot-bridge over a creek. It was evening and I did not see the badger until he hissed at me. I was the one who left the plank, and I did it fast, with the badger snapping at my bare heels. A ducking was to be preferred to having the badger fasten his teeth into a heel.

Badgers will make return trips to the holes they have dug. Jack rabbits and cottontails often use the holes for dens and a return visit may result in a meal of rabbit. I once watched a big hawk drive a jack rabbit into a badger hole. He only stayed there about a minute, so I was sure the badger was in the hole. The rabbit was willing to take his chances with a hawk but not with a badger. This proved a wise choice as the big jack was able to reach a plum thicket before the hawk could dive on him.

A few ground squirrels are taken before they reach their holes, but usually they are too fast for the short-legged badger.

BADGER   *Warren E. Garst*

It is when they duck into their burrow that they are doomed, unless they have an escape exit. If the badger finds a rattler he will eat all but the head.

The badger is a plains animal. He likes prairies and slopes more or less open. He has little to fear from other predators, though there are instances where a coyote has killed a badger, perhaps an individual in poor health or weakened by age.

On cattle ranges the badger is hated by cowboys. Many a rider has been spilled when his horse stepped into a badger hole while chasing a steer. The slopes on our Dakota farm were always dotted with badger holes. One of our range horses badly wrenched a shoulder by stepping into a badger hole while running down a hill.

A badger may come upon half a dozen drowsy skunks who have taken up winter quarters in a hole the badger has dug. Their stink bombs have no effect upon him. He will dine for a week or more on skunk meat.

A badger may cache some of the rodents it kills. I am not sure it remembers where the meat is buried, but it probably does. I have found badger caches in which the gophers had lain until they were little better than dried mummies.

A badger prefers open, dry plains but he can swim across wide rivers and lakes if need be. The badger's score is heavily on the credit side so far as man goes, even though it does at times damage irrigation canals by digging holes in the ditch banks while burrowing for squirrels. My father appreciated the help he got from the badgers in controlling the flickertail gophers. He never killed a badger.

The badger's pelt often ends up as an imitation silver fox fur. The badger's white-tipped hairs are often glued throughout the hair of other skins to make them look like silver fox skins. These appeal to women who cannot afford genuine fox furs. There was a time when all good shaving brushes were made with badger hair as bristles.

The raising of a family follows the usual pattern for most wild animals of its size. The den will be dug some five or six feet underground. There, the babies are cared for until they are big enough to go hunting with their mother. Few of them come to harm because the mother will face any killer who approaches her brood and attack without hesitation.

The range of the badger pretty well covers the west, including the coastal states. It is a solitary wanderer and will be found scattered over the desert and the lower mountain slopes, but never in groups and in pairs only during the mating season.

The badger is easily identified by its shape and markings. Also by its short legs and stumpy tail. It has a pointed nose, small ears and black and white markings on its face. Its long, shaggy hair is silver gray in color.

Wild Pig

All of the pigs in this country, except the peccary, are imports from foreign lands, including the wild boars roaming some rugged parts of the Monterey, California area, which were imported from the Black Forest of Germany. The peccary is unlike our placid barnyard hog. It is smaller, usually weighing no more than forty pounds when fat. And he is more nervous and active than domestic hogs.

Of course all pigs have traits in common. The hogs we raised when I was a boy used to run loose to forage on the gleanings from the flax and wheat fields. They developed some of the traits of wild pigs. I remember I once caught a very little pig in a gopher trap. When I tried to release it, the pig squealed lustily. Instantly the whole herd of some twenty pigs descended upon me squealing and frothing at the mouth. If they had caught me I am sure they would have torn me apart. In this, they acted about as savagely as a herd of salt-and-pepper-colored peccaries if you tried to catch one of their young.

When excited or aroused, the peccary gives off a very disagreeable odor which is a warning to other peccaries to be on the alert. The musk comes from a large gland in the arched back of the pig. Wherever a herd goes in the thick Arizona and New

Mexico bush, they leave scent trails which no doubt give information to other wandering herds.

After years of selective breeding our barnyard sow will give birth to a dozen or more pigs. A peccary sow has not had this careful breeding; she may have twins, but two is her limit.

Peccaries run in bands of up to twenty-five animals, males, females and youngsters. They move about energetically and are continually exchanging grunts and barks which can quickly change to loud warning sounds if danger threatens. When an alarm is sounded they bound away, grunting loudly with every jump.

Peccaries never get fat like farm hogs; they just run the fat off. But they are like domestic hogs in that they will eat anything edible. They root for tubers and roots and will snap up toads, snakes and lizards. They like manzanita berries, mesquite beans, cactus fruit. In areas where there are oak trees they will get almost fat on acorns. A peccary eats cactus fruit, thorns and all without any discomfort.

Peccaries have never learned to go without water as many desert dwellers do. The banks of the scattered water holes on their range are sure to be rutted by their hoofs. Trails will radiate from such watering places in all directions.

Their desert companions are the buzzards who keep an eye on the herd, hoping that one or more of the pigs may be injured in a stampede. Their defense against cougar, bobcat and coyote attack is mass retaliation. If a lone peccary is cut off from the herd and attacked he will back up against a rock or a log and fight savagely. If an attacking coyote or bobcat is surrounded it is torn to bits and devoured. When brought to bay by dogs, peccaries often kill some of them.

Our northern peccary is smaller than the white-lipped peccary of South America, and they are not as aggressive. Many stories have been told about peccaries attacking a man on foot or on horseback. Most of these are probably exaggerated. A herd of these wild pigs, if alarmed, will take off in the direction they

PECCARIES   *N. Paul Kenworthy, Jr.*

are headed and that might be toward a man. If a man caught a small pig, its squeals might bring the herd.

Unrestricted hunting almost wiped out these wild pigs in the early days. In those days they were called javelinas, and are often called by that name today. Now regulated hunting has raised the number of peccaries. The sport is a difficult one because this small pig is an elusive target and hard to kill. It requires a well-placed bullet to bring down a javelina. During a hunt many wounded pigs probably drag themselves off to die, hovered over by a flock of buzzards.

The meat of the peccary is dry and tough but not unpleasant to the taste, if the pigs have been feeding on oak mast. The first thing to do before dressing the game is to remove the musk gland which, if left in place, may ruin the meat.

Hunters who collect trophies have the heads mounted and the

tanned hides make good decorations. A mounted peccary head has a savage and rather sinister look. In Mexico the hides are made into very durable jackets and gloves.

The tusks of a peccary do not curve like those of a wild boar but they are sharp and serve as excellent weapons of defense.

Fossil remains show that the peccary of prehistoric times was bigger that its descendants living today. The original peccaries probably migrated to America from Europe and Asia about a million years ago.

Peccaries are born wherever the mother may be when the time comes. She will seek seclusion and shelter but she and her twins will join the herd as soon as the little pigs can run, which will be within a few days after birth.

The way of life of the peccary is one of nervous movement, a constant search for food, sociable hours spent in the shade of a mesquite tree, eager treks to waterholes. This fellow is always looking for better pastures over the next hill.

The Antlered Tribe

High on a mountain-side just below timberline a buck mule deer stands polishing dry skin and hair from a rack of hardened bone by rubbing his antlers against the rough bark of a tree. Those mature antlers are his pride and joy. The season is October and there is more than just a hint of frost in the air.

All through the summer this big fellow has bedded down meekly with several other bucks while small blood-filled and hair-covered nubbins on his head sprouted into antlers. These grew with amazing speed, rising and spreading at a rate that would seem impossible. The bucks had picked a spot high above fly-infested marshes and valleys because the blood-filled growth remains tender until it starts to harden. The bucks had never ventured into the timber where branches might injure the tender antlers. Their days had been spent browsing, building up their strength, feeding the lusty, growing antlers. They have been meek creatures, with no fire or drive. Now the big buck has changed. His chest muscles have swollen, his eyes are alight with fierce fire. He snorts and glares around him as he starts striding down-country. His weapons are ready and like a knight of old, he seeks battle. Far below, the does are waiting and he is eager to match his power with other bucks for their favor. Others like him are striding down ridges with antlers swaying at every step, neck scruff bristling, nostrils flaring.

He moves through timber and as he breaks over a ridge and starts down into a valley, he quickens his pace to a trot. In a meadow below, half a dozen does are feeding. They raise their heads and prop their big ears forward as they watch his approach.

Then out of the timber below the does strides another antlered knight. The first buck swings off course and slows his pace to a strutting walk, heading toward the approaching buck. When only a few yards separate them, they halt and stare defiantly at each other. They both charge with antlers lowered. They come together with terrific impact, and twist and wrench, each seeking to get past the other's guard and sink lances of bone into the body of the adversary. They grunt as they back away for another charge, then crash together again. If one of them slips or lowers his guard he will receive a deadly thrust which may pierce a vital organ and send him down, a helpless target for the thrusts of his opponent.

I have found bucks with horns locked. They lay dead from starvation, and I once photographed a pair of dead bucks who had entangled themselves in strands of barbed wire, ending their feud helplessly bound together. Few of the battles end in fatalities, the loser generally will limp away and the victor will give his attention to the does.

Buck deer make no attempt to hold a harem together as a bull elk does; they dash wildly from doe to doe, pausing only to challenge any other buck that appears. They give no thought to food or rest. By the time the mating season is over, they are racks of bones held together by their thick skins. Toward the end of their wild weeks of romancing they become weak and surly. It will take months of browsing to fill them out and nurse their bodies back to the strength needed to face the cold and snow of winter. Their savage anger will have cooled into the meanest dispositions possible to find.

This western deer is called a mule deer because of its big ears which stand much higher and broader than those of a whitetail deer. It was natural for the first explorers who saw them to be reminded of a mule. The mule deer's range overlaps that of the whitetail on the east and borders the range of the blacktail on the west. The body is stocky and heavy. Mule deer have been taken that weighed four hundred pounds; the average will be nearer two hundred. I was once invited into a hunting camp on a ridge above Soap Creek in Colorado. The hunters had one deer hung up which they thought was not a mule deer at all. The head and ears and the branched antlers were those of a mule deer but the body was at least twice as big as those of the other bucks hanging beside it. It was the biggest mule deer I have ever seen. My guess was that it would weigh at least seven hundred pounds. I asked the man who had shot it to let me know how much it weighed when he got it to a scales. He probably didn't weigh it because I never heard from him.

When startled, a mule deer's head comes up and it props its big ears forward, becoming an alert and beautiful animal. It will bound away with high leaps that seem powered by coil springs. It will sail over brush and rocks, each bound clearing four feet or more vertically and covering as much as twenty feet of ground if the deer is really in a hurry, as it would be if a cougar were rushing it. It can maintain this speed for as much as a quarter of a mile, slowing down when the pace has winded it.

I once rode with a crew of cattlemen on a deer hunt. The Spann brothers, who raised white-faced cattle above Gunnison, Colorado, would spot a buck on a sage-studded slope and go after it, shaking out their saddle ropes. I shall never forget those mad chases down a treacherous, sage-spotted slope. The buck always pulled away fast at first, then slowed down enough so that a rider could overtake it and drop a loop over its antlers.

I wangled an invitation for Art Carhart, a writer friend, to go deer hunting with the Spanns. He came back so used up that it took him a week to recover, and during that time he needed a cushion under him when he sat down. When on a hunt with the Spanns, I always brought up the rear. Even the nine-year-old son of one of them rode a wild pony and stayed with the men when they charged down a slope after a buck.

After the rutting season is over the bucks join the does on the feeding grounds. During December they drop their antlers. It seems a great waste of time and energy to grow such magnificent weapons and then only keep them for a few months. With their antlers gone, the bucks become as harmless as the does.

Winter is a deadly enemy of the mule deer. They prefer to live in high country were snow is usually deep. It buries their browse, and during the weeks of loose deep snow, before the surface crusts, they flounder from one willow thicket to another. At times they find wind-swept ridges and slopes where the snow has been blown away, uncovering low bushes and shrubs. Their refuge in the old days was the valleys, but these are all farmed today so they must forage higher up. In many western states food is put out for them during the winter.

An old buck shows no chivalry toward the does or fawns. At an early age, he develops an overbearing attitude toward them. But the leader of the winter band will be a wise old doe, probably barren.

When spring comes, the does are in no hurry to get to the high meadows. They drift upward at a leisurely pace. The timberline bucks hurry to the high meadows as soon as the deep snow melts.

The deer is a browser, eating the leaves and twigs of shrubs and brush. In the summertime the browse will be buckbrush, sage, oregon grape, the leaves of the scrub oak, choke-cherry, buffalo berry and other berry bushes. They are fond of mushrooms and in the mountain areas of Colorado and Utah where showers are apt to be a daily occurrence this tasty food is abundant.

About two hundred thousand deer are shot in this country every fall. This makes man the deer's worst enemy, but cougars

BROWSING DEER   *National Park Service*

BLACKTAIL FAWN   *James R. Simon*

kill many during the summer and winter. After the deep snow
crusts so that the cougar is able to move over it swiftly, he may
kill one or two deer a week. But the cougar is not a wanton killer.
He kills what he needs to keep his belly filled, and returns to the
carcass until he has stripped it of meat with the help of coyotes,
foxes and white-footed mice. Bears will kill any crippled or weakened deer they can find, but are not likely to pull down a healthy,
alert deer.

When fawning time arrives, the doe seeks out a secluded spot
for her nursery. She will pick out a dense thicket where she can
hide the fawn while she grazes or goes to a stream for water. The
fawn instinctively knows that it must lie curled up and unmoving
until she returns, its spotted body blending with the shadows cast
by leaves overhead. This is the most critical period in the life of
a deer. If the fawn can survive until it is able to bound at its
mother's side, it may live a fairly long life. Nature has given it
some extra protection, in that the new fawn has no scent that can
be detected by a predator. A cougar or a coyote may pass within a
yard of where it is hidden and not detect its presence. If the fawn
is a buck its chances of death from a bullet after it reaches the
antler stage are perhaps five to one. Many states permit hunters

to shoot only bucks with at least a two-prong spread of horns. That means the youngster will reach the age of two years safely if he escapes from predators.

I believe coyotes kill more deer than cougars because there are so many more of them. They are capable of pulling down even a grown doe. I once watched a pair of golden eagles attack a fawn on a winter feed ground. This happened in western Colorado on an open bench where the state game department had scattered cotton-seed cake for the deer. The eagles took turns diving down and striking at the fawn. It staggered along, trying to reach a stand of leafless aspens and was still making some progress when it passed out of sight into a draw. I checked but found no signs of a kill. The winter had been an unusually bitter one and the eagles were probably desperately hungry.

The mule deer population has increased in some areas until it is a problem, and steps have had to be taken to reduce the numbers of deer. In some states a hunter is allowed to shoot a doe. We will have these graceful creatures with us for many years. I admit that I am prejudiced in favor of this big muley deer. I grew up and rode the range in mule deer country.

Like the antelope, the whitetail deer flashes signals with its white, flaring rump patch as it dashes away through the woods. No other big game in America is as widely scattered and eagerly hunted as the whitetail.

This deer overpopulates certain areas where it is found. It is a polygamous animal and the does usually have twin fawns which may help cause overcrowding.

The fall running season of the bucks is about the same as I have described for the mule deer. The bucks are credited with being more aggressive and pugnacious than the mule deer bucks.

Whitetail fawns will not always stay hidden as do the mule deer fawns and the mother never visits them except to nurse them. Most of the time she is too far away to hear a bleat of distress. If sighted when they have left their bed, the twins will drop to the ground and lie still, and thus they are doomed; even a fox can easily kill a fawn. By staying away from her twins, except at meal time, the doe avoids calling attention to the location of the nursery. At the end of four weeks the fawns will be able to run with their mother.

Deer follow trails when going to water or salt licks. These may be well marked. They like to follow ridges and use them to descend to rivers or lakes. The antlers of the mule deer are sprung wider than those of the whitetail and are straighter. The whitetail's rack points slightly more forward and does not branch.

The rangers in Yosemite Park warn tourists not to pick up a fawn they find wandering about. Persons who know nothing about baby whitetails may think the fawn lost and want to take it to a ranger. Once this is done, the fawn will be abandoned even though the ranger does return it to the spot where the tourist found it. The doe will not accept it. The park rangers have a condensed milk fund you can contribute to for the purchase of milk to feed "bummer" fawns.

In some fruit-growing areas orchards have to be fenced against deer and the fence has to be mesh, hog or sheep fence. I have seen a doe go through a five strand barbed wire fence while traveling at high speed. It seemed impossible, but she went through without losing a hair. Of course, this is not always the case. I have seen evidence that showed clearly where a deer had not been so skillful. That doe was probably familiar with the fence which might have been across her route to water.

The enemies of the whitetail are the same as those of the mule deer. But the balance of nature does not seem to work as well with them as with others of the species. It might be better if they had more enemies.

These graceful creatures do much to liven the woods. Just to see them is a joy and I do not have to be looking along the barrel of a rifle to get a thrill out of seeing them.

The tall pines and redwoods of the Pacific coast rainbelt furnish shelter for the blacktail deer. He is a very small deer with a broad, black tail. Years spent in the moist dampness of the coastal ranges has darkened its coat.

Shy as a flickering shadow, the blacktail prefers to keep within the shelter of dense undergrowth whether on flat land or steep slopes. Its range follows the rain and fog belt along the coast and inland to the edge of the mule deer's domain where they sometimes meet and cross during the running season.

On the upper part of our twenty-seven-acre ranch in the Santa Cruz Mountains of California, we had three blacktail deer but seldom saw them. Of course they ranged beyond the seven uncleared acres they seemed to call home, but that jungle of brush and poison oak seemed to be their favorite daytime hideout. It was isolated; no one molested them there.

I knew there were three of them because after a rainy night I would find the imprints of their small hoofs in the yard and on the road leading past the barn. They used our access road as a trail. There was a vineyard just below the jungle where they hid out. It was an acre plot which had been planted to many varieties of grapes. The blacktails scorned the big, juicy malagas and other table grapes, also the wine grapes. They liked the little seedless raisin grapes and cleaned up most of them every fall. I was happy to share with them as there wasn't enough of any one variety to make the vineyard a commercial venture but hundreds of pounds more than one family could use.

The little deer were not molested but they did not get tame. If they had been mule deer we would have seen a lot of them as soon as it became clear that we would not harm them. I would see them sometimes late in the evening on their way down to a creek for water. In state parks they do become very tame. In California's Big Basin park with its stands of huge redwoods, the blacktails wander through the camping area cadging food. They like almost anything a person eats.

The bucks have beautiful racks of antlers, small but well

formed. The antlers branch the same as a mule deer's. These deer have black foreheads and undermarkings.

The blacktail does not bound as mule deer do; they run swiftly, ducking under the big shrubs which grow too high to be leaped over, and they stop often to listen. I have been told by woodsmen that a blacktail can tell if an approaching horse carries a rider by listening to the sound of its hoofbeats. Mounted horses may bring danger, one running loose is not to be feared.

The bucks drop their antlers in January and start new ones in April. Within four months the lances of bone will be hard and smoothly polished. Protecting them while they are in the pulp stage must be a problem for a buck who has to make his way through thorny brush. I have never seen a blemished or deformed rack of antlers on a blacktail and have concluded that they have solved the problem better than the mule deer who has to stay away from timber when his antlers are in the velvet.

Habits of these deer vary to fit the region where they live. In the north along the Alaskan coast, where mountains rise almost out of the ocean, the blacktail lives on offshore islands. Here bitter cold and deep snow make life a struggle during the winter, and only the strongest individuals survive. South through Washington, Oregon and California life is much easier. California blacktails do not face anything more rigorous than winter rains.

The mating moon shines down through the needles of the giant redwoods during September. The blacktail bucks keep on the move and there are occasional skirmishes between rivals. If a doe shows no interest, the buck wastes no time in coaxing her; he hurries off to find a doe who will be interested.

Fawns, from one to three, arrive between April and July. They will have more spots on their reddish brown coats than mule deer fawns. Their infant period is much like that of the larger deer.

Forest blacktails eat no grass. Little of it grows on the shaded forest floor. They are strictly browsing animals. They like mountain ash, wild lilac, dogwood, hazel brush and many other shrubs.

Oak leaves furnish browse the year round because the live oak is never leafless. When the acorns fall the blacktails get fat.

His enemies, aside from man, are the usual predators: in the north, wolves, bears and lynx cats; in the south, cougars, coyotes, bobcats and once in a while a great horned owl will attack a fawn. During the rainless California summers when forest and brush are tinder dry, fires often sweep over the range of the blacktail and kill many of them as well as destroying their cover and browse.

The blacktail is an accomplished swimmer. Those living in the coastal area from British Columbia to Alaska are amazingly venturesome, swimming across channels of rough water between islands. In some of these channels the tides run so swift and rough that a man in a rowboat may be swamped. But a blacktail will be able to make the crossing.

Because of the difficulty of hunting in the tangled growth along the Pacific coast, the blacktail numbers are not seriously depleted by hunters. The hunters mostly head into mule deer country where there will be open parks and meadows and unforested ridges. There the bucks will feed in the open or may be driven from cover. We will always have this graceful little deer with us, slipping through the green twilight of our forests. This is as it should be; the blacktail adds to the beauty of our western countryside.

October is a time when the monarch of the deer family comes into his own. Wapiti the elk strides forth, his shoulders swelled, his nostrils flaring, his body fired by lust and fury. He blasts his bugle call of defiance to the whole world as he strides down a ridge with his magnificent rack of antlers laid back, his head thrust forward. During this period the big bulls are dangerous. Wild bull elk have been known to attack a mounted man and to tree a man on foot. There is a case on record where a bull elk tossed a pack-horse over a cliff into a canyon. The horse was instantly killed. I remember watching a big bull elk who had

ELK   *Yellowstone National Park Photo*

broken out of a pasture on a Wyoming ranch. He was standing close to a dirt road which served as a highway to Neiber, Wyoming, and it was plain that he was looking for trouble. A red Ford Model T van chugged past doing its best speed on the up-hill road. I remember it had a big Bull Durham tobacco sack painted on one side, the favorite cigarette tobacco of the western cowhands. The bull raised his muzzle and bugled loudly, then charged after the Ford. The van probably was loaded down with tobacco. The driver put on all of the speed he could muster and barely made it to the top of the hill helped along by the antlers of the bull who was prodding at the back door of the Ford. Once on the down-hill stretch, the van raced away from the bull, who halted, winded, and stood shaking his head savagely. He finally hurled a defiant bellow after the red Ford and trotted away.

Battles between these giants are on a magnificent scale. There is a regular ritual which is followed just as knights of old followed rules when tilting. At this season all of the big bulls whistle as well as bugle. The two-year-olds try but are seldom able to voice more than a high squeal; because of this they are known as "squealers." But it is the loud notes or the bugle which bring the knights together.

A bull striding down a ridge toward a valley where he is sure he will find cows, hurls his challenge across the slopes. It is answered by another bull. When they emerge from the woods and see each other, they squeak with rage and stride toward each other, and seconds later they crash together with a resounding thump. They grunt and squeak, each trying to hurl the other off his feet. They may fight all over a meadow until the weaker is thrown off his feet and gored. Most of the battles end with the vanquished bull limping away to nurse his wounds. These duels are much more savage than fights between buck deer.

Something should be said about the bugle call. It is a clear, far-carrying call, starting on a bugle note that is low, rising in pitch and dropping suddenly into a chilling scream, ending in a deep grunt.

Elk heads are considered prize trophies. A fine set of antlers will have a spread of over fifty inches, and have twenty or more points. With hundreds of bulls shedding magnificent racks of antlers one would expect areas like Jackson Hole in Wyoming to be littered with them. They are not as durable as might be expected, but you may still see fences and hedges of bleaching antlers in Utah, Montana and other mountain areas.

The natural enemies of the elk are few. Cougars kill some calves, bears will kill sick or weak animals and calves. In gray wolf country the big wolves pull down elk just as they do moose. A bull elk in his prime and armed with his antlers would kill a bear. In the fall a bull elk will attack any animal no matter how big. Man, of course, is the enemy to be reckoned with. Many bull elk were once slaughtered for two of their teeth which were fashioned into cuff links or watch fob charms and highly prized by members of a fraternal organization that bears the name of this monarch.

For years hunters thronged into the area below Yellowstone Park and slaughtered hundreds of elk as they left the protection of the park. This became known as "The Firing Line." The elk were often avenged when hunters shot each other, and not always by mistake. Several shootings came about because of disputes over the carcass of a dead elk. Of course, these shoot-outs occur to a lesser degree in localities where deer are plentiful. I recall the first morning of a deer-hunting season on Soap Creek in western Colorado. We had driven high into the mountains and staked out on a ridge. As soon as there was light enough to make out the outline of an object, rifles started blasting. It was as though an invading army had moved into the valley below and was staging an attack. We had no trouble in getting our bucks; those wild men below just sent them loping up the ridges. Bill Caulkins, a friend of mine, was once blasted at from three sides as he led a pack horse down a trail. He had lashed his buck to the back of his horse with the antlers sticking up. Bill halted the attack by firing back. Even a city greenhorn knows that a buck won't start shooting back at you.

We should not leave the enemies of the elk without mentioning insect terrors. What the elk dreads are the swarms of flying attackers who sting, suck blood and actually attach themselves to the elk's skin. Such a one is the "deer-tick." It has wings in the adult stage, but once the tick is attached to the elk it drops its wings and settles down to suck blood. These pests drive the elk herds to high, wind-swept hills, deep water or to mud-wallows where they can cover themselves with an armor of dried mud.

In the winter, snow is the deadly enemy. When it lies deep on the slopes it covers the elk's natural food and makes travel from one yard to another difficult. In traveling through snow that is five or six feet deep, the elk move in single file, each using the track of the elk ahead. When the lead elk is exhausted it drops back and another animal breaks trail. I have followed such trails. At first glance it appears that only one elk has passed that way, so carefully do they step into the tracks made by the elk ahead of them.

In the Gunnison area of western Colorado, heavy snow always drives the elk down into the hay meadows. This is an area so high that no crops except timothy hay are grown. It is cattle country. The huge meadows will be dotted with hay stacks. The only way to keep a big bull elk off your hay stack is to build the stack on a platform as the ranchers do in Jackson Hole in Wyoming. The elk will make matchwood out of a stout aspen pole fence and even tear down barbed wire. If the elk would be content just to fill his paunch, the ranchers might not fight back, but an elk has to get on top of a stack and tear it apart. He is not a natural hay-eater and probably thinks there should be some twigs or boughs concealed inside the stack.

The Colorado ranchers were responsible for the return of elk to the state. They had been ruthlessly killed off, none escaping. I remember, years ago, helping to move six cow and two bull elk into the mountains of western Colorado. Those ranchers and cattlemen wanted to see elk again in their hills. I counted seventy elk in one band on a slope above the hay meadows of the Spann ranch on the North Fork in Colorado. The rancher had left two stacks unfenced. They were located at the foot of the slope where the herd was. The Fish and Game Department officials told Spann to shoot a bull and the rest would take off, when he requested protection. He was very fond of elk meat and not averse to hanging an elk in his meat house. He shot one, but the rest of the herd did not run away.

Along with watering places and salt-licks the elk always seek out spots where the mud is salty. They will lick salty places but they like salt flavored mud to eat.

Elk do some strange things at times. They do a circle dance, prancing around in a big circle and sometimes breaking into a frenzied gallop. This seems to be the only kind of play indulged in by the mature members of the family.

The mating habits of the elk differ from those of the deer. A big bull will gather many cows into a harem and hold them together. He will fight off any young bull or old rival who tries to steal any of them. He is as jealous of his harem as any bull fur seal.

In the spring, the cows will seek rich valleys above the winter feed grounds and linger there awaiting the arrival of their calves. The bulls will move to higher country to protect their sprouting antlers.

For some time after they are born the calves will be hidden while the mother browses. They lie in a thicket pretending to be logs, or rocks or bumps of earth. Even their white patches help to hide them, appearing to be splashes of sunlight reflected from hummocks of earth or some other inanimate object. It is only their bright eyes that give them away. They have to watch anything that approaches them. Even after starting to follow their mother she will hide them if she sights an enemy. The calves start browsing when they are about six weeks old. But they are not weaned until October or November and they may stay with their mother for another six months.

The females will mate at the age of three; the males are apt to wait another season. Young bulls spend a lot of time practicing being tough; they practice on each other.

To my way of thinking, elk hunting is a very tame sport. It is like shooting a rancher's cow. True, the hunter may secure a fine rack of antlers, but the glass eyes staring out of the head of a mounted elk always make me shudder. I made my last hunt thirty years ago. I was high in the mountains of Colorado, in rugged country where there were plenty of elk. Sitting on a log in a thicket I watched three different bull elk walk past and did not fire a shot. The old rifle-crazy urge was not there. Perhaps it wasn't all love of nature. It would have taken three days to get a carcass out of that canyon.

There are many places where you can watch wild elk. Try a winter trip on skis into high cattle country. You may get to pat a snow-bogged elk on the rump, but stay away from the front end; their big hoofs are armed with sharp edges that are powered by husky legs.

The moose is found in coniferous forests where there are streams, marshes and lakes. Their range is limited in the United States. Some are found in Alaska, Minnesota, the Maine woods, central Wyoming and in Idaho. They may be seen and studied in Yellowstone National Park.

No one would mistake a moose for anything else. His size, ungainly appearance, ample muzzle, throat bell, shoulder hump and flattened antlers set the bull moose aside from all others of the deer family. He is the largest antlered animal to walk the earth. He may stand eight feet high at the shoulders and weigh eighteen hundred pounds. Big as he is, he can fade into the forest as fast as a cougar.

A bull moose differs little from a deer or an elk when under the powerful urge to mate. He is as savage as either, and he is bigger and more powerful. During this period he is ready to fight any rival. He listens for the sound of approaching hoofbeats, the crashing advance of another bull or his deep grunts. If he hears a rival, he is not cautious; he moves to the encounter crashing through branches, smashing his antlers from side to side furiously, battering tree trunks. If his rival is equally pugnacious a mighty battle will follow. The ground will be torn up, trees flattened and brush trampled down. Antlers are cracked and broken. The defeated bull may be left as a feast for wolves or other predators. However, many times one of the bulls makes off as fast as he can go.

The cow moose takes more interest in courtship than the does or the cow elk. She gets excited and calls often in a hoarse

BULL MOOSE   *Hugh A. Wilmar*

voice, inviting any bull within hearing to come and pay court to
her. Her calf will be hanging about but that will not upset her
plans. When a bull appears, he is likely to spend at least a week
or two on a honeymoon. He is satisfied with one lady at a time
and does not collect a harem as the bull elk does and he does not
rush from cow to cow as the buck deer does.

In May the cow will decide to get rid of her yearling calf. She
is thinking about a new arrival. She may treat him very roughly
until, in fright, he makes off or she may just slip away from him
and get lost in the woods.

She may have twins, rarely triplets, but she usually gives birth
to one calf. The two will be inseparable for a year, the close relationship ending when a new calf is expected.

A yearling moose is a grotesque, awkward animal possessed of but very little sense. One might expect that after a year of watching his mother he would have learned something. But when it leaves her care it seems to have learned nothing. All it can do is to wander about making mistakes and inviting trouble. The only thing that saves it is that it does know how to pull up marsh roots and feed off the foliage of trees. It would be likely to walk right up to a bear and be startled out of its wits if the bear took a swing at it. But it is very likely to grow up and follow the natural instincts of a moose.

A moose is a curious animal and can be decoyed by a hunter who is skillful at imitating the natural calls made by the beast. But it can move very swiftly and silently through littered timber where a man cannot help but make snapping sounds every time he puts a foot down. Moose have been known to vanish completely and silently when an observer glanced down to check the trail.

Marshes which would bog down a deer or an elk offer no barrier to a moose. He can wallow through even if the mire reaches to his shaggy rib cage. If he has a long way to go, he just pauses for a rest every so often, unworried and relaxed.

The bull moose grows heavier antlers than any of the others of the deer tribe. A record rack may spread seventy-five inches. The broad bony structure with its many short prongs along the leading edge add to the beauty. Heads of this sort are highly prized.

Both bull and cow have plenty of courage. A mother moose will attack a bear, if he shows an interest in her calf, so furiously that he will have to take to a tree. The bulls are usually rather mild-mannered except during the mating season. At that time they can be dangerous and like the bull elk they may attack anything, even a truck or a tractor. Many a man has been treed by an angry bull moose.

Moose usually feed on high leaves and twigs. They can reach up to nine feet to get at the fodder, but sometimes they get down and move along the ground pulling short, tender grass. They also like to feed in marshes where they pull up lily roots and other roots of water plants, shoving their muzzles deep under the surface and coming up with them dripping. They leisurely swallow the roots they have pulled. The moose spends much of his leisure time chewing his cud. He seems to get a lot of satisfaction out of grinding up the food he has stored inside him.

The pronghorn antelope is an animal which has combined many of the features of the goat and deer. Like the goat it has a gall bladder, and scent glands; like the deer it has four teats and a coat of hair with underlying wool. It has hollow horns with a bony core like the goat, yet as with the deer, these horns branch, and they are shed each season.

Thousands of years before man used a heliograph, the pronghorn was using one to flash signals across the plains. The antelope's heliograph is well designed. A band of pronghorns in a valley will see white signals flashed from a hilltop and will know that a hunter or a predator has been sighted, and be on the alert.

The mechanism of the heliograph is adapted for its needs. The antelope has a white area on each buttock. The hairs on the outer edge of the patches are four inches long, becoming shorter in the center, all snowy white and normally lying flat, pointing to the rear. Among the hairs there is a gland which secretes a fluid having a musky smell. At will, the pronghorn can make the long hairs stand out while the other hairs are directed forward. Sunlight is reflected from this flare as the antelope bounds away flashing his signals.

The antelope is undoubtedly the swiftest runner of all our western big game. Its speed is several miles per hour less than that of a race horse but it is faster than the ordinary greyhound, though champion greyhounds have been known to overtake a pronghorn and pull it down.

This swift runner takes pride in showing his heels to the less speedy. He overtakes and passes a herd of fleeing deer, just for the fun of it. Any pretext may send him off on a wild run along with his comrades. This is true of our western antelopes today, just as it was reported by early-day hunters and trappers. Pronghorns have been known to race with a mounted horse. In one case a horse was pulling a buckboard and the antelope whisked across under the horse's nose.

An antelope can cover a lot of ground at a single leap. Being a plains animal, the pronghorn never has learned to make high, vertical jumps. Certain types of mesh fences may have helped the antelope to improve his high jumping, but ordinary barbed wire is passed through, even though the strands be only a foot apart, and this can be accomplished while the pronghorn is moving at lightning speed.

The antelope is not without voice; it may be a grunting bleat used by a mother to call to her kid. Adult animals express themselves in a short whistle or snort when alarmed, or give a bark of curiosity.

The eyes of the antelope are large and beautiful. Its vision is highly developed and adapted to sweeping vast expanses of prairie where objects can be seen for miles. Its eyes serve it better than its nose or ears. "Liver-eating" Johnson, an expert hunter, once said that while you are training your glasses on a pronghorn to make sure it is an antelope, the buck will be counting the cartridges in your belt. When stalking antelope, the hunter should not make the mistake of thinking the band will not see him even though they be two or three miles away, and visible to the hunter only through his telescopic sight. If he wants a shot, he had better keep himself hidden. All hunters agree that your chances of slipping up on a band will be nil if they spot you.

But they have one weakness which has led to the downfall of many, offsetting their matchless speed and vision. Often the pronghorn refuses to accept what he sees. A man concealed in a thicket must be examined. A buck may dash off, halt to look back, then return for a closer look, thus exposing himself to a bullet. In the old days, before the tribe learned about man, they could be "tolled" close enough for even a smoothbore musket to bring them down. This was done by waving a piece of cloth tied to a stick over the bush where the hunter lay hidden. I doubt if this would work today.

Like deer, antelope will make a trek to a stream or waterhole once a day. They travel in the heat of the day rather than at dusk as the deer does. A band will approach a waterhole with caution, knowing that predators who cannot run them down will resort to ambush. If all is clear, they will drink deeply. In desert areas of the southwest, the antelope takes advantage of the water stored inside such plants as the barrel cactus. These furnish both food and water.

The antelope has the usual list of predator enemies, being one of the hunted. The gray wolf, one of its ancient enemies, has vanished from the plains, but coyotes are more numerous and can catch antelopes, as I have noted in the chapter on coyotes. The most dangerous enemy is the hunter's rifle; next, oddly enough, come sheep, for these four-footed locusts destroy the winter range of the antelope. There was a time when the Public Domain, aside from our National Forests, was open to unrestricted grazing. Sheep men would hold big herds on areas until there was nothing left. I recall tramping over a ridge above Somerset, Colorado. It was the dividing line between cattle and sheep range. Sheep were grazed on the eastern slope, cattle on the western slope. The eastern side was denuded of grass and shrubbery. It was barren and eroded. On the western slope grass grew almost knee high and shrubbery flourished. Controlling sheep grazing on the Public Domain has improved the antelope's winter pastures and this means an increase in pronghorn population.

There was a time when golden eagles killed a few of the young and even attacked grown antelopes, but the number of these winged hunters has diminished. They have been cleared from the skies of Texas by pilots flying light planes and armed with shotguns. This resulted from a bounty placed on golden eagles by ranchmen. Idaho has most of the golden eagles left in the west;

ANTELOPE

Yellowstone National Park Photo

California has a few. Idaho protects them with strict laws. The antelope cannot outrun a diving eagle who will come down out of the blue at terrific speed. Maurie Nelson, one of the leading experts on eagles, says that he has timed one of his eagles in a dive at over a hundred miles per hour. He believes this eagle could attain a speed of almost double that figure. The eagle will drive a pronghorn out of the band, generally a young one. It will come plummeting down on the youngster and knock it to the ground, fastening its talons into the neck of the victim. A golden eagle has incredible power in its huge talons. I once saw an eagle fasten its talons upon the shoulder of a dog that had ventured too close to the post where it was chained. If the dog had not been rescued promptly it would have been badly injured as it was unable to free itself from the eagle's grip. In Asia shepherds have used this eagle to catch wolves. The eagle will strike and hold the wolf until the herder arrives with a spear to dispatch it.

Toward the end of September the pronghorn families break up. The bucks sense the coming of the mating season and become very restless, though at this time the females are not interested in romance. This restlessness takes the form of aimless expenditure of energy. A lone buck may run back and forth at top speed, going nowhere. The passion of the bucks takes definite purpose when the females begin to respond, and many battles take place between the males. These are not mere skirmishes; the bucks go into savage rages, just as do males of the rest of the deer tribe. Any animal as agile and fast-moving as a pronghorn is bound to do a great deal of feinting and thrusting when engaged in a fight. One would think the turned points of the horns would make them ineffective weapons. Actually they are deadly daggers as well as protective shields.

A buck gathers as many does as he can into a harem and defies rivals who try to steal any of them, at the same time stealing some himself if he can get away with it.

When spring comes the bands break up. The sexes separate at this time and the does scatter, seeking seclusion. The doe commonly produces two kids, occasionally there will be three. The mother hides her babies for a few days, visiting them often, and hovers nearby scanning the expanse of prairie.

The doe knows that at this time the kids give off no scent and that she can smell a creeping coyote. If a coyote comes along, she ignores it. The coyote may think he has found an unwary doe and start toward her, hoping to get close enough to spring. She lets him get close, but not dangerously so, just enough to rouse the hunter's lust. She suddenly whirls and runs away, not too fast because that might discourage the coyote. In this way she leads him far away from her hidden kids, and soon puts on a burst of speed that leaves the coyote far behind. Once out of the coyote's sight she circles back to her lookout spot near her babies.

If the mother has to, she will fight valiantly for her kids and an aroused doe will be a match for most coyotes. She packs a big wallop in her slender forelegs which are armed with sharp hoofs. Now that the gray wolf is gone, the mother loses few kids to the wild dog tribe.

For a time the kids will hide at a signal from their mother. But they soon develop antelope speed and can race away from danger at her side.

Early in September the band closes ranks again, does with kids drift in and the bucks arrive. There will be all sizes, sexes and ages mingled together. The cycle of pronghorn life is about to repeat itself.

Careful protection, closed seasons and limited bags have brought the antelope back to most of the western states. It is not uncommon to see a band grazing on a sage-slope close to a highway in any of our Colorado Plateau states. People who live in the west have come to appreciate this graceful speedster of the desert and prairie, more for his grace and beauty than for his chops and steaks.

Moving herds of caribou are reminiscent of the days when a traveler could stand on a hilltop and watch herds of buffalo stream down the slopes of western hills. There is this difference, the caribou is not headed toward extinction as the herds of wild buffalo were. There is no reason for military leaders to encourage their destruction for the purpose of starving Indians into submission, nor is it likely that they will be slaughtered for their hides or tongues. Herds of caribou on the trek compare favorably with the mass movements of the bison. They have been known to form an unbroken line four miles long, moving ten to fifteen abreast. This is a pretty good showing. I first saw them while flying over northwestern Canada and Alaska.

They swim rivers they come to and move over all obstacles with a steady purpose. No one ever really knows where they are going or why. One day there will be a flood of these awkward-looking animals with thick, hairy muzzles and maned necks; the next day they are gone and the woods or tundra deserted. Their range is most of northern and western Canada and Alaska, which gives them plenty of space to wander around in. They may overrun an area and leave, not returning for several years. Many reasons have been advanced for their migrations. I feel the best one is a lack of food. Lichens, their favorite food, grow slowly; an over-grazed area may require as long as twenty years to recover.

Both male and female caribou carry antlers. She is the only female member of the deer family which grows them. The bulls have magnificent racks often measuring as much as sixty inches along the beam. No two sets of racks are exactly alike. The points may be up to a foot long, and flattened at the base. The female's rack will be smaller but she will retain her antlers longer than the bull.

When the caribou's robe is prime, it is beautiful, but during the shedding season the animals resemble moth-eaten rugs. Loose strips of hair hang down, streaks and patches of hide will be bare, revealing a dirty, black skin.

There is a good reason for the caribou's feet being big. The animal has to cross spongy tundra, mud and snow and the split hoof spreads out to give more surface. A bull caribou has twice as much hoof-spread per pound as a bull moose, who is also a wader in mud and snow.

There are two kinds of caribou, the woodland caribou and

the barren-ground caribou. The habits of all members of the tribe are quite similar with a few modifications brought about by the nature of their surroundings.

Several million barren-ground caribou roam over Alaska and the Yukon. There the herds are basically intact, but the woodland caribou seems to have suffered badly, though they are holding their own in western Alberta.

The way of life of the barren-ground caribou is of necessity different from that of our deer. In a land where night darkness does not come for weeks during the summer, the caribou has to feed by daylight. During the long winter, with its lengthy night, the bulls separate from the cows and band together. They are essentially a herd animal and will seldom be found alone.

The caribou has been an important source of food for the Eskimo ever since the first Eskimo penetrated the frozen tundra country. The Eskimos even get their salad from the paunch of the caribou. They eat the partly digested lichens from the paunch, and the digestive juices furnish salad dressing.

Before they had rifles the natives devised ingenious ways of securing their meat. One method played upon the animal's sense of curiosity. Armed with a spear, the hunter would pull a caribou skin over him and hunker down in sight of a herd. Caribous are as curious as pronghorns. Soon several of them would approach him slowly, with muzzles extended. The native did not move so the caribou edged closer, bent upon a thorough check. At the right moment the hunter thrust his spear into the animal.

In May or June the cows who are to drop calves drive the yearlings out of the herd. These youngsters form bands of their own. The barren-ground caribou usually has only one calf. It is born wherever the cow is when her time arrives just as domestic calves are born.

At this point in its life the calf is in danger of being caught by wolves who lurk close to herds during the borning season. At an early age, a calf can outrun a man, but not a gray wolf, and unless it can reach the safety of the herd or a stream it will be pulled down. Again the grim law of the wild that the helpless perish, the strong survive. A great many calves prove that they belong to the ranks of the strong; they survive.

During the summer there is much food available and the herd gets fat. By the end of the short summer the bulls are getting ready for mating. They act much as any bull or buck acts under the driving urges of the mating moon: their necks swell, they fight savagely with each other, and many are badly injured. A badly wounded bull becomes easy prey for the gray wolves as does a pair whose horns have become locked. Unable to separate, they weaken and the gray ones feast.

Bull caribou gather harems which include weaned calves and yearlings as well as cows. The bulls are very active in holding the harem together and in fighting off rivals. They eat little during these weeks and are very active, so that by the time the mating period is over, they are in very poor condition. Luckily the bull does not have to depend upon layers of fat to keep him warm, he has a heavy robe which will defy temperatures of fifty degrees below freezing.

Caribou appear to be rather stupid animals. They are easily shot and are often approached while resting; most of them will be asleep but some are always awake. They seem to wait for the other fellow to give the first alarm. But the caribou is a kindly fellow, living, for the most part, a placid and unexciting life.

It is a joy to find a wild animal that has missed the slaughter which has desolated the plains and mountains of most of America. Our ancestors found a land teeming with big, wild animals, splendid creatures. In a matter of years, after the railroads crossed our western plains, the countless millions of buffalo were reduced to a few fugitive creatures. Animal drives slaughtered thousands, and the killing went on until the western plains were virtually silent and vacant. True, we are finally trying to save the few left. But I rejoice because the northern caribou can still be found in their millions.

Mountain Climbers

Anyone who is squeamish about heights will be chilled by watching a bighorn sheep climb a cliff. To the casual observer, the cliff face seems to offer no ledges or crannies sufficient to offer a toehold. True, almost all cliffs have some slope, few are actually perpendicular. And almost every cliff offers a sheep ladder to the bighorn. He will go up a granite wall in five or six-foot leaps with as much unconcern as he would show bounding over level ground. Two to four-inch projections, little shelves, a thin ribbon of white quartz, all spotted as he leaps upward, form the rungs of his ladder. He exhibits perfect muscular coordination, proper timing, and steel nerves.

Everyone knows that climbing down a cliff is much more difficult than ascending one, but the bighorn never seems to have heard of this rule so carefully recognized by other climbers. A drop of twenty feet is taken at one leap, perhaps to a small ledge and from there another twenty or twenty-five foot leap to another narrow ledge or to the ground below. The legs of the ram act as shock absorbers, bending, taking up the shock as the two hundred pound body hits solid rock.

An entire band of bighorns has been known to bound down the face of a cliff one hundred and fifty feet high and only eight or ten degrees off perpendicular when pursued by hunters. No other mountain dweller can match the bighorn at going up and down steep places. The white goat is a better climber, but he is a cautious and careful climber, not given to wild leaps. Compared to him, the bighorn has wings.

The bighorn has the equipment to accomplish his feats of climbing. He has a quick, calm brain, muscles like steel springs and feet equipped with great, soft pads which can grip any surface.

The home range of the bighorn is rugged mountain country, the kind found in the Rocky Mountains and the Cascades and High Sierra. He ranges high up during the summer, lower when the heavy snows arrive. He has adapted himself to all of the mountain country from Mexico to Alaska. In the dry desert mountains he goes without water from streams or waterholes, getting it from the cactus plants, as many desert animals do. In the north it drinks mountain water daily. There are a number of species, the main ones being the Dall or white sheep of Alaska and the Rocky Mountain Bighorn. They vary in size and color but otherwise are all quite similar in habits.

All predators prey on these sheep, gray wolves in the north, cougars, coyotes and bobcats in the south, but few of them can capture a bighorn in its craggy homeland. It is only when the bighorns descend to the open grassy slopes that they are in danger. Man with his telescope-equipped rifle is the exception; against him the swift climber has no defense. An old ram likes to stand on a pinnacle from which he can survey the surrounding country and that makes him an easy target, unless he can spot the killer before he has time to draw a bead. If he sees the hunter, he will be off and that is apt to be the last time the stalker will see him.

BIGHORN   *Yellowstone National Park Photo*

He can easily move into country so rugged a man cannot climb the cliffs.

During the summer, the rams loaf in bachelor clubs. In October the Rocky Mountain rams cease to be placid. They start quarreling and by November are off seeking ewes. They chase the ewes continually and sometimes as many as half a dozen will be after one ewe. They seem crazed, and the exhausted ewes may have to seek refuge on a ledge or in a cave. Some rams gather a few ewes into a harem; others simply rush about paying court to any ewe they can find.

At this time the rams fight many duels. They have a set of rules which must be followed. They approach each other and stand side by side, but facing in opposite directions. Grunting and snorting, they lash at each other with their sharp hoofs, keeping this up for some time. Suddenly they wheel and charge with lowered heads. Two three-hundred-pound rams will come together with an impact which should crush both skulls. There is a loud explosion and they back away shaking their heads, and seemingly not injured or even shaken. Without pausing, they charge again. The battle may end quickly or it may last an hour or more. Seldom is a ram injured and after they exhaust themselves, they may walk off side by side, their wrath cooled. By the time the duel is over the ewe they were fighting over is likely to be off with another ram.

Even after the mating moon wanes, the old rams often stage butting contests just to work off energy. In these bouts there is little fury; they are mostly displays of muscle and vocal grunting.

During the winter the bighorns seek shelter in caves as do the white goats. They are the only two members of the horned game class who habitually seek shelter in caves to escape snow and wind. They usually bed down close to the entrance of a cave. This is likely to be a precaution which allows them to get out of the cave fast if a cougar comes along.

June is usually bright but not warm in the high country. At this time, the ewes leave the band and seek shelter in sunny nooks where the cold wind blowing off the snow banks above timberline does not strike them. Here twins will be born and it will be a critical time for the lambs. They must be accepted by their mother at once or she will not accept them at all. She accepts them by cleaning their hair carefully, licking each lamb from head to foot. If tender mucous parts are not cleaned at once, deadly blow-flies will deposit eggs and the lamb may die when the maggots start working. If one of the lambs becomes separated from the ewe she may refuse to accept it later and it will starve to death. But generally the ewes are loving mothers, cuddling the twins and lavishing tender care on them.

For several days the lambs remain hidden, though from the first hour they are able to stand on their feet and move about. For a month the lambs will not follow their mother to distant watering places, but will bed down and await her return.

When the time comes for them to accompany her, she shows great concern, knowing that her little ones can easily be carried off by a bear, a cougar or a coyote. She approaches the stream where they will drink cautiously, pausing often to sniff the breeze. Having drunk, they hurry back to the rocky breaks where there is safety. Among the rocks even a lamb is hard for an agile cat to corner. It will leap nimbly from rock to rock and even up the face of a cliff.

The lambs nurse for two months, then start eating browse and grass. During the summer they will not see their fathers. It will be November before they meet them, and that meeting will end their association with their mothers. They have to keep out of the way of the crazed rams.

Man's sheep herds, driven into the high country for summer pasture crop off much of the bighorn's grass and shrubbery, and his rifle takes a toll. Hunters go to a lot of trouble to secure heads with big, curving horns. A good head will have horns up to forty inches in length with a girth of eighteen inches or more. It was the curling horns that first attracted the attention of early explorers to this sheep. Coronado, when seeking the golden city of

Cibola in 1540, reported seeing bighorns. He described them as sheep as big as horses with very large horns and short tails.

I remember seeing them while fishing on Spring Creek on the western slope of Colorado. They would come down from the game refuge on Mill Creek to graze on new grass. The old rams would mount big boulders and stand watching me, usually at a distance of less than fifteen yards. Their lack of fear of man probably came from their having lived all of their lives in the refuge. Later I fined a poacher for shooting one of that band. At the time I was a judge and never wasted any sympathy on a poacher of bighorns.

The bighorns of the southwest have been practically exterminated by persistent hunting. They were cleaned out before shooting them was outlawed. Now they can be hunted only in the states of Idaho and Wyoming and the number of tags issued entitling a hunter to kill a bighorn is very limited. They may gradually repopulate some of their old range.

The mountain goat is called a goat because he acts and looks something like a goat, but he is actually an antelope with heavy legs and shoulders, and horns shorter than those of the pronghorn, which do not spiral but are straight and have no prongs. They are sharp-pointed and arm the mountain goat with deadly weapons. These horns are black in color. It may have been his long beard, similar to that a billy goat wears, that got him his name. The beard is white and gives this white mountaineer an air of solemn dignity. The mountain goat's coat is of coarse hair which gives him poor protection against cold rain or snow. When the cold fall rains come, the goats seek shelter in caves. They do the same thing when snow storms and blizzards sweep over the peaks and ridges.

Like the bighorn it keeps to high, rocky terrain where it is safe from most wild killers. Again, man with his rifle is the most deadly enemy. Mountain goats are one of the favored attractions in Glacier National Park where they have come to be quite tame.

This white goat is no traveler except up and down. He may live out his whole life without traveling five miles from where he was born. Its mileage up and down cliffs and slides is a different thing.

The mountain goat's way of life is much like that of the bighorn sheep, except that he is not a reckless climber, his pace is unhurried, except when chased by wolves or attacked by a cougar, then it may scramble fast to reach a ledge where it can make a stand with its rump against a stone wall. Woe be to the wolf who leaps upon that ledge, it will be impaled on the sharp, slightly curving black horns and hurled off the ledge.

A band of white goats has been known to show no concern at all while being stalked by gray wolves. Usually they travel in bands and simply seek high ground where they have an advantage if the wolves close in. However, they are careful; one old goat usually stands sentinel while the others graze. Gray wolves are not as great a menace as cougars and lynx cats, both stalkers who slip up behind their quarry and leap on its back, or hurtle down from a ledge, depending on power and shock to bear down the goat.

If surprised on a ledge from which there is only one exit, an old billy goat will lower his black lances and charge even a man. The right of way will be his, one way or the other; usually the intruder, be it even a man, takes his chances on diving off the ledge. Like the mountain sheep, the white goats mate in November and December. The rams may collect several dozen ewes. They become wildly excited as the bighorn rams do, but there seem to be fewer battles between them.

The young are born in late May or early June. There is usually one kid but there may be more. They are sturdy when born and soon move about. They learn about rocks at an early age by jumping over them and on top of them. They are weaned in August but stay with their mother until the following May. They may recognize her and remember her until they are at least three years old. By the time the young rams are five years old they will be able to hold a harem against an older ram.

A fox has been known to travel with a band of goats, nipping at their heels and being butted by them, all in play, it would seem. However, the relationship would certainly be strained if the fox tried to play with a small kid.

Old billy goats never seem to lose their dignity. They march stiff-legged around each other when sparring. They depend upon their sharp horns rather than their skulls to inflict damage.

Winter will find them on wind-blown ridges and slopes where the snow has been swept away. An occasional band may be trapped by that terror of the mountains, a snow-slide which may strike without warning, and descend with express train speed, filling a gulch or a canyon with snow, uprooted trees and huge boulders. If the canyon walls are too steep to be climbed and no ledge can be reached, the band will be wiped out. I doubt if many are destroyed this way. I have seen few cliff faces a white goat couldn't climb.

On level ground, a man might overtake a fleeing goat if he was a fast runner, but once the goat reaches a rock slide and starts leaping from boulder to boulder, forgetting its usual dignified pace, the man would be left far behind in minutes. One thing which baffles killers, including man, who lie in wait to ambush a white goat is that a goat seldom takes the same trail twice. Many times a band of white goats traveling together will scatter and each pick a different route over a ridge.

Sheer cliffs and great heights have no effect upon this fellow. He can stand a few inches from a thousand foot drop and gaze peacefully into the chasm below. He has no fear of slipping off into space because he has suction cups on the sole of each foot.

It has been said that golden eagles carry off small kids. I have made a careful study of these eagles and am convinced that they cannot get off the ground with any prey heavier than six pounds. I am sure an eagle might strike and kill a larger kid but he would have to devour it on the ground and in the process have to battle the mother.

White goats are subject to such ailments as pneumonia, infections of worms in the stomach and other stomach ailments. But they are a hardy lot and usually avoid pneumonia by seeking shelter in caves before their coarse hair gets soaked with rain or wet snow.

It seems likely that they will continue to prosper in their sky-high castles well beyond reach of hunters both human and wild. The trophy hunter will get a few and so will the cougar and the Canada lynx but many others will survive.

Like Bats
out of Hell

If you perch on a rock on a summer evening in front of the entrance to Carlsbad Caverns in New Mexico at dusk, you will see a sight that cannot be duplicated anywhere in North America, probably in the world. You will watch a flight of bats pouring out of caverns as fantastic as Dante ever described. They are leaving their roosts on the ceilings below for their night-time flight.

They operate on a schedule which does not vary much. The park rangers have kept careful records and know that the bats have synchronized their watches, or what pass for watches with them. When flight time arrives one or two old Mexican free-tails loose their grip on the rough ceiling and soar toward the entrance, zig-zagging out into the evening sunset light.

A murmur goes up from the expectant watchers seated with you on the rocks. Up along the face of the cliff above the caverns the leaders soar. Perhaps a minute later a puff of bats swirls up out of the yawning pit below. They come by the thousands, like a flight of Monarch butterflies descending upon Carmel, California. They have a regular flight pattern but many of them swerve away from it. These may be young bats who have not yet learned the pattern, but they quickly make sweeping arcs and join the flight. They will pour out of the caverns for better than half an hour, filling the sky with swirling black dots. They are headed toward the river-bottom areas where mosquitoes and other night-flying insects breed. Here is something you have to see to believe.

Most of the members of the flight will be Mexican free-tail bats, but they have many cousins who have come to live with them; at least seven other varieties will be in the flight, including the lump-nose, pallid, silver-haired, and hoary. Horned owls have been known to roost inside the caverns and come out while the bats are leaving. With thousands of bats swirling up out of the depths, it would seem that an owl would have little trouble in catching a bat. But bats are equipped with a sonar system which detects approaching objects. As they swerve and bank, they keep squeaking loudly and the sound bounces off any solid object near them warning of the danger of trees, rock walls or live bodies. The owls will put on a wild show as they try frantically to grasp a bat. In the end the owl is likely to be successful. There are so many bats that some unlucky ones may not have room to maneuver.

Sparrow hawks and sometimes a red-tail will attack the hordes of fliers. The little sparrow hawk seems to have better luck than the owl, being able to make tighter and faster turns in the air.

The bat is a mammal in a class by itself. There are some two thousand kinds of bats scattered over the face of the earth. They are found in every land area except the polar regions. There are three main families found in North America and these are split up into a number of species. But the general physical structure is similar wherever you find a bat.

Our American bats are small animals equipped like any other mammal except that they have real wings, membranes attached to what would be legs in a squirrel or a mouse. Instead of feet they have hooked claws. They have rows of sharp teeth, a pug nose and a definite chin. The pug nose carries the sonar system upon which the bat depends when hunting and in avoiding objects which may block its path of flight. Tests proves that a bat does not have to see to avoid wires, limbs or any other object. Another thing which places the bat as a true mammal is the fact that its young are suckled.

It is interesting to speculate on how the bat was able to do something no other mammal, except man, has been able to do: fly. Suppose we take a tree mouse that has spent all of its time leaping from limb to limb, never running around on the ground, sleeping with its head hanging down. In order to lengthen its leaps it might beat its legs wildly. One thing is certain, if the bat started out as a mouse, he had more determination than any mouse we know today. Its urge to fly must have kept it trying for thousands of generations. Perhaps a half million years from now the flying squirrel will join the bats in Carlsbad Caverns. The flying squirrel seems to give us a hint of how the bat developed into a flier. The flying squirrel has developed the leg membranes and also the radar-like ability to dodge limbs while gliding at night.

Down through the ages the bat has exerted considerable influence upon man. Man's reaction to bats was such that the little creatures got a very bad reputation, they were sought by witches as a potent ingredient for brews; in Egypt bat blood was used on infants to prevent the growth of hair. A bat was attached to the ankle of an expectant mother by a hair from the tail of a cow. This was supposed to make childbirth easier. Bats were considered Satan's cherubs. They flitted about down in Hell, ducking through the sulphur fumes and smoke, accompanying his majesty when he left the lower regions to prowl. Why an inoffensive little creature like a bat should be doomed to an eternity in a place reserved for sinners has never been explained.

Even in modern times, in some places today, women believe that bats will fly into their hair and that evil things will happen to that woman thereafter. I asked a ranger at Carlsbad Caverns about it. He assured me that in all of the years bats had been

BAT   *National Park Service*

pouring out of the caverns, flying low over women's bare heads, there hadn't been a case recorded where a bat flew into a woman's hair. Occasionally a bat off-course will collide with a person, but it just bounches off and goes on its way. I saw one hit a boy on the cheek. It bounced off and landed on the shoulder of another boy; from there it took off. All of this happened in a few seconds. The boys were delighted but if the bat had struck a woman who was afraid of mice, there might have been a scene.

The term "batty" is often applied to people who are a bit off in the head. That person has "bats in his belfry." A woman we dislike may be called "an old bat."

Through the years, in song and story, bats have been considered supernatural creatures endowed with evil genius. In the book of Deuteronomy, Israelites are forbidden to eat bats, among other "unclean birds."

Today we know enough about bats to make us laugh at the ancient beliefs. But, as with snakes, some of the stigma and super- stition lingers on. Actually, aside from the blood-drinking vampire bat, all bats are harmless to humans and indeed one of man's best friends. Think of the tons of mosquitoes destroyed every night by the flying thousands from Carlsbad Caverns. Each bat flying down over the lowlands will eat half its own weight in insects during a night. The same is true of your own back yard; bats will destroy thousands of mosquitoes each night, if you are lucky enough to have a few in the neighborhood.

If you could hear as well as a bat you would be able to hear sound waves of 50,000 cycles per second. Bats give voice to sound waves with this high frequency. But they have many other sounds they make, some of which the human ear can pick up.

Bat guano, the droppings of the bat, once sold for as much as $90 per ton. A few optimists in Texas built roosts to lure the bats from which they could harvest this valuable fertilizer. The diet of the bats makes this fertilizer high in nitrogen. Over a hundred thousand tons of guano have been shipped from the deposits in the New Mexico caverns, which were a hundred feet deep and a quarter of a mile long. This deposit is being replaced at the rate of about an inch a year.

Baby bats are born in a maternity ward which consists of a rock wall or the limb of a tree. They are saved from falling to the ground when they emerge into the world by being caught in an apron of membrane their mother has spread to receive them. There may be one or two babies. For a while they will cling to her breasts when she flies out at night to seek food. They quickly become too heavy to be carried in flight. But she will be able to manage until they have reached a weight slightly above her own. No small bird could equal this feat.

At the age of two weeks the mother starts hanging them up by their hooks on a limb when she goes hunting. There is a genuine love lavished upon the babies. The mother will attack any jay or cat which threatens her young. There are instances on record of a mother which landed on a person who was carrying away her babies.

At the age of three weeks the youngsters start practicing flying and very soon they join the nightly forays and catch their own meals.

The life span of a bat probably does not exceed three years, two might be closer. In captivity bats have lived as long as twenty years; the reason for the difference may be that the energetic wild bat burns himself out by his high-powered efforts each night.

Look for bats in the evening when the night hawk, commonly called a "bull bat" starts his zooming flights. Outdoor lights in yards will bring them to harvest the myriads of bugs which gather around such lights.

Many of us have boyhood memories of encounters with bats. I remember exploring a cave in the rim rock above the Clark's Fork River in Montana and finding bats roosting on the ceiling, clustered together in a furry mass. I also remember being out in the evening and having bats swoop down low over me, lured to me because I was always accompanied by a plentiful supply of mosquitoes. The thing to do in case a bat dived at you was to swat at it with your old felt hat. I remember one evening when I was out with Dad while he was milking Old Brin, our brindle cow. A bat came diving down, undoubtedly attracted by the swarms of mosquitoes and flies which pestered Old Brin, but it was a challenge to me. I started swiping at the bat with my hat as it swooped down. Finally I made a direct hit and swatted the bat into Dad's milk bucket. The pail was brimming with foam-covered milk and the bat made quite a splash. I saved myself from serious trouble after Dad had fished the dripping bat out of the milk. Dad settled for a compact. No mention was to be made to Mom that I had knocked a bat into the milk pail. Mother had some very old-fashioned ideas about bats.

I placed the bat on top of a fence post where it could lick the milk off its fur. That wild bat is probably the only one to have a meal of cow's milk. It was a very angry bat and had to be handled with a handkerchief and a stick. It was ready to use its sharp teeth on my hands.

Neither Dad nor I ever thought of killing a bat. I recall that mother's defense against bats was a broom. Once in a while one of them would get into the house, lured to the screen door by the hundreds of flies that settled there to roost at night. When one got inside the kitchen, steps had to be taken. My sister, armed with a turkey-feather duster, held the screen door open and shooed the flies away, while mother tried to head the bat that way with the broom. The bat, using his radar to avoid the broom and other objects in the room, swirled and dived. Mother was continually frustrated because she could never swat a bat. There was always one thing she did before attacking the bat; she always donned her sunbonnet. She never took a chance on having a bat get tangled in her mass of red hair. Eventually the bat would discover the unobstructed open door and escape.

I did learn a lot about bats by being around them and searching out their roosting places. I learned that they are not unclean animals. I never saw a bedbug on one of them, though everyone said they were bedbug carriers. Years have passed and I have studied many bats. I still don't know how they managed to learn to fly when no other mammal can do it.

Relics of the Past

The opossum mother is one animal who does not have to make a den for her young, she carries the den with her, a pouch similar to that of a kangaroo. If she feels the need for a house for herself she fashions a den of sorts. Opossums had their beginning back in the Mesozoic Era, during the age of reptiles. They are one of the few animals to survive down through the millions of years since that period ended. There is only one other such animal living in America, the armadillo.

This ten-pound possum, with its long naked tail, is not a very handsome beast. It gives one the impression of seeing a huge house or dock rat. It is a rather dull creature and probably hasn't learned anything new in the last few million years.

The arrival of the young and how they survive is a strange story. When they arrive they are premature. Their birth occurs thirteen days after the mother mates. They will be smaller than a bumblebee, and will not exceed a fifteenth of an ounce in weight. Their eyes and ears will still be developing inside the skin, and their bodies will be transparent enough so that all the organs inside can be seen. And they are not born inside the pouch. In order to reach it they have to make a perilous journey.

The moment they are born, they set off unassisted by their mother, instinct guiding them upward to the pouch opening. They have to pull themselves over her hairy stomach with their tiny forefeet. Even after they reach the snug safety of the pouch their troubles may not be over. A mother possum has twelve teats and there may be as many as eighteen babies born. In that case six of them will starve to death because once a baby fastens upon a teat, it does not let go for weeks. This may be nature's way of eliminating the weaker members of the brood; the stronger are sure to reach the pouch first. They grow fast and within two months will be as big as mice, but long before that they start peeping out of the pouch for a look at the world around them. Soon they are riding on the mother's back, clinging to her coarse fur, sometimes twining their snaky tails around hers. Childhood with mother is brief; they leave her when they are three months of age.

Nature has rationed the possum to two litters a year; otherwise the woods would be full of possums, in spite of the fact that predators find them easy victims.

The first concern of a young possum is to find a place where it can live. The possum is not a skilled digger, so it seeks any vacant shelter it can find and makes a few repairs on it, then settles down. It may even move in with a skunk or an armadillo, creatures not given to protesting against uninvited guests. In fixing up the den the young possum gathers grass and loops its tail around the bundle, then drags it to the nest.

A possum does not stake out any particular area as its hunting ground; other possums may wander about on the same plot without being challenged. Possums eat anything that can be eaten, flesh, fruits and berries, stink-bugs, ants, crickets, beetles and grasshoppers.

Eating and a brief time of mating are the only interests of a possum's life. His world is limited to an area only a few acres in extent. He may have a flurry of excitement when he is faced with any of the many hazards and dangers which beset the life of a possum.

Next to the hazardous journey up to his mother's pouch, the first few months after leaving the mother are the most critical in his life. Dogs, coyotes, bobcats, hawks, in fact all of the larger predators, find a young possum easy prey to kill. The possum is not a fighter and will offer little resistance to attack. It is apt to play dead if attacked, falling limply on one side. Its heart-beat will be reduced and it will appear to be lifeless. This has given rise to the term, "playing possum." This may be a state of true shock, but if the attacker is fooled and goes away, the possum recovers quickly. I have a feeling that only dogs are fooled by this trick, as they would not kill a possum to eat it. A bobcat or a coyote would go ahead and eat the possum.

Wooded streams appeal to the possum, but it will live in any area where there is brush and woods for shelter. It is usually met in the evening or at night, seldom leaving its nest during the day. Possums are found along the Atlantic coast westward to Texas and Colorado and along the Pacific coast.

It hunts as readily in treetops as on the ground. The hind feet are better hands than the forepaws, because they have a flexible big toe. This toe can reach any of the other toes, so the opossum handles his food with his hind feet. His long scaly tail is also useful. A possum may dangle by his tail from a limb.

The first possums to reach the west coast were brought there and turned loose or escaped from their owners. They multiplied rapidly and are now found scattered over most of the western states. The first wild ones appeared in Oregon and California.

The color of the possum is usually gray with dark underhair, which has long white guard hairs; albinos are not rare. The pointed muzzle and naked tail make the possum easily recognized.

Possums have remarkable vitality, and will recover from

wounds that would kill an ordinary animal. This tenacity to live is probably one of the reasons the race has survived so long, in spite of high infant mortality. Skeletons examined have shown broken ribs, legs and other cracked bones, all completely healed. The possum is accident-prone, but has the stamina to recover from severe injuries. Not being very intelligent, the possum has to be tough to survive.

In many places this scaly-tailed night-prowler is considered excellent eating. Served with yams it is relished by many people. It somehow never looks appetizing to me but then I never tried eating a roasted possum. Over three hundred thousand possums have been known to have been killed in one year in Missouri. Many of them, I imagine, went into the pot. The pelt seldom brings more than fifty cents, but quite a bit of the fur is used in trimming inexpensive coats.

I am not a great admirer of the possum, but I do champion his right to wander through the woods or to hang from a limb by his tail. If the meek are indeed to inherit the earth, the possum, I am sure, will find a place of importance.

The range of the armadillo does not extend very far north in America. It avoids severe cold weather. This little armored tank is literally a fire eater. It licks up fire-ants, scorpions and tarantulas. With one swipe of its long sticky tongue it can lick up seventy or more ants, each one trying to bite the tough-skinned tongue.

This armored pig shuffles on his way, dressed like a knight in chain mail. Only the ears are naked. It is encased, fore and aft, by bony plates that are joined over the ribs by nine flattened hoops. One plate covers the head to the tip of the snout. The tail is protected by rings of bone. Even the legs are covered with hard scales.

This little monster has interesting dental equipment. Provided with such excellent armor, it is weak on offensive fangs. It has no front teeth. It has molars but no pre-molar canines, and the molars have no enamel on them. Using the food-getting tactics of the ant-eater it has little use for teeth. It is a creature depending upon defense and not offense.

The armadillo is a friend to nesting ground birds. It kills thousands of ants which often kill baby quail and other fledglings as they break out of the egg. Armadillos have been known to ignore a nest of bird eggs put into their cage. To the best of my knowledge, they do not raid birds' nests. Of course, there is usually a rogue in every family, and a few armadillos may acquire a taste for bird eggs.

It has been established that ninety percent of an armadillo's food is insect matter. I doubt if there is a crawling or flying insect it will not eat. Ant-hills are, of course, banquet tables. Sometimes it will eat puffballs and mushrooms.

This armor-plated fellow is descended from an ancient, pre-historic ancestor, but in order to survive it had to shrink in size. The original armadillo was as big as a rhinoceros. Remains of this monster armadillo have been found in South America. The shrinking process has required millions of years, but appears to have stopped well short of the vanishing point. In this country they came up from Texas and Louisiana and pushed north and east. Before there were bridges across the Mississippi River, they crossed it and are common in states bordering that river.

Extreme cold is the only thing that checks their spread. Cold spells they can weather in their dens, but extended periods of bitter weather kill them. If they do not freeze, they starve, be-cause their surface food is gone and they cannot dig into the frozen ground. It seems that the northern limits of their range have been reached.

Heat drives the armadillo underground, even though it does hunt by day. Long, dry spells will drive the insects it feeds upon deep into the ground where it cannot reach them. This will cre-ate a long lean spell for the armadillo.

In spite of his armor plating, the armadillo is a good swim-mer, but if the stream is not very wide it prefers to walk on the bottom. It may have to surface once or twice to get a lung full of air, but if it decides to walk, it walks.

The armadillo likes some shade but not enough to discourage the insects it feeds upon. It lives in grass meadows, patches of cactus or chaparral. It likes limestone areas where erosion has hollowed out caves it can use as homes. One armadillo usually has a number of dens, sometimes as many as a dozen. Shallow tunnels attract desert insects, millipedes crawl in as well as spiders and scorpions, all of which are welcomed by the sticky tongue of the armadillo.

In digging, the armadillo is no match for the badger but it does a very creditable job. Using its snout and claws it loosens dirt and shoves it back under its belly. When there is a pile accumulated it raises its back end and sends the dirt flying with its hind feet.

If attacked, an armadillo either dives into its hole or curls up inside its armor. If it gets underground no hunter can pull it out. It just wedges itself and the only way to capture it is to dig it out. It is hunted by all of the large killers; peccaries even hunt it. Men hunt it as game. The meat is delicious, especially when served with chili sauce. In East Texas it is often referred to as "the poor man's pig."

The armadillo is a sociable animal. They are often seen in bands. Adults usually live alone, but at times as many as five or six may use the same burrow.

It is difficult to tell a female armadillo from a male. They are the same size and look and act alike. The female usually gives birth to four young ones. One cell splits into four identical quarters and the young will be identical down to the last hair and scale, and all will be of the same sex. Mating takes place in midsummer and the young are born in February. Their eyes will open late in March. For a time their coats will remain soft and leathery. The armor cannot harden until the armadillo grows up, and during the growing-up period, the youngsters have little protection against their enemies.

Armadillos root for much of their food, plowing a furrow in loose soil or leaves, sniffing out bugs, worms and grubs with their keen sense of smell. They are diligent hunters, moving about at a trot or a fast walk. An armadillo's eyesight is bad and so is his hearing, in spite of his big ears. Enemies may slip up on an armadillo before he sees or hears them. Texas varieties do not curl up in their shells as much as do the South American armadillos when attacked. The Texas armadillo usually resorts to flight and it can run fast. If it can reach a thicket it will dig furiously and wedge itself into the hole it has excavated.

This little pig in armor has been holding his own, but he has probably reached the limit of the regions where he can live and prosper.

POST-SCRIPTUM

This is not a scientific book. It is a record of the journey through life of a sentimental fellow who has always had a curiosity about living things; a great respect for wild creatures, big and small. Often that respect amounts to real affection and sometimes to admiration.

Each living creature is governed by its needs, and by the pattern laid down in the seeds it came from. I leave to the professors the definitions. I know that all of the wild animals are kin to man. This kinship should be respected.

Every animal I have observed was an individual, a complex and wonderfully sensitive miracle of life, created for a reason and to fill a place for a span of a few months or a few years.

I hope this book will arouse in a few readers the realization that man does not own the earth, he just shares it with other creatures; and that our wildlife does not ask for much from us. If we destroy the wild creatures we will make a dreary place out of the land we live in. We will steal from our children's children a rich heritage, a kinship which can only be found in the great outdoors.

I know we are all in a great hurry. We rush about our daily affairs, too often counting that vacation a success which puts the most mileage on the family car. Thus many of us cheat ourselves out of the best things in life, things that are free for the taking; an hour in the woods, a day in the mountains, a chance to become acquainted with the teeming population of a meadow, the sweep of a slope with mule deer bounding over it, high benches where antelope flash their white heliographs. Why not slow down and share an hour with nature's children?

I believe that more and more people are turning to the simple ways of the wild during the present time of stress. There is an awakening desire to preserve our wildlife. With man standing on the brink of a horror of his own making, the deep woods, the parks and the sanctuaries offer a refuge from stress. In the lives of the wild creatures you can find a serene sureness of purpose. They live as God intended them to live. May He go with you when you enter their world.

INDEX

Italic Numbers Indicate Main Reference